Mary Harrod is Assistant Professor in French Studies at the University of Warwick. She is co-editor of the collection *The Europeanness of European Cinema: Identity, Meaning, Globalization* (I.B.Tauris, 2015) and has published book chapters and journal articles in the areas of European and US cinemas and television, with a focus on gender studies, transnational cultural exchange, language and the relationship between aesthetics, spectatorial engagement and ideology.

'Mary Harrod's investigation of the French rom-com over the past two decades is a tour de force. In her unlayering of the complexities of contemporary socio-sexual life as revealed in the rom-com, she clearly delineates the French specificities of this most transnational of genres. Not only does she demonstrate how the rom-com provides an accurate social barometer of human relationships in contemporary France, in so doing she also makes clear the relevance of an academic study of this much neglected genre which speaks to the social culture of its time around such challenging issues as love, marriage, divorce, parenthood, gender and queer relations, and the impact of new technologies and legislation on human connections.'

Susan Hayward, Modern Languages Department, University of Exeter

'Mary Harrod's wide-ranging survey brings out the many contradictions and tensions of the contemporary French rom-com. With its focus on shifting gender roles, the importance of the family unit, and the relationship with the US rom-com, this book is essential for an understanding of popular French cinema.'

Phil Powrie, Professor of Cinema Studies, University of Surrey

'Harrod's groundbreaking book puts French romantic screen comedy into stimulating analysis, making a compelling case that this popular genre is vital to understanding France's recent filmmaking.'

Tim Palmer, Professor of Film Studies at the University of North Carolina Wilmington, and author of *Brutal Intimacy: Analyzing Contemporary French Cinema* (2011) and *Irreversible* (2015)

From France with Love

Gender and Identity in French Romantic Comedy

By Mary Harrod

BLOOMSBURY ACADEMIC
LONDON • NEW YORK • OXFORD • NEW DELHI • SYDNEY

BLOOMSBURY ACADEMIC
Bloomsbury Publishing Plc
50 Bedford Square, London, WC1B 3DP, UK
1385 Broadway, New York, NY 10018, USA
29 Earlsfort Terrace, Dublin 2, Ireland

BLOOMSBURY, BLOOMSBURY ACADEMIC and the Diana logo
are trademarks of Bloomsbury Publishing Plc

First published in Great Britain 2015 by I. B. Tauris
This paperback edition published in 2021

Copyright © Mary Harrod, 2015

Mary Harrod has asserted her right under the Copyright,
Designs and Patents Act, 1988, to be identified as Author of this work.

For legal purposes the Acknowledgements on p. xi constitute
an extension of this copyright page.

All rights reserved. No part of this publication may be reproduced or
transmitted in any form or by any means, electronic or mechanical,
including photocopying, recording, or any information storage or retrieval
system, without prior permission in writing from the publishers.

Bloomsbury Publishing Plc does not have any control over, or responsibility for,
any third-party websites referred to or in this book. All internet addresses given
in this book were correct at the time of going to press. The author and publisher
regret any inconvenience caused if addresses have changed or sites have
ceased to exist, but can accept no responsibility for any such changes.

A catalogue record for this book is available from the British Library.

A catalog record for this book is available from the Library of Congress.

ISBN: HB: 978-1-7845-3358-8
PB: 978-1-3502-2514-5
ePDF: 978-0-8577-2666-7
eBook: 978-0-8577-3990-2

International Library of the Moving Image 31

Typeset by Aptara

To find out more about our authors and books visit
www.bloomsbury.com and sign up for our newsletters.

For Marion and Jeric.

Contents

List of Figures ix
Acknowledgements xi

   Introduction 1
1 Romantic Comedy – and its Discontents 14
2 Romance Today 28
3 Gendered Identities in Love 81
4 Family Affairs 129
5 Genre, Style and Transnationalism 166
   Concluding Remarks: Rom-Com into the 2010s 208

Notes 215
Bibliography 221
French rom-coms 1990–2010 with Box-Office Admissions 241
Index 247

Figures

1. Boxed in: urban living gone awry as Amelie and neighbours dine alone. © UGC — 32
2. Post-modern intimacy in *Irène*. © M6 Droits Audiovisuels — 43
3. Sex and spirituality in *Dieu est grand, je suis toute petite*. © Mars Distribution — 52
4. The mistress as object in *Ils se marièrent et eurent beaucoup d'enfants*. © Pathé — 61
5. An ordinary adulteress? Yolande Moreau of *Quand la mer monte*. © Pirates Distribution — 64
6. Screwball intimacy in *Ils se marièrent et eurent beaucoup d'enfants*. © Pathé and StudioCanal — 69
7. Screwball intimacy in *Ce soir, je dors chez toi*. © Pathé and StudioCanal — 70
8. A figure of fun: Alain Chabat in *Prête-moi ta main*. © Optimum Releasing — 95
9/10. Fetishistic views in *Ma femme est une actrice* and *L'Art (délicat) de la séduction*. © Pathé and CTV International — 97
11. Enslaved to the beauty myth forever in *Laisse tes mains sur mes hanches*. © ARP Sélection — 102
12/13. Caricatural gay melodrama versus a 'serious' consideration of queerness in *Pédale douce* and *Crustacés et coquillages*. © Pathé and Peccadillo Pictures — 124

14 Domestic disharmony: contemporary life closes in
for Hugo and Ariane of *De l'autre côté du lit*.
© Warner Home Vidéo   155
15 Sabine Azéma is the exotic face of romance in
La Bûche. © Pathé   160
16 Foregrounding performance in *L'Arnacœur*.
© Revolver Entertainment   203

Acknowledgements

My heartfelt thanks go to all those who have supported me before and during the six-year process of this research and writing, which encompassed the birth of two children. These include my wonderful (step-/)parents Marion, Jeric and Ian; my husband Hugo, who sat through films in the wrong genre and language, provided an astute sounding board and was generally a romantic hero in all the ways that matter; my children Elodie and Kit themselves; and Tanya and Henry Harrod for their priceless help in looking after them. I also wish to thank colleagues, several of whom have contributed to the genesis of the book, including many people from King's College London whose approaches have helped shape my own and who have supported me in numerous other ways, especially Sarah Cooper, Michele Pierson, Richard Dyer and Belén Vidal, as well as current colleagues from the University of Warwick. I am indebted to the Arts and Humanities Research Council for funding the research, Peter Graham and Nick and April Bueno de Mesquite for the enormously generous loans of their flats in Paris, Yvonne Tasker, Steve Wheeler, Carrie Tarr and Phil Powrie, as well as whole the editorial board of *Studies in French Cinema*, for excellent feedback on earlier drafts of part or all of the book, Philippa Brewster and Anna Coatman at I.B.Tauris for their interest in and helpful suggestions for it and especially Raphaëlle Moine, for inspiring the research, for her positive and perceptive reactions to my work as a whole and for going out of her way to promote it in France. I also thank the librarians of Senate House and the Maughan Libraries; my students, who have brought new and rich perspectives;

and many extraordinary personal friends who continue to inspire me in all sorts of ways. But my biggest thanks of all go to Ginette Vincendeau, whose guidance and kindness have exceeded all duty and who has been absolutely instrumental in the romance of learning that gave rise to this book.

Introduction

French filmmaking and love stories have often gone hand in hand. However, a form of film more readily identifiable with the internationally recognisable rom-com genre than were earlier examples has proliferated in France since the 1990s. On the one hand, this development can be seen in the context of the increasingly transnational nature of cinema. On the other, the phenomenon coincides with a period characterised by an identity crisis unprecedented in human history, one with both a global reach and specific resonance in France, provoked by the movement away from clearly delineated gender roles (Badinter 2010: 12). Since romantic comedy is a genre focused on coupling culture, its French variant can be expected to respond to this crisis. This book seeks to examine the factors behind and implications of the spectacular rise of the rom-com in France in the 1990s and 2000s, as it pertains to the film industry and to the issue of generic definitions, as well as more generally in terms of representations.

In probing the significance of the contemporary French rom-com, this study not only takes stock of a new development; it also represents an intervention into the field of French film studies, in that popular cinema (and comedy in particular) originating in France has to date suffered from neglect by scholarly research. According to Richard Abel, 'most historians would agree that it was the French who almost singlehandedly created film comedy' (1984: 220). Moreover, Susan Hayward has shown how the genre has consistently outperformed others in the domestic market and, specifically, been a key factor in the national mainstream cinema's success since 1990, accounting for at least 50 per cent of domestic box office takings to 2002. Since then, too, the genre has year on year accounted for the lion's share of production (between 20 and 35 per cent) and comedies have featured in similar proportions in the nation's annual box office top 20. No wonder, then, that Hayward remarks on the need for 'an extended analysis of the processes and ideological function of French comedy', at the time of her writing and still nearly two decades later 'conspicuous by its absence' (2005 [1993]: 304–6). By analysing one subgroup within French comedy – and, as we shall see, a significant, pervasive and commercially impactful one – this research represents a contribution towards redressing the balance between French comedy's enormous popularity and its widespread exclusion from academic enquiry.

Prominent precursors to the current French rom-com trend begin appearing as early as the end of the 1980s, with a film by feminist popular auteur Coline Serreau, hit inter-class romance *Romuald et Juliette/Mama, There's a Man in Your Bed* (1989), leading the way. Serreau's film doubtless influenced the wave of female auteur rom-coms appearing in the 1990s, directed by the likes of Chantal Akerman, Josiane Balasko, Catherine Corsini and Tonie Marshall. By the start of the 2000s, other directors of both genders were making rom-coms that not only achieved domestic success but also relatively substantial international distribution, bringing greater global visibility to the genre. These include *Le Fabuleux destin d'Amélie Poulain/Amelie* (Jean-Pierre Jeunet, 2001), *Décalage horaire/Jet Lag* (Danièle Thompson, 2002), *Prête-moi ta main/I Do* (Eric Lartigau, 2006), *Hors de prix/Priceless* (Pierre Salvadori, 2006), *De vrais mensonges/Beautiful Lies* (Salvadori, 2010) and *L'Arnacœur/Heartbreaker* (Pascal Chaumeil, 2010). These successes cemented the genre's firmly established status as a relatively common form of French production by the end of the 2000s. So much so, in fact, that the term *comédie romantique* has become standardised in press and marketing campaigns and even filtered down to made-for-television films (see for example Germain 2010). Nonetheless, the fact that as recently as 2008 the two French film scholars to remark on the trend, Raphaëlle Moine and Brigitte Rollet, were still describing it as nascent (Moine 2008) or even 'an extremely rare and recent phenomenon' (Rollet 2008: 92) suggests that the speed with which the traditionally foreign genre has caught on has been so dizzying that commentators have had trouble keeping up. This makes a scholarly exploration of the contemporary French rom-com timely.

Two further, more specific factors in the rom-com's French efflorescence emerge from this summary: the number of female directors working in the national industry, and the genre's commercial potential. As concerns the first of these, a cursory look at the appended rom-com filmography of the 1990s and 2000s suggests that at least a third of films (more in the 1990s) were directed by women. This is a high figure even in the context of a country where female directors have been responsible for between 14 and 19 per cent of overall production during the period (compared with 9 per cent in Hollywood in 1998, falling to only 5 per cent in 2010).[1] Although filmed romantic comedy was not originally conceived as geared to female audiences in particular, it has consistently been theorised as a genre with specific relevance for women, given their historical circumscription to cultural narratives of heterosexual coupling and family life, and thanks to the substantial roles the format has offered actresses. Moreover, as several rom-com critics have noted, recent decades have seen a turn towards assigning to rom-com a more exclusively feminine address in the context of post-*Pretty Woman* (Garry Marshall, USA 1990) Hollywood (Garrett 2007: 121; Ferriss and Young 2008a; Burns 2011).

Mobilising the tropes of romantic comedy has certainly been a factor in the considerable box-office revenues garnered by French women directors, particularly in the 2000s (see also Harrod 2012: 227–8). Indeed, the second immediate explanation for the genre's burgeoning at this particular time in France concerns precisely the explosive success of the global (primarily Hollywood) genre in the 1980s and 1990s – including in France, where films like *When Harry Met Sally* (Rob Reiner, USA 1989) and *Pretty Woman* attracted massive audiences (1.9 and 4 million tickets sold respectively).[2] It is unremarkable that French producers and directors should seek to emulate such profitability in their home market, not least given comedy's popularity during eras characterised by the kind of social division and, latterly, financial crisis that France has known over the period in question. The fact that French comic genres do not typically require huge budgets (by contrast with the situation in Hollywood and with other popular French genres such as heritage biopics [*La Môme/La Vie en rose* (Olivier Dahan, 2007), *Coco avant Chanel/Coco Before Chanel* (Anne Fontaine, 2009), *Yves*

Saint-Laurent (Jalil Lespert, 2014)] and special effects films [*Micmacs à tire-larigot/Micmacs* (Jeunet, 2009)]) makes them all the more appealing for commercially-oriented filmmakers.

However, this exclusively industrial angle does not tell the whole story. Rather, this study subscribes to the widely held view of genre as 'a functional interface between the cinematic institution, audiences, and the wider realm of culture' (Krutnik 1990: 57). This perspective does not ignore the complexities involved in speculating about exact relations between film texts and the social world, and specifically the limitations of top-down, 'mass society' theses, which have tended to portray establishment institutions as foisting ideologies upon uniformly uncritical consumers of popular and media culture. These limitations have been foregrounded by now familiar but nonetheless highly significant 1970s studies by such media scholars as Ian Jarvie (1970; 1978) and Andrew Tudor (1974) (or, in a French context, albeit less explicitly and fully, Pierre Sorlin [1977]), as well as the 1990s' turn towards reception studies, which seek to take stock of audience members' individual profiles, circumstances and ability to actively interpret films. While such approaches distance themselves from earlier readings that assumed uncomplicated recognition of single patterns of meaning, they nonetheless acknowledge the ongoing value of – inevitably subjective – critical analyses of film texts from a socio-historical point of view. As Tudor has put it: 'In dramatising [a society's] traits the movies participate in a continual and complex social process. [...] They are both reflection and cause; a link in a closed circle' (1974: 218). In accordance with the recognition that films both reflect and feed back into social change, this research attempts to sample and shed light on this circular dynamic, and thus contemporary French cultural history, as it is manifested through the phenomenon of national romantic comedy. In so doing it hopes to elucidate the reasons for and implications of the rom-com's appropriation by French filmmakers in the 1990s and 2000s, as well as the ways in which the genre contributes to film's widely recognised role in establishing cultural norms – in this case notably, if certainly not exclusively, 'defin[ing] and demonstrat[ing] socially sanctioned ways of falling in love' (Wright-Wexman 1993: ix). In order to begin to ask more specific questions about the genre, however, I will first elaborate on precisely what are the characteristics of the films that have led to the emergence of a French rom-com genre.

Corpus and Contexts

The notorious difficulty of generic definition may be particularly acute when it comes to rom-com. Brian Henderson (1978: 1) has suggested that several major generic inventories do not include it as a distinct category because the frequency with which romance and comedy occur across Hollywood production makes this genre extremely hard to pin down. This situation is compounded by the term's liberal use as a highly 'saleable' marketing label as much as any reflection of a film's content. Nonetheless, various theorists have hazarded attempts to categorise the genre. These range from extreme generalities (Krutnik's [2002: 133] argument that rom-com pivotally hinges on the question of love) to 'master' definitions (Jeffers McDonald 2007: 9) that are by their nature constricting. One structural feature that recurs in descriptions of the genre and is relevant to pinning down the key traits of the recent French trend is the broadly equal allocation of narrative space to male and female characters (see for example Neale and Krutnik 1990: 139; Rowe 1995: 109). Celestino Deleyto (1998: 137) has qualified this observation with the important caveat that in practice one point of view tends to dominate. Nonetheless, such textual architecture may be viewed as relatively egalitarian in comparison with that of most other Hollywood genres (female-centred melodramas providing an important exception), which, historically, have privileged a focus on men.

The contrast with French cinematic history is even starker. According to Moine (2008), the closest French cinema comes to romantic comedy in the classical era is the *comédie boulevardière*, or vaudeville comedy. These comedies were generally structured around the amorous adventures of a male character: a star performer, usually from a theatre background, for whom the stories – often theatrical adaptations – were vehicles (see Sellier 1999a). Films starring and directed by Sacha Guitry are emblematic. Female characters in this schema were subordinate, smaller roles played by performers who were less well-known, and often much younger, than the men with whom they were paired, making them prime examples of the on-screen portrayal of 'incestuous' coupling identified with the films of that period by Ginette Vincendeau (1988). The contrast with the contemporaneous Hollywood screwball comedy, animated by feisty heroines and powerful actresses, is apparent. For Moine, the major differences between these two filmic frameworks for the exploration of heterosexual love explain the relative absence of US remakes of French films into romantic comedies (she counts only three rom-coms out of more than 70 US remakes of French films ever).

Various scholars have similarly identified incestuous and/or misogynistic tendencies in both classical and New Wave French cinema (Burch and Sellier 1996; Sellier 1997[3], 1999b; Vincendeau 1992). As Vincendeau (2000b: 113) suggests, it is the relatively equal allotment of narrative *subjectivity* that has been seen to typify rom-com that even 1960s French cinema was still some way off tolerating. This has for the most part continued to be the case in mainstream comedy at any rate, up until the emergence of the current spate of rom-coms, with male duos reigning even more supremely in France than in Hollywood. Thus since 2000 alone exemplary male buddy comedies – with openly misogynistic elements – including *La Beuze/The Dope* (François Desagnat and Thomas Sorriaux, 2003), *Brice de Nice/The Brice Man* (James Huth, 2005), *La Doublure/The Valet* (Francis Veber, 2006), *Bienvenue chez les Ch'tis/Welcome to the Sticks* (Dany Boon, 2008), *Rien à déclarer/Nothing to Declare* (Boon, 2010) and *Intouchables/Untouchable* (Olivier Nakache and Eric Toledano, 2011) have all featured in the box-office top ten.

The contemporary cycle of films represents a major change in this regard: it is principally their promotion of female points of view – as well as a light-hearted approach to love viewed at once as miraculous transformation and yet also as socially contingent – that identifies them with the global genre and renders appropriate their analysis from within its purview. Additionally, many films include explicit acknowledgements of their debt to Hollywood, through intertextual references.

The promotion of female subjectivity by the French rom-com, taken in conjunction with female filmmakers' widespread participation in the genre, clearly says something about changing gender roles in contemporary France – as indeed does a high proportion of narratives of female rebellion (as well as, in the 2000s, of male riposte). Such observations begin to add detail to the schematic suggestion made earlier that the genre arises in part from women's greater access to professional equality in the film industry. As suggested, the ways in which the genre mediates social anxiety arising from such changes is a key concern of this analysis; but it is nonetheless as well to state clearly from the outset that the genre's explosion is itself viewed here as a measure of acutely heightened tensions around the role of men and women, in couple formations and in society as a whole, in contemporary France. This is perhaps no surprise in a context where gender equality has historically lagged significantly behind that of the US or Britain. For example, French women were not allowed to manage property and income until the early 1900s, nearly a century after most of their North American sisters, and they did not achieve suffrage until 1944, a full quarter of a century behind the latter. In more recent years, too, relative equality in some spheres has been coupled with a firmly embedded loyalty to the notion of gender difference in other aspects of life. For example, a major feature distinguishing French from anglophone schools of feminism historically has been the former's focus on championing feminine specificity, as opposed to stressing equality. This emphasis on 'the feminine', and concomitant celebration of motherhood has arguably posed relatively few challenges to existing designations of gender roles: as Christine Bard (1999a: 304) has chronicled, '[those advocating a 'feminine identity' were accused] of excessively reinforcing difference to the overall benefit of patriarchy'.[4] At the same time, while marriage in Western culture has been in 'crisis' for well over a century, it is generally acknowledged that second-wave feminism and the attack on traditional values of the 1960s provoked particular disturbances in the conventions of marriage and intimate relationships. France's historical allegiance to the Catholic Church may initially have fortified the institution of marriage more solidly against the challenges posed within its borders by liberalism than was the case in Britain or the US. In recent years, though, France has had the lowest per capita annual marriage rate of any country in Europe (around 50 per 10,000 citizens [Hampshire 2008: 398]). In other words, there appears to have occurred in France a delayed reaction to the liberal gains achieved elsewhere over 30 years ago; it is my contention that this reaction is strikingly visible in the unprecedentedly high rom-com output of the last 20 years.

This sense of social backlash is visible in a certain 'nervousness' about romance in the French rom-com that is akin to a sensibility visible in North American culture in the 1970s. Indeed, a distinctive characteristic of the current trend is the prevalence of 'dark' elements, associable with both the melodramatic and realist traditions. Looking further back into French literary history sheds additional light on the texture of the contemporary film genre: importantly, a mistrust of laughter is exemplified within France's literary and especially dramatic canon by a bias towards narrative-based definitions of comedy (Frederick 1973; Greene 1977) and an adjuvant tendency to include relatively sober material within the category (see Neale and Krutnik 1990: 13–4). Moreover the tendency to mix comedy and drama is still in evidence in French film criticism today, through, for example, the prevalence of the label *comédie dramatique* or dramatic comedy – much more common than the closest English-language equivalent *comedy-drama* (or occasionally *dramedy*). It is not by chance that when Geoff King (2002: 10) seeks to illustrate global comedy's potentially melodramatic penchant, he invokes a French film, Serreau's *La Crise/ The Crisis* (1992).

In rom-com, while Hollywood narratives from *Sleepless in Seattle* (Nora Ephron, USA 1993) to *500 Days of Summer* (Marc Webb, USA 2009) are no strangers to melodrama – indeed its presence in the genre may even be on the increase in recent years (Jeffers McDonald 2007: 85) – it is true that this mode appears to a striking extent as the default second register of the French genre. *Se souvenir des belles choses/Beautiful Memories* (Zabou Breitman, 2001) is a salient example of this tendency, with the romance being played out in the setting of a mental institution, between a woman with a degenerative brain disease and a man suffering from amnesia after accidentally killing his family. The rom-com's traditional 'happy ending', with the man declaring his love, is undermined by the use of slow-motion and asynchronous sound to evoke the woman's experience of his words as disconnected. Nonetheless the film's rom-com identity is acknowledged by Rollet's inclusion of it in a list of films of the current French cycle (2010).

The force of recognising overtly incongruous elements as common in the French rom-com is to broaden the scope of the corpus I propose to analyse here. That is, while on the one hand a crop of films substantially different from predecessors appears in the national cinema in the 1990s and multiplies in the 2000s, it is simultaneously the case that my study relies on a flexible understanding of rom-com itself. This creates space for the analysis of films not necessarily ostentatiously identifiable with the global label 'rom-com' in a highly self-conscious way alongside those that are: a two-pronged approach to probing the significance of films that engage with contemporary social reality around coupling culture in France. This is consonant with rom-com studies globally, where heterogeneity characterises the genre at the synchronic as well as the diachronic level. Pushing the boundaries of the genre in this way reveals the specific new directions being taken by its French version: what happens when the French rom-com *à l'américaine* is fully locally integrated, becoming rom-com *à la française*.

To summarise, my interest in the French rom-com spans both purely generic contexts and the social – domains that bear on one another. A major line of enquiry for the research is concerned with the genre's French specificity, including how this may evolve over the period and the extent to which the genre is naturalised and/or exported, with repercussions for understanding global film traffic. Thinking about the rom-com's identity raises questions too about the stars who populate it and how we might assess its representational politics. Specifically, my statements about female authorship in the French genre, as well as the newness of privileging female subjectivity to any extent in national comedy, beg several further questions about exactly *how* the two genders are constructed in films. Is it appropriate to see the rom-com as a particularly feminised genre in France and, if so, in what sense? These questions transcend the simple issue of any split in focus and point of view between the genders, pairing this structural issue with analysis of both story arcs and specific narrative and aesthetic details. In this vein, how does the genre negotiate major contemporary social shifts, particularly those most obviously linked to gender? Notable here are the decline of marriage, the linked extension of singlehood and female autonomy and the increased range of acceptable gender roles today – particularly the rise of the professional woman, which in turn has profound implications for masculinity and for the family, a key unit of social organisation. Do films broadly reflect and embrace such shifts or do they resist, critique or downplay them, as comedy has often been accused of doing? Finally, how are the articulations of these questions inflected by considering production and reception contexts, including films' status as auteur or mainstream fare – which suggest slightly different target audiences – as well as the issue of gendered authorship? By considering questions such as these and how their answers may evolve over the period in question, the study is centrally concerned with feminism – indeed, takes a feminist approach – while not being exclusively limited to such an optic. It ultimately hopes to pinpoint some of the ways in which the French rom-com has been mediating and shaping perceptions of many key social trends over the past two decades or so, both at home and globally.

Methodology and Structure

Given its focus on the relationship between film and society, this research walks a delicate line between textual and contextual detail, while pointing to links between the two. At the same time, within film analysis it seeks to strike a reasonable balance between picking out meta-trends across texts and the desire to be more than an encyclopaedic overview of a large body of films. This means it ranges from, on occasion, relatively scientific statements about narrative and aesthetic patterns, to fuller explorations of the possible implications for spectators of concrete textual constructions, the latter through both fairly extended analyses embedded in subsections and separate, even more thoroughgoing case studies of individual films. With respect to both these strategies, while I have already rejected the structuralist framework whereby narrative patterns equate to fixed textual meanings, and am closer to the approach of discourse analysis, with its central emphasis on polysemy and personal circumstances (such as being a female, UK-based researcher) bringing connotations to bear on interpretation (see Ali 2012), I nonetheless propose certain theoretical subject positions, or readings, for consumers of the films in question. Without suggesting such interpretations are the only possible options for viewers, certain popular texts characterised by a high degree of narrative explicitness do seem designed to elicit preferred or dominant readings (see Hall 1980). At the same time, my interpretations are supported by reference to production and especially reception data. The latter are privileged over the former because this analysis is more interested in how films interact with a range of viewers than in authorial intentions, and they typically take the form of press materials, since ethnographic audience studies – including even admissions figures broken down by age or gender – do not by and large exist in France. In other words, the analysis is at the interface of historical materialist and more purely theoretical, textually-based stances.

In terms of organisation, the remainder of this book is divided into five chapters and concluding remarks. Chapter 1 surveys the principal directions taken by scholarship on romantic comedy and related genres, including via literary and cultural studies. It begins by examining relevant global scholarship in romance studies; it then discusses work from this context on filmed rom-com itself; next it scrutinises francophone research on the French rom-com and related genres; and finally it returns to focusing once more on exogenous, anglophone perspectives, now on the contemporary French rom-com itself. In Chapter 2, I begin examining the corpus itself, here by focusing on romance's role in contemporary society, globally and especially in France. In the first half of the chapter, this involves putting romance into dialogue with other important societal shifts relating to demographic patterns and to identity in the late twentieth and early twenty-first century, as they are negotiated by the French rom-com; in the second, I interrogate the ways in which romantic discourse itself has evolved in films of the corpus. Chapter 3 attempts to isolate the ways in which specific, gendered identities – that is, feminine, masculine and alternative positions – are configured by the genre and how such constructions may be determined by and bear on the roles deemed acceptable for and by French people today. In Chapter 4, I approach rom-com from the point of view of its articulation of concerns about the French family today: an archetypal *topos* of the domestic popular cinema. Finally, Chapter 5 places the French genre in a transnational context, both in the sense of interrogating in more detail its relation to Hollywood predecessors (both actual and perceived, including via a reception analysis focusing on reviews and other press relating to films) and also by probing its role in feeding back into transnational generic flows, and therefore mass consciousness. It might be noted that the study thus follows a circular logic at both macro and micro levels of structuration. Not only does it track the appropriation and then re-export of a foreign genre by France, but its apprehension of films' role in reflecting and feeding back into social norms underpins comparable dynamics within several individual chapters. As for the concluding remarks section, this both draws together findings and briefly considers the contribution to these of films that have appeared since the period of the research was concluded at the end of 2000s – a less than four year interlude during which the genre has multiplied beyond all expectations, such that every week the new crop of films in theatres appears to include at least one rom-com.

Regarding periodisation, it is worth noting that my choice of individual case studies for this book reflects the fact that it is at the end of the 1990s and especially post-2000 that the home-grown rom-com really begins to take off in France. These studies also illustrate the way in which box-office data is an important criterion, but not the only one, for singling out films for analysis. Thus while *Amelie* and *L'Arnacœur* were huge global hits, *La Bûche/Season's Beatings* (Danièle Thompson, 1999) was a more modest, largely domestic success. This is partly because I am also interested in generic development itself: an evolution whose interrelation with wider culture is complex. For example, texts with smaller audiences can still make great impact on film culture and therefore influence other directors in ways that filter down into broader patterns. The growth of the home-video market has also attenuated the importance of box-office figures. Finally, it is also the case that a poor box-office performance can be telling about social attitudes. For all these reasons, films have in general been chosen for more sustained analysis through a combination of considering their impact in a quantitative way but also for the relevance of the themes they explore and indeed the different market positions they occupy – within a broadly popular framework, seeking to counterbalance academia's prioritisation of art cinema. All the same, auteur films are far from ignored: examples like *Vénus Beauté (Institut)/Venus Beauty Salon* (Tonie Marshall, 1999), *Quand la mer monte/When the Sea Rises* (Yolande Moreau and Gilles Porte, 2004) and *Les Chansons d'amour/Love Songs* (Christophe Honoré 2007), to name just a handful, receive considerable attention in various places, in part because of their possible influence within the industry and their prominence in cinephilic culture, as well as the crossover appeal they may have, including due to winning prizes. In any case, admissions figures are provided for all films included in the appended filmography of rom-coms 1990–2010.

Finally, a note on bibliographical and filmographical references. In the first case, while source details throughout the book are as complete as possible, a number of daily and weekly press references do not indicate a page number. This is because they were obtained from the database at Bifi (Bibliothèque du Film) in which the scanning of articles has deleted page numbers. Readers wishing to consult the full articles are directed to the Bifi Library (51 rue de Bercy, 75012 – Paris), which offers fast and convenient online access to the material. The Bnf, Bibliothèque Nationale de France (Site François-Mitterrand, Quai François-Mauriac, 75013 – Paris) holds full issues of the papers. For film references, within the text I have opted, the first time a film is mentioned, to give the full French title and English translation where available, along with director details and year of production.

The country of production is included only when this is not France (or France in combination with others). For subsequent references only the French title (or a commonsense abbreviation) is given. For non-French titles, I have given only the English-language title.

1

Romantic Comedy – and its Discontents

This chapter is concerned with definitions of romantic comedy and the specificity and status of its French variant. As we shall see, however, the chapter's central theme is the deprecation of rom-com as an object worthy of study and its consequent scholarly neglect, globally and in France particularly.

Romantic Comedy in a Global Context

There are reasons to believe that romantic comedy as a genre may be especially well equipped to negotiate external cultural developments. As Roberta Garrett has recently observed in a discussion of the contemporary global genre, over the years key rom-com studies have offered 'a degree of critical consensus [...] concerning the historical specificity of and formal distinctions between cycles such as the early comedy of remarriage (1920s–1930s), the screwball comedy (1930s–1940s), the sex-comedy (1950s–1960s) and the nervous romance (1970s)' (2007: 96). In other words, throughout its theorisations rom-com has typically been seen as *by definition* a genre dealing with the shifts in gender roles and relations that have occurred during different periods. To understand why, we must look beyond the cinema to literary and cultural studies scholarship on comedy and romance.

Literary and Cultural Studies Approaches

The comic component of the rom-com's identity is important in understanding the genre's social relevance. A running theme of the many and diverse literary theories of comedy put forward since the Classical period is the latter's essentially social status and import. This relevance is perhaps most obvious when it comes to satire. In France, critiques of contemporary regimes, philosophies and mores by writers like Voltaire and Diderot are exemplary. But even the most seemingly trivial jokes frequently rely on immediate context for their import. Freud himself, often accused of an ahistorical bent, cannot avoid tying his discussion of the varying conditions in which innuendo might occur to social class, historical era and especially gender, when he designates certain jokes a way of oppressing women (Freud 2002: 96–7).

If context is all-important when it comes to comedy, comedy can be profoundly revealing about the social world in which it is produced. Not only does 'comic insulation' (Palmer 1987: 45) – the protective layer afforded by comedy's apparent frivolousness – allow it to broach topics that might be taboo in more 'serious' registers; comedy in fact tends to accumulate around such sites of difficulty or anxiety, as jokes exploit the tension generated by these. This makes comic texts potent mediators of a society's norms and values, both official and internalised.

As for romance, this term presents a dualistic profile, as both cultural and fictional narrative. The ubiquity with which the notion of romantic love appears in recent Western fiction is certainly a measure of its enduringly irresistible allure. As observed in a study of literary romance in twentieth-century France, despite the cultural shift away from marriage towards 'more sequential and complex family structures', an investment in love as a mutual commitment based on passionate desire and affinity is a major feature of contemporary culture (Holmes 2006: 115). So much so that, as global rom-com scholar Deleyto puts it, 'we have forgotten that [romance] is [...] an "invention" of a group of Provençal poets at the end of the eleventh century' (Deleyto 2003: 167). His discussions here and elsewhere (2009a; Evans and Deleyto 1998) focus on this discourse's capacity for adapting to circumstance, as is apparent in various other interventions on the subject (see for example Foucault 1981; Giddens 1992; Pearce and Stacey 1995: 12). Michel Foucault's work as a whole has emphasised the way in which even the most apparently 'unreal' (one meaning of *romantic* in common parlance) stories feed into dominant attitudes, while sociologist of romance Anthony Giddens (1992: 45) – moving away from Foucault's stress on the overpowering and totalitarian nature of the ideas and models circulated by discourse – has suggested that it is narrative's very fictional status that may allow its consumer to use it consciously as a hypothetical model. Certainly it is often within the field of romance that apposite examples of the influence of ostentatiously contrived fiction upon the social world present themselves. To cite one, historians generally agree that novels were the principal means by which a romantic conception of marriage became widespread in nineteenth-century North America (May 1980: 75–6) – the same tendency satirised contemporaneously in France by Flaubert's *Madame Bovary* (2002 [1856]). In contemporary French cinema, the realisation that 'romanticism and realism can co-exist at different levels of our subjectivities' (Jackson 1995: 56) is already a hallmark of many auteur films and is particularly highly visible in the contemporary tendency towards imaginative 'autofiction' in films by female directors from Maïwenn to Mia Hansen-Løve, as well as in many rom-coms.[1]

Romantic fiction's potential power to infiltrate cultural discourse has not always predisposed it to enthusiastic scholarly or critical appreciation, any more than has comedy's superficially light-hearted approach to serious subjects. Instead, the rom-com has suffered as a genre from being written off as irrelevant or pernicious, sometimes both at the same time. This is inextricable from the prejudice operating towards most forms of popular diversion as 'only entertainment' (Dyer 1992) – especially genres perceived as 'feminine', as part of misogynistic currents operating in patriarchal society. In some ways paradoxically, though, second-wave feminism has been pivotal in shaping critical attitudes to the romance genre for several decades in the postwar period, condemning narratives which tend to idealise the heterosexual couple as a tool of patriarchal oppression (see for example Beauvoir, 2004 [1949]; Millet 1969; Firestone 1979 [1971]; Greer 1971). However, works like the literary studies of Tania Modleski (1990 [1982]) and Janice Radway (1991 [1987]), or Ien Ang's (1985) influential study of the pleasures of viewing the soap opera *Dallas*, have subsequently rehabilitated romance as a forum for women to explore their identities, emotional lives and life experiences. Such work does not overlook the limitations arguably imposed by the happy ending around coupling constructed by the traditional romance (a point to which I shall return), reasserting the universal law of kinship and a power structure in which woman has always been subordinate; hence Radway concludes that for women romance represents 'a minimal but nonetheless legitimate form of protest' (1991: 222).

A similar battle over the progressive or revisionist status of female-oriented romance has been waged in the post-feminist period around the phenomena of 'chick-lit', 'chick television' and 'chick-flicks'. Scholars such as Yvonne Tasker and especially Diane Negra (2004; 2008; Tasker and Negra 2007) have suggested that within these genres, whose current manifestations are thought to have proliferated following the success of the British novel *Bridget Jones' Diary* (Fielding 1996; see Ferriss and Young 2006: 5), any positive value for female viewers is severely attenuated, in ways that are bound up with the centrality of romance to chick texts. Other analysts of chick culture have placed more emphasis on the substantial pleasures and specific forms of empowerment such narratives offer to female consumers (Ferriss and Young 2008a: 4). Notably, several commentators on the global blockbuster book, television and film series *Sex and the City* have foregrounded its celebration of female desire and friendship (Henry 2004; Akass and McCabe 2004; Jermyn 2009). While it is undeniable that rom-coms are structurally predisposed towards endorsing heterosexual coupling, and I agree with the view that many post-feminist fictions promote values that are disempowering for a broad spectrum of women, my own position with regard to the politics of romantic comedy is in some respects closer to these latter studies. I seek in any case to interrogate the variegated and complex stories of the French rom-coms under examination in order to assess fully their textual and contextual specificity and historical inscription.

Rom-Com as a Cinematic Genre

The *Sex and the City* film franchise provides a prime example of texts around which critical discourse has tended to conflate as more or less synonymous the chick-flick and the rom-com (see Mortimer 2010: 1). While both of these epithets infantilise and trivialise the associative resonances of the films to which they refer through their perky, monosyllabic rhymes, chick-flicks are even more likely to be written off as of limited interest. The film genre designated by these terms brings with it a specific history of cinematic studies.

As suggested, critical denigration and neglect have also pervaded scholarship in this area, perhaps even more than in the case of written romance. This situation is in part a function of the culturally illegitimate status of comedy within staged fiction as a whole, which Moine (2002:

27–8) has in France dated back to Aristotle's designation of it as a low form. In film studies, though, further double standards apply. Firstly, earlier comedy has been the subject of considerably more literature than more recent texts. This may be partly ascribable to the fact that social relevance becomes easier to pick out with hindsight. Kristina Brunovska Karnick and Henry Jenkins (1995: 2) have also pointed out the facility with which comedy, frequently defined by an infantile, ludic quality, becomes a site for nostalgia, perhaps further influencing scholars' positive attitudes towards comedy of past eras. Additionally, biases in favour of auteurs mean that figures like Buster Keaton or Jacques Tati (who directed as well as starred in their films, a less common tendency in today's vertically integrated era) receive the most praise and attention from both critics and scholars.

Within rom-com studies specifically (and probably talking comedy as a whole), it is certainly rom-coms of the classical 'screwball' era that have received the greatest attention in film studies. This cycle of films has been the subject of studies by Stanley Cavell (1981), Wes Gehring (1986), Bruce Babington and Peter William Evans (1989), Tina Olsin Lent (1995), Kathrina Glitre (2001), David R. Shumway (2003b) and others, with some generic inventories privileging only this version of romantic comedy (see for example Schatz 1981: 150–85). These analyses bring out the rom-com genre's heterogeneity, since within merely one cycle an umbrella term has brought together films as diverse as didactic social comedy *Sullivan's Travels* (Preston Sturges, USA 1941) and domestic farce *Adam's Rib* (George Cukor, USA 1949), through features ranging from a utopian dissolution of class divisions (ibid) to the promotion of play as an expression of intimacy, reflecting new, post-Victorian ideals of companionate love (Lent 1995; Ruiz Pardos 2000) and a concomitant loosening of restrictions on female freedom, both within texts and through the rise of a slew of actresses to billing on an equal footing with men (Gehring 1986: 5; Rowe 1995: 146; Sarris 1998: 98).

Scholarship on more recent rom-com is equally varied but sparser. These features speak respectively to the lack of critical consensus over the contemporary genre's definition, and its typical status as an object worthy of cultural suspicion and scorn. However, some scholars, in attempting to identify the rom-com, accord relative centrality to the possibility of increased equality across the two genders in the genre's structural focus. In contrast, many scholars writing from feminist and other perspectives about cinematic romance in general (as in literary studies) have focused on the happy ending of the Hollywood romance as more or less forcing conservative ideologies upon its viewers (Fischer 1989: 243; Neale and Krutnik 1990: 145). While this overstatement was most common in the wake of 1970s post-structuralist-influenced theory, it has subsequently been seriously challenged through the expansion of cultural studies in the 1990s and the move to return agency, historical contingency and social identity to the film viewer. The fact that the happy ending is still commonly associated with rom-coms – Classical definitions of comedy, after all, hinge upon this feature – has allowed negative attitudes to persist; for instance, Rollet's article on the French rom-com sees the global format in terms of a narrative structure based on obstacles to overcoming supposedly inevitable union, to which she attributes an 'implicitly reactionary ideology' (2008: 94). Yet not only has work in film studies emulated the move elsewhere to interrogate romance for the pleasures it can offer female audiences (Stacey 1990) (as Rollet acknowledges [2008: 96]), but Rowe (1995: 8) has defended the rom-com in spite of its default ending, drawing on Mulvey's (1985) essay 'Changes: Thoughts on Myth, Narrative and Historical Experience', in which (revising earlier statements) she suggests that the importance of narrative's potential lies not in its final resolution but in the upheaval that precedes this. There is evidence this may be particularly true for comedies, given the fact that these films are frequently sold on their humorous moments, as opposed to story elements (King 2002: 87). Similarly, many comedies acquire a cult status that involves repeated viewing and a focus not so much on the ending as on particular sequences. In any case, as I will illustrate, the centrality of the happy ending to romantic comedy has been exaggerated and it is certainly of limited usefulness for the contemporary French genre.

Returning to the question of how to conceive rom-com beyond ideology, most incisive is Deleyto's 2009 *The Secret Life of Romantic Comedy*, in which he argues for a re-envisioning of genre as a whole and rom-com in particular in terms not, as traditionally, of belonging, but of participation. Borrowing from a wide range of sources including George Lakoff's cognitive theory of categories, chaos theory and most importantly Jacques Derrida's theory of genre, Deleyto argues convincingly for an approach to genre that is both more ambiguous and more pervasive than those traditionally taken in film studies. In his model, all texts can be seen to participate in one or several genres, without these generic affiliations providing the limits of their definition (Deleyto 2009a: 1–17).

Deleyto is equally eloquent on the importance of this wide-ranging approach for analysing rom-com. As he notes, of all genres this one is frequently held up as the most trivial and crassly commercial: he cites a recent *Sight and Sound* review referring to 'a conviction-free romantic comedy aimed at the teen market' (ibid: 2), while a definition of romantic comedy as 'the most vile, insipid, sanity-destroyingly horrible genre in the history of cinema' thrown up by an internet search on the urbandictionary.com site is equally typical and even more vitriolic. This definition goes on to illustrate the misogynistic association between women and strands of popular culture viewed as execrable, by suggesting that '[the rom-com] exists solely for the entertainment of obnoxious, highly sentimental housewives who feel that their gender must consign them to this terrible fate'.[2] More relevant to Deleyto's argument, though, is its citation of consistency of formula as one of the negative features of rom-com. This exemplifies his claim that the rom-com is the victim of a circular argument whereby it is seen to be typified only by those highly conventional films including the most conservative perspectives and therefore it is designated the most conventional and conservative genre. Instead, he argues:

> The genre of rom-com can [...] be seen as the intersection of three, closely interrelated elements: a narrative that articulates historically and culturally specific views of love, desire, sexuality and gender relationships; a space of transformation and fantasy which influences the narrative articulation of those discourses; and humour as the specific perspective from which the fictional characters, their relationships and the spectator's response to them are constructed as embodiments of those discourses (ibid: 45–6).

Deleyto goes on in the same passage to explain that the breadth of this definition illustrates why so many films use rom-com conventions, without necessarily being primarily identifiable with the genre, and that even the absence of one of these features does not necessarily invalidate the appropriateness of the paradigm.

In stressing generic hybridity, within film studies Deleyto's approach is comparable to the new genre criticism of writers including Richard Maltby and also – as he recognises (ibid: 5–6) – Neale and especially Rick Altman. Such models complement his own by focusing on the functioning of various genres within one film. At the same time, Deleyto goes beyond these theorists' work in seeing genre as *primarily an analytical tool*. Providing a kind of limit case for genre itself, this paradigm might appear to beg the question of the appropriateness of delimiting the corpus examined here in generic terms at all, given the wide sweep of texts I will be referencing. It is true that the choice of films discussed in these pages – along with the wider rom-com filmography of the period provided – while not arbitrary, proceeds from a number of informed choices and cannot claim to be an exhaustive enumeration of French films of the period that use rom-com conventions. The filmography, instead, lists films of the period under analysis in relation to which the rom-com analytical toolbox proves particularly useful.

Romantic Comedy in France

Romantic Comedy in French Film Studies

In France, not only is there no branch of film studies equivalent to the originally Anglo-American category of genre studies, but romantic comedy specifically has been seen as simply nonexistent in national filmmaking until very recently. Yet, given the broad understanding of rom-com offered in this chapter, one could in fact argue for approaching many pre-1990 French films from the perspective of the genre. Salient candidates might include the Belle Époque films of the late 1940s and the 1950s directed by Jacqueline Audry and others, usually considered costume dramas in the *tradition de qualité*, whose critical neglect has been signalled by Geneviève Sellier (2005) and more recently Hayward (2010); some New Wave films – especially those which are less well-known like *Les Jeux de l'amour/The Games of Love* (Philippe de Broca, 1960) and *Ce soir ou jamais/Tonight or Never* (Michel Deville, 1961), also analysed by Sellier (2010) from the classic rom-com perspective of their negotiation of anxiety about female emancipation, but also some films by François Truffaut and even Jean-Luc Godard; and a number of other films from the 1960s to the 1990s by, in addition to de Broca and Deville, such directors as Jean-Paul Rappeneau, Jacques Demy and Eric Rohmer (see Harrod 2014).[3]

Such scholarly lacunae are inseparable from the snobbery around genre in general and comedy in particular that exists in many French cinephilic institutions. This is partly bound up with the ongoing legacy of both realist (see Hayward 2005: 98) and auteurist models there (see for example Prédal 1993: 54). Regarding the former, the status of filmic realism as itself reliant on formal and other conventions is now almost truistic in global film studies (see Hallam and Marshment 2000: 97–121). In any case, stylisation and blatant contrivance have already been shown to be exceptionally poor indicators of fictional texts' interrelation with and bearing on the external world.

As for the promotion of individual, idiosyncratic auteur styles, originally by the New Wave, it is easy to see how this clashes with the appeal to familiarity on which narrower conceptions of genre rest – despite the centrality of genre filmmakers like Alfred Hitchcock in elegiac New Wave writings about Hollywood. Moine (2002: 7) further constellates the rejection of genre with a general Gallic tendency to divorce films from their context. Indeed social relevance, especially gendered, is a facet routinely neglected by aesthetically-oriented work even on relatively popular auteurs like Demy, Truffaut or Rohmer. Romantic comedy is likely to suffer at the hands of critics bent on abstraction, notwithstanding the potentially more 'universal' elements of romantic discourse, because of its simultaneous, often comic, appeal to specific cultural knowledge.

Nor is bias against comedy limited to academics in France. For instance, the genre is frequently excluded from prestigious film awards like the Palme d'Or and the Césars. One particularly striking omission concerns the fate of 2008 smash hit comedy *Bienvenue chez les Ch'tis*. Despite attaining the record for the highest grossing French film ever in France, the film was almost absent from the Césars (and certainly from the even more unapologetically art cinema-oriented Cannes awards). In rom-com, it is more often those films positioned at the auteurist end of the spectrum, usually involving some stylistic experimentation – and often more consonant with a realist or melodramatic mode than with comedy – that achieve greater recognition. Exemplary are the Césars won by bitter-sweet, naturalistic ensemble piece *Vénus Beauté (Institut)* (Best Film, Best Director, Best Writing and Most Promising Actress for Audrey Tautou) or understated but intermittently visually surreal romance *Quand la mer monte* (Best Actress for Yolande Moreau, who also directed the film). Such prejudice is further replicated transnationally through distribution: even at London's Institut Français, whose film library is used primarily by Gallic expatriates for home entertainment, auteur films are more likely to be stocked than truly popular fare.

A further reason for hostility towards rom-com specifically emerges from this research: its original association with the USA. As Darren Waldron and Isabelle Vanderschelden (2007: 8) have argued, suspicious attitudes towards popular cinema have only been exacerbated in recent years by a French critical tendency among cinephilic critics, such as Jean-Michel Frodon in articles in *Cahiers du cinéma* from 2005 onwards, to equate commercial filmmaking with 'a multifaceted crisis' linked to inflated production costs and shorter cinema runs. The spectre of Hollywood looms large behind this negative perception of so-called multiplex culture. This negativity is itself partly a question of France's relatively Leftist politics; in any case the nation has a long history of cultural and trade disputes with the USA centred on the cinema. Pascal Ory (1989) has shown how postwar Franco-centrism developed in the 1980s into cultural-centrism. Lucy Mazdon (2000: 6–8) has moreover charted the way in which a French tendency since World War II to use the US as a foil against which to define itself led, through the issue of culture, to a mobilisation of anti-American discourses, in particular around the 1993 GATT trade agreements, in which cinema featured prominently.

At the same time, conversely, as Moine (2002: 27) has also noted, the elevation of comedy from other countries is another not uncommon discourse (see for example Audé 1989). Rom-com directors including Ernst Lubitsch and Howard Hawks were prominent among those Hollywood genre filmmakers venerated by the *politique des auteurs* and US rom-coms are still sometimes championed by the French press where domestic ones are not. This situation appears illogical in a context where the possibility of defining French cinema in any sense against Hollywood is complicated by the fact that:

> The practice of combining generic features drawn from a national cultural tradition with a form, references and generic paradigms that are at least perceived as belonging to a globalised neo-Hollywood model, constitutes one of the defining tendencies of contemporary French popular cinema. (Moine 2007a: 36)

King has further pointed out that the global dominance, since the Great War, of Hollywood *comedy* makes it difficult to pinpoint distinctly national dimensions, 'so strongly has the Hollywood version become associated with the fundamentals of the form' (2002: 164). This is also true of rom-com, which has been perceived as quintessentially American, thanks partially to the US' place at the forefront of the move towards gender equality.

Another major perceived threat to indigenous cinematic quality via popular output is television. Well-known scholar René Prédal's work is exemplary, asserting that the small screen is 'contaminating' and 'sucking the lifeblood' from a cinema already beleaguered by 'the hegemony of US production' (2008a: 36; see also Sorlin 2005). And once again such prejudices are likely to apply in great measure to (romantic) comedy, since a high proportion of not only artists but also filmmakers have moved into this genre from the arena of television in France in recent decades (Rollet 2010). These are often women, including such commercially successful figures as Valérie Guignabodet (*Mariages!*, 2 million tickets sold), Isabelle Mergault (*Je vous trouve très beau*, 3.4 million) and Lisa Azuelos (*LOL [Laughing Out Loud]*, 3.6 million).

The latter observation reflects the fact that many of the same cultural biases rampant in global discourses around rom-com apply in French film studies. The fact that women often come to popular filmmaking in France through television speaks to their exclusion from high French cinephilic culture (see Vincendeau 1987: 9), adding specific appeal to popular genres for them. Indeed, the final nail in the coffin for any specifically French history of romantic comedy studies has been the absence of cultural and gender studies as distinct disciplines in French academic institutions. While I have suggested that it is within this framework that many analyses of the genre have emerged in anglophone contexts, no equivalent has existed in France until very recently – despite the contributions of France-based scholars like Beauvoir, Emmanuel Levinas, Hélène Cixous, Monique Wittig, Julia Kristeva and Luce Irigaray to theories of gender. This bespeaks conservative attitudes towards the issue, explaining the absence of references not only to rom-com but also to romance itself even in books dealing specifically with genre in a French context (see Rollet 2008: 93).

It is important to note, however, that in the past two decades gradual changes have slowly begun to emerge in French scholarship. Moine's pioneering contribution to contemporary global and French genre studies is undoubtedly the most significant body of French scholarship relevant to this study – alongside, less directly, Sellier's cultural studies approaches to French cinema of earlier decades. Moine's extended studies (2002; 2005a) are highly significant in eroding longstanding boundaries – notably the opposition of auteur and popular cinema itself, as problematised by her (2005b) essay examining the emergence of the label *comédie d'auteur*, or auteur comedy, in the national press in the early 1990s. Such iconoclastic, cultural studies-informed approaches are also in evidence in the work of French scholars who write in both French and English, including, in addition to Rollet, Vanderschelden and Vincendeau. All these scholars' contributions to critical thought are helping to bridge the chasm that has, over the years, separated some aspects of French and anglophone critical thought.

French Romantic Comedy in Anglophone Film Studies

Despite the large body of anglophone work on French cinema, it is still the case that here too a very small proportion has focused on rom-coms or even comedies, with medium-brow genres like the thriller or the heritage film more likely to come under scrutiny.[4] As Jenny Lau has noted, 'the analysis of comedy is an exceptionally difficult task because the recognition of humour depends heavily upon understanding of the complex dynamics involved in the interaction of the symbolic, such as gestures and icons, linguistics and so on, which are defined by their own social and cultural tradition' (quoted in King 2002: 156). Equally, despite recent rom-com exports, the local referentiality of stars and narrative situations remains a barrier to popular cinema's international exhibition, alongside French cinema's 'arty' image (see Palmer 2011: 54, 117–20). Add to this global prejudices against rom-com, and the paucity of anglophone scholarship on the French genre comes as no real surprise.

By contrast, the French grotesque tradition has been one area accorded some interest in comedy, typically distracting attention from the gendered aspects of humorous film narratives (for example Gordon 2001). This blindness is frequently linked to the male buddy duos which are prevalent in national comedy (see for example Forbes 1992a: 177–84; Harris 1997), in that such a focus tends to ignore buddy films' generally sexist portrayal of female characters, who are objectified almost as a rule. It does, though, incorporate a degree of interest in the importance of stardom to comedy, picked up in the 2000s by Vanderschelden (2005), examining *beur* actors' increased opportunities for substantial success in the genre. Here the rom-com has contributed to the trend, with example cases including Moroccan-born Gad Elmaleh and to a lesser extent the half-Algerian Dany Boon, who – along with Gallic rom-coms stars like Alain Chabat and Edouard Baer – are among the highest paid French actors.

The fact that all these actors are also stand-up comics illustrates intersections between romantic and comedian comedy. Indeed, the space the genre creates for women is particularly significant in light of comic theory's stress on the cultural power of joke-makers. Of course, comedians' status is subject to considerable variation even within films clearly built around their performance, notably depending on their involvement in the screenwriting and directorial process, and the linked balance between their characters' construction as either teller or butt of the joke, or between the combination 'identification and distanciation' (Neale and Krutnik 1990: 149) typically identifiable with comedy. But in general the accession to a position of relative (discursive) power of groups – notably women – traditionally seen to be disenfranchised within patriarchy is a remarkable and positive development (see Tarr with Rollet 2001: 166–7).

The same understanding of jokes has led to many comic theorists noting that one of the major ways in which social groups define themselves is through shared humour, in turn suggesting why the issue of inherited comic forms may be a particularly sensitive one in a nation with a great comic heritage, where the perception of national culture under threat is widespread. It is significant, too, that French culture is often seen as menaced specifically by the USA, the same nation from which the rom-com notionally hails. In this genre, nationalism is a clear candidate for the 'other less orthodox satisfactions' of identity for which Frank Krutnik (2002: 142) and others have argued the genre can be an alibi. For all these reasons, the rom-com's significance for French identity, conceived either nationally or transnationally, is a master theme of this study.

It is therefore appropriate to conclude this survey by citing an analysis of French rom-com from a US perspective. The genre is present in all but name in observations by Suzanne Ferriss and Mallory Young about the development of a new European form of romantic chick flick, following the Anglo-American 'prescriptions' for such films. Interestingly, while for Ferriss and Young the pertinence of the anglophone paradigm resides in 'a far more sanguine view of love' than that of European forebears, 'with surprisingly feel-good endings', these scholars suggest the 'European' contribution discernible in their examples is the element of naturalism This study also provides a welcome, industrially-informed overview of movements in European cinema and specifically the disintegration of the old perceived dichotomy between European art versus US commerce, due to the transnational influence of not only Hollywood but also American indie culture, as well as the mass-crossing of European 'talent' to North America and the surprisingly high volume of European films receiving wide US distribution (Ferriss and Young 2008b: 176–7). This chapter thus contains the germ of my own key concern: to consider the specificity of the French rom-com while understanding its ultimately markedly transnational position – and in particular position*ing*.

2

Romance Today

In this chapter I attempt to place what is broadly understood by the notion of romantic love more fully in its contemporary French context, as it is manifested in and through romantic comedy. I begin in the first section by examining those influences on the genre that might be seen as exogenous, in other words aspects of social change that remain relatively separable from perceptions of love relationships for couples per se, but that nonetheless impact on them in various ways. Grouped together under the umbrella concept of today's 'cold climate', these include new living arrangements (and specifically the move away from community and family that has gathered pace, especially in urban conglomerations, since the Industrial Revolution), as well as the 'dehumanisation' of work in the post-Fordist era and the effects of new technologies on courting rituals. Secondly, such changes encompass the far-reaching effects of the so-called death of God, as well as the more recent rise of Allah, on attitudes towards coupling. In the latter half of the chapter I examine the French rom-com's interaction with changes that have been more fully internalised in ideas circulating around love and relationships themselves. Here the term 'post-romance' designates the complex nexus of discourses, both incorporating and transcending traditional romantic ideas, that inform contemporary notions of the couple and of intimate relations between its members.

Love in a Cold Climate[1]

If, as proclaimed by Anna Gavalda's best-selling 2004 novel and its César-winning 2007 film version, 'togetherness is everything'

(*Ensemble, c'est tout*), then post-modern life, with its increasingly fragmented social organisation, is teetering on the brink of the abyss. The re-imagining of space since modernity has been a major focus of academic enquiry over the last half-century or so. Post-modern histories and theorisations of changes to the organisation of social space chart the way in which urban living's challenge to traditional community structures has accelerated since the 1980s, largely due to the technical revolution, an idea popularised by the metaphor of the global village. In conjunction with the changes such developments have wrought in the world of work, this spatial reconfiguration has meant that face-to-face physical encounters are ever rarer and anonymous communication has become normalised. The perceived resulting disintegration of interpersonal relationships has been a major focus of recent Western fiction as a whole, notably in the strain of social realism prominent in French auteur cinema of the 1990s, associated with such directors as Robert Guédiguian, Erick Zonca and Bruno Dumont. It is also remarkable that in an increasingly mobile world, romantic relationships have themselves gained considerable significance as a determinant of living arrangements, in contrast with parental and familial links.

As for the decline of religion in the West, while this predates the rise of urbanism, it is the combination of the two that has, arguably, left many human beings consigned to solitude, adrift in a cold modern world. This has clear repercussions for the status of romance today, most obviously providing a compelling explanation for the discourse's increasing cultural prestige. Thus, in a French context, philosopher Gilles Lipovetsky (1993: 316) describes the (post-)modern 'era of emptiness' in terms of 'individualism à la carte, hedonistic and psychological, elevating intimate fulfilment to the highest goal of existence'. The comforting presences of both God and community have, in other words, both been replaced by The One, placing huge stress on the love relationship. This is reflected, too, by legislation: in France, the 1999 PaCS (Pacte Civil de Solidarité) laws – a milestone in the history of romantic unions in a Catholic country – ratified desire alone as a sufficient basis for a relationship (Holmes 2006: 115).[2] Additionally, since the events of 9/11 mobilised the possibilities of the shrinking world to annihilative ends, there has been something of a resurgence of interest in religion, notably Islam, but secondarily, in response to this, perhaps also in Christianity (Wheatley 2014). Indirect though their relationship to cinematic romance may seem, these new developments too are making their mark in different ways on the French romantic comedy.

Post-Industrial Pairings

The loneliness of singlehood is a subtext of many contemporary rom-coms and French examples are no exception. In several cases, this is directly premised on fragmented urban lifestyles; and typically, it is women who are perceived as suffering most from the disintegration of interpersonal structures in post-industrial life. At the same time, urban solitude goes hand in hand with urban freedom and the rom-com also evidences recognition of the new opportunities for romance afforded by life in post-industrial cities. The genre thus frequently envisions the metropolis as a playground of possibilities, typically peopled by what *Elle* magazine journalist Dorothée Werner (1996) has described as a perpetually infantilised twenty-something (and now perhaps also thirty-something) generation. The preeminent, early example of this form of thematically highly post-modern rom-com, also setting up a number of specific subtrends associated with such an optic, is *Amélie*. For this reason and in view of its probable role in catalysing the rom-com's French appropriation (see Rollet 2008: 92), I have chosen to open this chapter's more text-based section by analysing it in detail.

Case Study: Le Fabuleux destin d'Amélie Poulain/Amelie (Jean-Pierre Jeunet, 2001)

Directed by crossover popular/auteur director Jean-Pierre Jeunet, who was until then known for fantastic, visually sumptuous collaborations with Marc Caro, *Le Fabuleux destin d'Amélie Poulain* was by and large French-funded, including through contributions from television channels Canal + and France 3. Drawing over 8.5 million spectators into French cinemas and taking more than $33 million at the US box office alone, the globally distributed mega-hit at home represented not just a financial success but a social phenomenon. Despite sparking considerable critical controversy thanks to a now infamous article by *Inrockuptibles* editor Serge Kaganski accusing it of promoting a socially and ethnically cleansed vision of France (Kaganski 2001), the iconic Parisian rom-com was embraced by politicians across the spectrum, who publicly declared their love for the film and organised personal screenings of it (Vincendeau 2001: 22). So influential was *Amélie* perceived to be, in fact, it has been credited, by a feature in *Biba* magazine, with leading to a communitarian tendency in French cities like Paris and Lyon, through the establishment of residents' associations and the resurgence of small-scale local commerce in the wake of its release (see Austin 2008: 160).

Since rom-com was not yet recognised as an indigenous genre in France in 2001, French reviewers and commentators – unlike those in the US and Britain, including in readily available online critiques – did not describe the film in such terms, and nor have any of the various scholarly articles (including Rosello 2002; Scatton-Tessier 2004; Ezra 2004; Moore 2006; Morrissey 2008; Bazgan 2010) and one book (Vanderschelden 2007) dedicated to the film considered it substantially from a generic perspective. Nonetheless, *Amélie* is a romantic fairy-tale set in a digitally reconstructed Paris, in which the eponymous female protagonist actively seeks out apparently blissful fusion with an idealised (she has never spoken to him) love object, pornographic DVD rental shop employee Nino (Mathieu Kassovitz). The couple are finally paired atop a scooter for a final sequence whose grainy, home-video look, upbeat music and fast editing style encode ebullient happiness: '[as] the end of the film [...] brings the hitherto star-crossed lovers together, the sheer predictability of their union, the "fabulous", storybook fulfilment of Amelie's "destin", recalls the ending of countless Hollywood films' (Ezra 2004: 309).

The film has, however, simultaneously been correctly identified as 'well anchored in its socio-historical and cinematic period, exploiting the same issues of loneliness and isolation found in recent French new social cinema' (Scatton-Tessier 2004: 197). This is most obvious in the narrator's account of loner Amelie's cold upbringing, during which her increased heartbeat due to excitement during a physical examination by her emotionally distant doctor father leads to mistaken fears about a heart condition and a cloistered, subdued childhood which has left her inept at relating to others. More generally, the voiceover and dialogue emphasise language's limited power to reveal people. Hence the narrator's method of introducing characters by a list of dislikes and dislikes, or a scene in which Amelie's colleague Gina acquaints herself with Nino via the nonspecific verbiage of proverbs, while Amelie's father is explicitly depicted as asking her the same old questions and failing to listen to her. Visually, too, Jeunet's use of crane shots as

Figure 1. Boxed in: urban living gone awry as Amelie and neighbours dine alone. © UGC

well as mirrors and glass 'symbolically enhance[s Amelie's] isolation' (Vanderschelden 2007: 49–50). It is the desire to overcome this alienation that propels the plot's trajectory towards romantic union. In other words, the film subscribes to the rom-com format epitomised by *When Harry Met Sally*, where romance is prescribed first and foremost as a bulwark against loneliness.

Amelie's solitude is portrayed as deriving in large measure from fragmented post-modern, paradigmatically urban, life. The failure of her own family to nurture her emotionally (also due to her mother's untimely death) is figuratively extended to Nino's experience by an ironic interjection in relation to the latter's habit of putting back together passport-style photos ripped up and discarded by strangers and collecting them in an album. Thus the narrator recounts Amelie's reaction to this curiosity as, 'Some family album!'. Indeed, families as a whole are conspicuous by their absence (Morrissey 2008: 107). More generally, the film is explicitly nostalgic for the extended community of Montmartre it depicts as in decline: Amelie's plots to improve the lives of those around her represent a refusal to accept compartmentalised living of the kind graphically illustrated by shots of her and other inhabitants of her apartment building engaged in everyday activities, simultaneously but on their own [Figure 1]. Wendy Everett has for her part described *Amélie* as 'fractal', or a 'filmic portrayal[s] of urban space which is no longer shaped by the linear mappings of modernity, but is posited as both entirely random and yet at the same time structured by complexity, simultaneity, and violent encounters' (Everett 2005: 159). Conversely, but equally negatively as regards the representation of contemporary urban life, for Jim Morrissey, Jeunet's film seeks 'fear[fully]' (2008: 109) to bring Paris' chaotic aspects to order by digitally recreating the city through an old-fashioned optic – one that has provoked numerous comparisons with the photographs of Robert Doisneau and the films of Jacques Prévert and Marcel Carné.

Rick Clifton Moore's discussion of the film's attitude towards post-modern technology meanwhile invokes the concept of 'machineness', to show that in several instances within the film 'mechanisation in work leads to mechanisation in relations' (2006: 15). Examples given include the automatism of a Metro employee who stares blankly when Amelie poses a philosophical question and asks for her ticket; the habit of Amelie's neighbour Collignon, retained from his working days, of punching holes, nowadays in leaves; and the painter Dufayel's obsessive repainting of the same thing. The film in this way affirms post-Marxist prognostics about the alienating effects of capitalism; as Charles Levin has put it summarising Baudrillard, '[man] defines himself through his work – give him back some real work' (Levin 1981: 12), and Amelie is no exception, introducing herself to Dufayel with the uninspiring label of her job as a waitress. It also suggests the limited place of Art in hypermodernity, since both Dufayel's and the writer Hipolito's activities are restricted to dilettantism and a seemingly fruitless search for 'truth'.

Moore further points out the false note sounded by *Amelie*'s all but obligatory (in rom-com) happy ending, Indeed, our heroine has undergone no major personality change since orchestrating her meeting with Nino through a series of manipulations so convoluted he calls her a 'borderline sociopath' (Moore 2006: 16). The narrator's explanation of both characters' longing for the sibling they never had desexualises their relationship. Even in the final sequence of implied congress – during which they exchange no words – their interaction is remarkably chaste, as they ritualistically kiss each other, for example, on the eyes, also affirming the film's celebration of the visible over the inner life. Moore notes that the post-coital shot of Amelie and Nino in bed together is captured from the same angle as an earlier one in which Amelie was shown to be disengaged in sexual encounters, suggesting that this betrays her continued lack of involvement. Although this comparison could in principle be seen to foreground contrast, rather than sameness, Vanderschelden (2007: 35–6) has similarly highlighted the film's repetitions and circular motifs, such as the merry-go-round and the insistent waltz on the sound-track. Not only that but the film's major secondary romance, between Amelie's colleague Georgette and regular customer Joseph, is already falling apart, as he tortures her with jealousy. Moore is therefore justified in dubbing the final sequence 'a series of seemingly incoherent (or irrational) images' (2006: 16–17). At this point, Jeunet's famous playful Flaubertian echo, '*Amélie* Poulain, c'est moi' (quoted in Vincendeau 2001: 25) becomes meaningful in a secondary, unintended way. For not only do the similarities between Amelie – manipulator of images and maker of myths – and the film director abound, but just as scores of rural French women ignored the ironies of *Madame Bovary*'s satire on readers of romantic literature and championed it as sympathetically recounting their lives, so those viewers who left *Amélie* feeling warmed inside chose to overlook the hollowness of its conclusion. Like many post-classical Hollywood rom-coms, then, at close inspection *Amélie* speaks paradoxically to the inadequacy of romance as a panacea. A statement by Amelie's boss, for whom 'passionate love [*les coups de foudre*] exists but it's manufactured – and there's a recipe', refers self-reflexively to the film's generic makeup.

However, Moore's discussion stresses overall the ambivalence to technology on display in *Amélie*, just as Morrissey's appraisal of the film's negative attitude towards the (pro-filmic) city of Paris is counterbalanced by Nicoleta Bazgan's claims that it in fact 'is a love story about Paris as well' (Bazgan 2010: 103). Aesthetically, the film revels in the possibilities afforded by modern technologies, and enormous vibrancy is imparted to the narrative by Jeunet's exuberant, digitally enhanced vision of Paris as a hyper-modern playground where poetic realism meets virtual reality. Moreover, as also noted by Scatton-Tessier (2004), dynamic mobility is presented in the narrative as the upside of the post-modern condition, as for example in the many fast-paced shots of Amelie traversing the city by Metro. The manic quality lent these sequences by their rapid editing may betray a desperate need for frenetic activity as distraction from the inner emptiness that threatens at moments of quietude (or on one occasion, for Morrissey, 'communicate a sense of nausea' [2008: 106]) but they also invite a certain breathless pleasure for the spectator transported to the four corners of Jeunet's colourful toy-town metropolis. Indeed, the viewer's relationship to the film here arguably becomes less analytical than experiential, in the manner of the theme park rides that feature in the film and as theorised by some scholars of digital cinema (Bukatman 1998; Balides 2004).

Amélie further reflects in a more positive way the recent shift in patterns of human interaction by having its couple actually meet in the Metro, an example of what Marc Augé (1995) has dubbed 'non-places', or places of transience too insignificant to be regarded as places. Augé cites Michel de Certeau's discussion of *spaces*, or busy public places, like those inhabited by the characters in these films, to suggest that to frequent such spaces is 'to be other, and go over to the other, in a place' (Augé 1995: 83): a fusional regression to the experience of infancy that psychoanalysis identifies as driving human desire for the other. Interestingly, Radway's (1991) ethnographically researched study of popular literary romance in 1980s North America draws on psychoanalyst Nancy Chodorow's work in order to argue for romances' status as a pleasurable re-enactment of the girl's Oedipal drama, with a positive conclusion appended. Her description relies in great measure on portrayals of heroines' loneliness prior to finding heterosexual love. Vincendeau (2005) has identified Audrey Tautou's star persona – largely but not exclusively since this film – with childlike innocence, while Scatton-Tessier (2004: 203) links the film's fascination with surface pleasures (such as skimming stones), or *petisme*, with immaturity. In the same vein, Moore (2006: 14) remarks on the narrative contiguity of Amelie's child and adulthoods and cites Ellul and R. Stivers' association of puerility with the kind of 'technological personality' he attributes to her. Her depiction certainly fits Freud's profile of the extremely submissive woman who is, for Moore, one possible result of a poorly resolved Electra complex (see also Roux 2001).

The frequently female-gendered nature of post-modern loneliness is perhaps *Amélie*'s most important legacy for the French rom-com. However, it sets up additional structuring themes and tropes for the contemporary genre, giving rise to categories for discussion in the rest of this section. These are, in addition to urban solitude, 'machine-ness' in work and social relations and the decline of traditional family and community structures in favour of contingent arrangements based on tenuous networks of more distant relationships, all of which become firmly entrenched features of French rom-coms over the next decade.

I. Solitude and the City

Amélie is only one of several French rom-coms to make an ambivalent generic virtue of the new experiences offered by increased mobility today in urban contexts that are given considerable prominence both aesthetically and narratively. For instance, several films of the genre produced in the next few years (as well as at least one earlier one, *Vénus Beauté [Institut]* [1999]), including *Décalage horaire* (2002), *Clara et moi/Clara and Me* (Arnaud Viard, 2004), *Où avais-je la tête?* (Nathalie Donnini, 2007) and *Je vais te manquer/You'll Miss Me* (Amanda Sthers, 2009), reflect the recent shift in patterns of human interaction by having a couple meet in places of transience – in these films either airports or, in *Clara et moi*, the Metro. Even more than *Amélie*'s Nino, who, in accordance with that film's preservation of some degree of community, worked in a local DVD shop (albeit for porn), these pairings represent a post-modern twist on the traditional notion of the girl next door – the girl, if you like, in the next-door seat.

On the one hand, there is something celebratory in the new potential for cross-cultural dialogue theoretically afforded by the encounters which all these films stage in liminal spaces of possibility – although, unsurprisingly for this genre, in all these examples the couple are both French, white and broadly middle-class. The pleasurably regressive qualities of the non-place in Augé's formulation are again reflected in these rom-coms' stress on wonder and fantasy – especially where characters' childlike aspects are emphasised, as in *Décalage horaire* and *Où avais-je la tête*, both of which are also indebted to *Romuald et Juliette* in having an uptight businessman rediscover childish abandon through a bubbly and somewhat chaotic female character. However, alongside their partial disavowal of contemporary isolation through blissful fusion across the wide gulf separating strangers, these narratives also speak to the disadvantages of anonymous existences. Notably, in Tonie Marshall's *Vénus Beauté*, for singleton Angèle, her work as a Parisian beautician appears first and foremost a refuge from the unwelcoming winter cityscape, thanks to Marshall's carefully constructed mise-en-scène. The credit sequence's neon pink writing against a black background, set to a mournfully twanging guitar, anticipates the contrast between the artificial lights of the salon's feminised space, where customers take a pause for themselves and undergo 'magical' transformations, and the cold, gleaming surfaces of sombre streets and public places. These are glimpsed fleetingly, in low-key lighting that leaves patches of blackness and often also filmed out of focus, suggesting an unknowable world only distantly related to Angèle. This sense of the faintly menacing otherness of the city is conveyed by the film's opening scene, which shows Angèle silently tidying up the salon for the night amid the space's trademark reassuring warm glow, still to the credit music and through the glass of the salon front, which is framed by a darkness threatening to encroach from all sides. As she finally turns off the lights to leave a cold blue hue, a biting violin joins the score at the same moment that the growling sounds and ugly forms of traffic invade the soundtrack and the foreground respectively, before she is whisked off on a bus. It should be noted that such a severe portrayal of Paris contrasts strongly with recent classically romantic portrayals of France's capital city in films designed for export such as *2 Days in Paris* (Julie Delpy, 2007) or *Midnight in Paris* (Allen, USA 2011). Nonetheless, depicting city life in a 'realistic' way is about more than targeting the urban audiences that make up the majority of cinema-goers in France (as elsewhere).

While Angèle meets her love interest in a train station, three years later in 2002 Danièle Thompson notes in interview that her playful use of a lost mobile phone to bring the central couple together in Charles de Gaulle Airport in *Décalage horaire* gestures towards the serious issue of the communication breakdown endemic in contemporary society (Baudin 2002). This is further (mis-)communicated throughout the film by the central male protagonist Félix's verbal confusion, as he speaks in a turbulent Franglais that is the product of his cultural disorientation as a Frenchman living in the USA. In *Clara et moi* the couple's first interaction or 'meet cute' (see Mortimer 2010: 5–6) (a phrase that again picks up on the regressive elements of romance) echoes Amelie and Nino's aphasia. Just as Montmartre's modern-day good fairy communicates with her love object through a trail of written messages, so Antoine (Julien Boisselier), seeing beautiful stranger Clara (Julie Gayet) opposite him on the train, opts to write a note requesting a date. Since the impossibility of expressing love through a language plagued by cliché is an increasingly explicit staple of rom-com (Krutnik 2002: 138–9), this neatly avoids the problem, emphasising instead the actors' faces, shot in endearing close-ups as shy smiles steal across them. This moment of emotional warmth stands out all the more – indeed it was commented on by several reviewers – for its contextualisation in a mise-en-scène whose chilly, grey-toned palette and naturalistic lighting, captured at times digitally through a hand-held camera, reinforces the social realist codification of the frequently drab Parisian setting. Similarly, the anchorage of events in the real world makes it still more surprising when, at their first date against the romantic backdrop of the Seine by night, in a daring act of generic contortionism, the couple burst into a romantic song complete with dancing. Even within the musical number, however, tonal disjunction is preserved, as the couple's thin voices, more Demy than George Cukor, accompany inexpert, rather tentative dance steps.

These chinks in *Clara et moi*'s romantic overlay, and the human frailty of Clara's wavering voice in particular, pave the way for a plot development which brings to the fore the dark side of today's cultural freedoms: Clara's diagnosis as HIV positive. Occurring suddenly and without foreshadowing, this development prompts the film to lurch for the remainder of its duration into a melodramatic register. Specifically, although Antoine decides after much soul-searching that his love for Clara transcends the material challenges posed by her affliction, in a shock ending diverging from the rom-com's typical levelling of difference, it is Clara who rejects Antoine, saying she does not believe he will make her happy, presumably because of his initial failure to support her following her diagnosis. What is interesting is the suggestion that it is precisely those freedoms that have brought Antoine and Clara together – and indeed are celebrated through intimate bedroom sequences replete with aestheticised views of Gayet's breasts – that finally prove the obstacle to their love.

In *Clara et moi*, then, today's anonymous urban encounter, emblematically figured as finding love in a non-place, functions ambivalently, as opening up new possibilities only at the cost of old ideals of chaste femininity. This conjunction of ideas constitutes an obvious point at which to return to, and address directly, the ways in which the fragmentation of post-industrial living is represented in gendered ways in the rom-com. Women's centrality in the romantic drama of solitude is reflected by the cultural currency in France of the notion of 'Bridget Jones syndrome' (Anon 2002b; Rollet 2010), while Érika Flahault (1999) has identified anti-feminist images of female solitude as frequent in the French media since the 1970s. In fact, *Clara et moi* is unusual in presenting a woman who, faced with a display of male egotism, opts to remain single. The fact that she is hosting a party when Antoine begs her to take him back suggests, refreshingly, that this may be a positive choice.

Amélie's insistence on the desolation of female singlehood in an urban environment is, however, more typical, and reinforced by rom-coms that both precede and follow it, including *Vénus Beauté* (1999), *Irène* (Ivan Calbérac, 2002), *J'me sens pas belle/ Tell Me I'm Pretty* (Bernard Jeanjean, 2004) and *Tricheuse/ So Woman!* (Jean-François Davy, 2009). *Vénus Beauté* is relatively subtle on this point, offering a telling contrast between female and male attitudes towards coupling relations, when Angèle promises a stranger sex in order to have him listen to her relationship troubles. The humour of her interlocutor's diffident but increasingly evident impatience arises from the fact that audiences are assumed to take it as read that men have little need for the kind of emotional connection the female character is attempting to achieve. Focused on a higher socio-economic stratum, both *Irène* and *Tricheuse* depict dissatisfied white-collar women (both in fact working in law). The more prominent earlier films stars Cécile de France as the eponymous heroine, whose dissatisfaction at singlehood is portrayed as both social (she finds her parents' ongoing enquiries about her love-life upsetting) and sexual (she fantasises about naked men whom she hardly knows). Like Tautou – and to some extent Gayet in *Clara et moi*, with whom she shares prominent gappy front teeth and a boyish haircut – de France is physically childlike, as reflected by press that has described her 'eternal role of little bird fallen from the nest' (Morain 2006b). This is further underlined in this film by her character's marked clumsiness and her consistent framing alone and overwhelmed by expanses of empty space around her. It is noteworthy that Irène does not even mingle with crowds on the Metro but travels in the self-contained bubble of a car, observing the world at a distance through a pane of glass. This post-modern version of the *femme-enfant* is, then, less a question of titillation in the manner of a Bardot than a means to visually express the vulnerability of the human 'atom' uprooted from community structures in today's metropolis: what one observer of Tautou has described as a 'modern fragililty' (Gili 2007: 28). Irène's solitude is only magnified by an expensive but soulless apartment, in a building where interaction with neighbours is limited to passing civilities. Her unhappiness and overt availability also belies a friend's indignant insistence, on the topic of parental pressure to marry, that families should realise that being single can be a choice – a comment which is echoed in frank reverse two years later by the hangdog female heroine (Marina Foïs) of *J'me sens pas belle* ('Being alone can be great – if it's a choice').

II. The 'Machineness' of (post)Modern Relations

In this section I examine more directly how the French rom-com mediates the impact of technological developments (beyond transport networks) on romantic relationships. In the first instance, I examine the recurrence of secondary themes around job satisfaction relating to the technological age, tending – as so often – to fall into gendered patterns. Secondly, I analyse a trend for rom-coms featuring anonymous communication networks as a forum for courtship.

Professional dissatisfaction is a common theme of French rom-coms. The topos of the failing artist or craftsman recurs in most of the films alluded to so far in this chapter, including *Clara et moi, Ensemble, c'est tout/ Hunting and Gathering* (Claude Berri, 2007) and *Décalage horaire*. Most directly concerned with the interrelation between romantic and professional identities, though, is *Mensonges et trahisons et plus si affinités/The Story of My Life* (Laurent Tirard, 2002), the first part of whose title (literally, *Lies and Betrayals*) refers to its male protagonist Raphaël's (Edouard Baer) job as a ghostwriter. A considerable proportion of the narrative is taken up with Raphaël's professional life, which is described as a failure and narrated with black humour, as when his work is slated by his publisher or when a footballer, whose biography he has been hired to write, tells Raphaël he finds his writing pretentious, but that he would prefer something in the style of Baudelaire! In secondary plots, too, one of Raphaël's best friends has explicitly 'sold out' by working for a large corporation, and later suffers a breakdown, while the other abandons a career in advertising for a more fulfilling one in photojournalism and, dying in an accident, is martyred to the cause of truth. The indivisibility of romantic and professional satisfaction as interweaving aspects of the construction of the self is made explicit in *Mensonges* through Raphaël's remark that for him writing and women have always been closely linked. This comment highlights the intersections between romance and Romanticism. What the two discourses share is their emphasis on the individual and his or her imagination. It is therefore logical that one way to endow characters in broadly realistically depicted worlds with the extraordinariness that makes them classic rom-com protagonists is through giving them artistic aspirations. The subtext of Raphaël's words to his newborn son at the film's close, telling him his father is (now that he has published an original novel) a writer, is that he is not just anyone but *someone*: in publishing his own work he has in fact attained the status of a character in not one but two grand narratives.

However, all these films make gendered assumptions about professionalism. Female professionalism is belittled, through a combination of female characters' consignment to relatively low-status jobs and/or a suggestion that work alone cannot fulfil women (see Negra 2004: 3), which is particularly germane for the concerns of romantic comedy. Thus Irène, who failed as a lawyer and became a high-level notary (*juriste*) answers to a much older male boss, who at times berates her unfairly; and the seeming meaninglessness of her corporate job is later contrasted with the artistic background of the man with whom the film comes closest to coupling Irène (although the ending remains open), musician turned painter-decorator François. Equally, while romance allows the male characters in *Décalage, Clara et moi, Ensemble, c'est tout* and *Mensonges* to access their creative potential, in the first two films lower-status jobs appear satisfactory for the female leads (a beautician and a train hostess respectively); *Ensemble* excludes the female character from the trajectory to professional satisfaction enjoyed by her two male counterparts; and in *Mensonges*, despite female protagonist Muriel's high-status position as an architect, the value of her success is undermined by the revelation of a previous suicide attempt following a break-up. Additionally, Muriel's perceived masculinisation through her job, underscored by images of her wearing a hard hat, appears to contribute to Raphaël's initial refusal to commit to her. Moreover, architecture still retains a lower status in a Romantic individualist schema than Raphaël's literary calling. In this example, faced with women's penetration of all professional spheres, the world of work itself is denigrated by negative comparison with artistic vocations still by and large held up as male property, especially in male-authored films. It is left, in fact, to female filmmaker Thompson to endow a female character with a desire for (creative) professional self-affirmation entirely outstripping romantic need in her most recent film *Le Code a changé/Change of Plans* (2009). Thus, Sarah, (Emmanuèle Seigner) voluntarily separates from her oppressive husband and attains success as a writer – although even here her authorship of children's literature remains outside the male-dominated 'high' literary canon. This diminution of female characters in professional roles in the rom-com is perhaps predictable given the genre's potential role in preserving the couple against the challenges female professionalism has posed to it.

Another detail shared by both *Irène* and *Mensonges* is their allocation of a role to anonymous communication networks in coupling. In *Mensonges* this is limited to a secondary romantic plot involving one of Raphaël's friends, who searches for love via the internet. But it is extremely prominent in the first film, which provides an extensive exploration of online courtship. Early in the film, Irène's nascent relationship with a white-collar colleague, Luca, is accorded greater attention than her interaction with François. When Luca tells her he is being transferred to Tokyo, the couple are reduced to internet communication. What follows is a wryly humorous comment on the dehumanising aspect of corporate life – and the technical revolution as a whole – which finds comedy where a film such as recent auteur polemic piece *La Question humaine/Heartbeat Detector* (Nicolas Klotz, 2007) found dark drama. Irène and Luca decide to have internet sex, using webcams, prompting some initial reluctance from her and a comical false start, when the screen freezes. Hilarity is likely to turn, though, to nervous laughter on the part of the viewer when the pair actually start to enjoy this new form of intercourse and, in a hollow parody of post-coital intimacy, are portrayed 'side by side' on her bed, but with Luca's face on the computer screen [Figure 2]. As much as Michel Houellebecq's well-known 1998 novel *Les Particules élémentaires*, this storyline presents an unsettling vision of a contemporary society demanding, in the titular words of Slavoj Žižek in an article inspired by Houellebecq's narrative, 'No Sex, Please! We're Post-Human' – and all the more so when it is revealed that Luca has lied about being in Tokyo because this is his preferred way of conducting his relationships.

Failed internet dates in *Laisse tes mains sur mes hanches/Leave Your Hands on My Hips* (Chantal Lauby, 2003) and *Je préfère qu'on reste amis* (Olivier Nakache and Eric Toledano, 2005) imply that searching for a compatible partner by such means is a game with difficult odds. More recently Josiane Balasko's controversial film *Cliente/A French Gigolo* (2008) explores internet dating via prostitution, by featuring Nathalie Baye as a seemingly well-adjusted, successful bourgeois businesswoman in her fifties, who hires male 'escorts' to romance and seduce her. Of

Figure 2. Post-modern intimacy in *Irène*. © M6 Droits Audiovisuels

particular note is her voiceover reflection that she first stumbled on the escort website by accident, and was attracted by the profile of a man who shared her still beloved ex-husband's name. This detail softens the anonymity of the experience, and the recollection as a whole aligns it with the more acceptable practice of internet dating; however this in turn underlines the businesslike aspect of all these ways of finding a mate. Balasko's film makes no moral critique of prostitution, depicting a real fondness, attraction and respect between Irène and Marco; but nor is this relationship finally posited as satisfying all Irène's romantic desires, as Marco eventually returns to his wife, leaving her weeping.[3]

A comparable trend for featuring not just internet but blind and/or speed dating also emerges in films of the 2000s, including *Mensonges et trahisons* (in the secondary romance), *Je préfère qu'on reste amis* (2005) and, in passing, *Célibataires* (Jean-Michel Verner) and *Prête-moi ta main*, both from 2006. Of course, the comic potential of the blind date has not gone unnoticed by the Hollywood rom-com either (recent examples feature in *Dan in Real Life* [Peter Hedges, USA 2007] and *He's Just Not That Into You* [Ken Kwapis, USA/Germany/Netherlands 2009]) and their presence can to an extent be seen as a pretext for jokes. Thus a split-screen montage shows *Prête-moi*'s Luis opposite an unappealing selection of the friends with whom his sisters have tried to set him up, culminating in a man. In *Mensonges*, Raphaël's corporate friend Max's experience of speed-dating appears discomfiting in the extreme, as his interlocutors' conversation veers from the banal to the excessively intimate ('I like theatre but not fellatio'). Worse, his own repeated opening gambit of quoting his salary is a parody of the reduction of sexual relations to commodification effected in Houellebecq's novels. Later, though, following Max's nervous breakdown – after attacking a woman he met speed dating – and then his subsequent re-sensitisation, Max discovers the 'true' worth of love as mutual appreciation and the familial values more traditionally endorsed by the rom-com genre, when he starts a family with an East Asian bride, having explicitly travelled to this part of the world with the purpose of helping a woman out of poverty. So *Mensonges*, too, for all its ambivalence about the realities of speed dating, in the end speaks of a slow move towards endorsement of highly contrived encounters as an increasingly legitimate means to find fulfilling love.[4]

The films discussed so far in this section can all be seen to explore the implications of the decline of traditional community and family, in turn linked to the rise of urban living and changes in work patterns. Despite the pleasures and convenience offered by city life, loneliness and professional dissatisfaction are structuring themes, most often but not exclusively for female characters. The absence of traditional communities also places greater emphasis on anonymous networks as a way to meet a life partner, a trend that is viewed ambivalently by the rom-com. In the examples above a virtual community temporarily replaces – and generally provides a poor substitute for – a real one. In several romantic comedies, though, the family is more directly replaced by a physically present but loosely structured network of friends and colleagues.

Coupling Choral

I. Familial Failings

In this section I take up an argument made by Powrie (2007) in a French context and María del Mar Azcona (2010: 6–7) in a global one: that an abundance of multi-protagonist films produced in the past 20 years responds in a reassuring manner to the *absence* of old-fashioned, close-knit networks. More specifically, Powrie sees the decline of the traditional family reflected in films that celebrate groups of associates, which he calls tribal or surrogate families. Such constellations of characters are strikingly visible in the rom-com. Moreover, it is significant that the failure of the family as a refuge or adequate support is frequently an explicit secondary theme of the contemporary French rom-com. This is true to some extent across the board, even in dyadic rom-coms. In *Irène*, for example, when the heroine is at her lowest ebb, in tears over a romantic rift and utterly alone, her mother telephones only to ask about a missing piece of clothing. Nonetheless, families on the whole appear either more conspicuously absent or much more heavily critiqued in tribal, or community, ensemble films of the kind theorised by Powrie.

Family absence is emphasised in a film starring Guillaume Canet and another directed by the actor-director. In Berri's *Ensemble, c'est tout*, a miniature community grows up in an apartment block. Franck (Canet) spends his weekends journeying by scooter to see his grandmother, apparently the only relative with whom he is in contact, in an old people's home. Later a utopian storyline sees her liberated, cared for by Franck and his neighbour, then flatmate, then lover, Camille (Tautou). The English title *Hunting and Gathering* gestures overtly to the trope of the tribe in the narrative. Rom-com elements also intermittently adorn a melodramatic backdrop in the top French film at the national box office in 2010, *Les Petits mouchoirs/Little White Lies* (Canet), wherein a group of friends (and in some cases their spouses and children) converge on a holiday house, while one of their number languishes in hospital in a coma. The way in which friends occupy a space traditionally reserved for family in the narrative is underlined by interpolated home-video footage of the group – including the invalid Ludo – on former holidays. However, the fact that Ludo dies without having been visited by many of those closest to him, as they are busy enjoying sun and sea, is a locus for guilt and resentment among the group, suggesting the limitations of friends as a substitute for family.

As in *Ensemble, c'est tout*, a grandmother stands in for the nuclear family in *Fauteuils d'orchestre/Orchestra Seats* (Danièle Thompson, 2006), which comments more directly on the pluses and minuses of family ties. This character provides a frame narrative through an opening voiceover in which she recounts a journey she made to Paris in her youth. The same journey is now being undertaken by her granddaughter

Jessica, played again by Cécile de France, as another childlike woman who prefers peach melba to alcohol. The community whose membership Jessica covets is that of the Parisian Avenue Montaigne theatre. However, her lack of connections and means force her to embrace an existence on its margins, secretly sleeping in a hotel room reserved for daytime use by a concert pianist. Elsewhere in the film, familial strife is dramatised through a storyline focusing on Jessica's suitor Frédéric and his father Jacques, who engage in Oedipal rivalries over women. However, the most coruscating vision of the patriarchal family is provided by gay rom-com *Pédale douce* (Gabriel Aghion, 1996), based principally around a cross-dressing bar-club secretly frequented by bourgeois businessmen. Here the critique resides in the throwaway detail that the bar's owner, Eva (Fanny Ardant), left home and has embraced an underground culture because her father raped her.

Imagining social networks as an idealised replacement for the deficient family, these ensemble narratives encapsulate the contradictions characteristic of romantic comedy today. However, their endings also endorse heterosexual coupling, the basic unit of the family structure. Thus *Ensemble, c'est tout* closes on Camille's announcement that she wants to have Franck's baby; *Fauteuils'* Jessica is paired off with wealthy playboy Frédéric; and even Eva of *Pédale douce* produces a child with her conservative lover Alexandre. The notion of friends or acquaintances replacing family is thus ultimately limited in the genre.

II. The Mosaic Film and the Chance Encounter

All the films discussed so far have the groups they depict converge around a locale, be it an apartment building, a theatre or a bar. Margrit Tröhler has suggested that multi-protagonist structures of this kind, involving characters who have some sort of connection antecedent to the events of the plot, and which she calls group (or ensemble) narratives, have proliferated in cinema globally from the late 1980s, principally in independent films such as *Life According to Agfa* (Assi Dayan, Israel 1992), *Bhaji on the Beach* (Gurinder Chada, UK 1993), *À la vie, à la mort/'Til Death Do Us Part* (Robert Guédiguian, France 1995), *The Ice Storm* (Ang Lee, USA 1996), *Made in Hong Kong* (Fruit Chan, Hong Kong 1997), *The Celebration* (Thomas Vinterberg, Denmark 1998), *Flowers of Shanghai* (Hou Hsiao-hsien, Taiwan 1998) and *The Swamp* (Lucrecia Martel, Argentina/France/Spain 2001).

According to her, the 1990s saw a growing trend for films constituting a moderate variation on the pattern. These slightly newer narratives depict characters with no pre-existing relationship, whose paths cross – if at all – due to random encounters. Tröhler labels these mosaic films and examples include *Short Cuts* (Robert Altman, USA 1993), *Beijing Bastards* (Zhang Yuan, China 1993), *71 Fragments of a Chronology of Chance* (Michael Haneke, Austria/Germany 1994), *Les Voleurs/Thieves* (André Téchiné, France 1996), *Amores Perros* (Alejandro González Iñárritu, Mexico 1999), *Code inconnu/Code Unknown* (Haneke, France 2000), *Magnolia* (Paul Thomas Anderson, USA 2000), *The Circle* (Jafar Panahi, Iran/Italy/Switzerland 2000) and *Babel* (Iñárritu, France/USA/Mexico, 2006) (Tröhler 2007: 209–13; 391; 344). Although Tröhler herself underlines the flexibility of her taxonomy – since some films, for example, start off as a mosaic then tend towards a group – the distinction is useful for thinking about different narrative structures' role in translating the fragmented aspects of post-modern life. In this section I will therefore consider a handful of French rom-coms that can productively be thought of as containing significant mosaic elements. I will moreover suggest on the one hand that this sub-genre's component elements, most notably the chance encounter, respond neatly to some of romantic comedy's formal and thematic exigencies; on the other, I will analyse precisely how films with this particular structure translate social atomisation.

In addition to *Amélie*, further mosaic rom-com instances include *Reines d'un jour/Hell of a Day* (Marion Vernoux, 2001), *Modern Love* (Stéphane Kazandjian, 2008) and *Je vais te manquer* (2009). As the dates of release show, these films have all been made in this millennium, and they are also all set in cities (usually Paris). The potential for the chance encounter to meld nicely with the classic rom-com idea of romance as miracle is illustrated by *Je vais te manquer*, as a reference to a romantic 'sign' in her horoscope leads a character, Lila, to mistakenly assume stranger Olivier's gestures to his daughter through the glass partition of the departure gate at Charles de Gaulle Airport are directed at her. She therefore abandons her flight and summons him to a tryst over the tannoy, which leads to an affair. The film also makes significant use of the kinds of formal bridges between storylines common in multi-protagonist films (Mar Azcona 2010: 39), as for instance when the same song playing on the radio connects different locations. At other times, speeded up footage adds to the sense of frenetic activity propitious both for comedy and also for apprehending today's multiply interlinked networks of human organisation, as several storylines unfold simultaneously.

The essential separateness on which the interweaving of human trajectories depends features as a greater source of anguish in both *Reines d'un jour* and *Modern Love*. For one protagonist of auteur Vernoux's mosaic rom-com, photo-shop assistant Marie, the violent encounters of the post-modern city range from being impregnated by a stranger (the groom) in a back room at a wedding reception, to crashing her car into that of a stranger – a wealthy woman on whom she vents anger at the inequalities of their respective economic situations. Unlike in *Je vais te manquer*, romance provides little solace from the chaotic vicissitudes of daily life, as another character Hortense's obsessive pursuit of her married lover leaves her looking a fool, while Marie is left to deal with the repercussions of her pregnancy alone. As for *Modern Love*, this pointedly named film represents the most extreme case of a mosaic narrative in the corpus, keeping its protagonists' interactions to a bare minimum. It ends with two characters, who have crossed paths just twice before, recognising each other vaguely and deciding to have a drink. This leaves the possibility of this new, reshuffled romantic permutation open.

Such loosely structured mosaic films vary considerably Powrie's model invoked at the start of this chapter, of surrogate communities replacing family. Instead, characters are left broadly adrift with little in the way of interpersonal support networks at all. I have already indicated that this mosaic tendency mirrors larger shifts in global filmmaking and as such – alongside multi-protagonist films as a whole to a lesser extent – it has attracted some theoretical attention.

III. Theorising the Multi-Protagonist Rom-Com

The rise of the ensemble format has in fact been cited as a transcultural phenomenon over the past two decades (see Thompson 1999; Tröhler 2000, 2007 and 2010; Bordwell 2008: 211), for reasons which Mar Azcona (2010: 6–7) links on the one hand to 'social, economic and political processes that have crystallized in concepts such as globalization, transnationalism, deterritorialization, and diaspora', and on the other to changes in the field of intimate relations.[5] The question of changes within intimate relations is one I return to in detail later in this chapter; my intention so far here has been, rather, to apprehend the contemporary French rom-com genre at its point of intersection with broader developments in social organisation focused around urban fragmentation. Thus the global trend for embracing ensemble structures in cinematic storytelling of recent years finds its echo in this national genre – where it simultaneously fits neatly with a longstanding French fondness for the film *choral* in popular cinema (see Bruyn 2006), linked also to the possibility of displaying many star performers.

It is worth noting, with regard to the social meaning of such films beyond romance, that not only does the idea of 'chorality' in cinema have some of its roots in Italian Neo-realism, and thus an impulse for socially committed filmmaking in the widest sense, in Hollywood it has been more often associated with art than mainstream cinema. Roland Barthes among others has questioned the centrality of the single protagonist in Western narratives, for which he blames the novel (1977: 108). Tröhler goes further in citing Gilles Deleuze and Félix Guattari's concept of the rhizome as the best model for multi-protagonist films tending towards mosaic organisation. The rhizome is described here as an accented structure in which any point can be arbitrarily connected to any other without hierarchical organisation, bypassing the traditional structures of power implied therein (Tröhler 2007: 391). In envisioning romance across relatively randomly organised plot threads, then, films like these may have the capacity to shake off some of the old status relations conventionalised by many dyadic (and triadic) rom-coms, and to go beyond the simplistic binary conceptions of central characters based on contrast, difference and otherness endemic in rom-com. Attempting to capture something of contemporary reality's overwhelming multiplicity and contingency, their engagement with existential questions surpassing romance itself is in any case markedly prominent. At the same time, keeping in mind Mar Azcona's (2010: 113–4) observations about iconic multi-protagonist rom-com *Singles* (Cameron Crowe, USA 1992) (on which the French *Célibataires* appears loosely calqued), it may be that ensemble films gain special appeal through an open structure, in which the viewer can be positioned as a further imagined member of the group of individuals depicted. In other words, such films may attempt to offset the loneliness they, at times, depict by instilling in the viewer a comforting sense of belonging – if only, paradoxically, through unbelonging – after all.

Romance, Religion and Race

The metaphorical absence of French fathers (i.e. patriarchal families) in many French rom-coms is complemented by an overarching absence in the genre of God the Father, or spiritual meaning. Yet sometimes religious issues, and more often unions between diverse ethnic religious identities, do feature. Indeed, according to interracial rom-com director Roschdy Zem: 'All couples are mixed couples' (Attali 2006). Romance has certainly provided a significant trope for the negotiation of difference in fiction historically, including across diverse cultures. Moreover, while for Tarr with Rollet (2001: 133) 'awareness of social divides' has deepened in France since the mid-1990s, the rise of religious fundamentalism globally, gathering pace since 9/11, has specifically brought categories of faith and race to the forefront of public attention – as most famously in France through the well-publicised *affaire du voile*, the debate arising (also since the mid-1990s) around the wearing of the Muslim *hijab* in schools. Without delving into the highly complex socio-political factors behind the formation of particular groups or the execution of individual acts of territory- and identity-staking, the rise of religion can be seen as a function of post-modernity in two senses: primarily because of the threats to racial and religious identities produced by mass population shifts and diasporas on the one hand and the globalisation of culture on the other; secondarily, catalysed by post-modernity's lack of meaningful frameworks for existence.

I. 'God is Great' – What About Love?

As hinted, religion itself tends to be a signficant absence rather than a direct theme in contemporary rom-coms. For instance, in *Vénus Beauté*, the only outdoor scene outside the bleakly depicted winter metropolis takes place outside the church in Angèle's home-town of Poitiers, following the Christmas Eve mass. Angèle, who has just been disabusing her aunts of their belief that she must 'know people' in Paris – ironically far from the truth of her urban solitude – immediately bumps into an old school-friend; and nor is it accidental that her idealised romantic hero lover is a sculptor who is currently working on a church altar. An exception to this trend is Pascale Bailly's *Dieu est grand, je suis toute petite/God is Great and I'm Not* (2001). The film stars Edouard Baer opposite Tautou, hot on the heels of her success in *Amélie* – although this film was in fact filmed three years earlier and delayed due to the withdrawal from the project of its original producer. The date is relevant, confirming that the film predates 9/11 by some years and cannot therefore be interpreted as a reaction to those events. Indeed, this film takes up those issues that underlie fanaticism at an earlier stage in its process of evolution, by positing romance and spirituality alongside one another as two possible palliatives for the malady of contemporary life.

Sex and spirituality are interwoven by posters for the film showing a half-smiling Tautou with her eyes – and jaunty eyebrows – raised heavenward, holding up a votive candle, but one strap of her little black dress off her shoulder and Baer looking on appreciatively from behind [Figure 3]. This association is reinforced by Michèle's (Tautou) first interaction with François (Baer), which leads to a passionate kiss in a church. Bailly cuts straight from this moment to a shot of the over-dosed Michèle falling off a chair onto Baer the next morning, still overlaid with the solemn Latin chants from the church, only subsequently returning to the interim night of passion in flashback. The suicide attempt, juxtaposed with religious themes, will only later be partially explained by reference to an abortion.

As the film progresses, Michèle lurches from attempts at devout Catholicism into a faddish interest in Buddhism (she tries to meditate but, comically, falls asleep) and her desperation to find serenity in any form emerges. Familial and spiritual troubles are conflated as her stepfather mirrors the role of saviour-rescuer played by God in Michèle's dream, when she wakes up – with blatant symbolism – atop her real father's gravestone. Nor does Michèle's professional life as a model fulfil her. Although work is not shown to contribute directly to her unhappiness, it is portrayed as so un-engaging that she spends most of her working hours reading books about spirituality, her job's empty theatricality underlined by Michèle's excessive postures and gestures as well as her highly stylised makeup and costumes, including outsize false eyelashes, arresting futuristic cosmetics and weird plastic clothing. When photographers do not end up deciding a shot is better with no models in it at all, a typical instruction is to 'look vacant'!

Figure 3. Sex and spirituality in *Dieu est grand, je suis toute petite*. © Mars Distribution

Complementing the narrative's mobility between multiple Parisian locations, the film's self-conscious form further conveys the existential restlessness displayed by Michèle. This includes an episodic and occasionally disorienting narrative structure, a home-video look created by a hand-held camera and numerous sequence shots, intercalated text, jump cuts, unusual camera angles (including overhead shots playfully suggesting God's perspective), along with the use of slow-motion and coloured filters. This formal heteroglossia mimics the facility with which post-modern magpie Michèle dips into different spiritual traditions according to her whim. In addition, occasional wipes and sepia tones combine with the 1970s look of many of the clothes and sets at the photo shoots to suggest a gnawing cultural nostalgia for times past.

While *Dieu est grand*'s engagement with Catholicism and Buddhism remains superficial, Michèle's later decision to convert to François' putative Jewish religion gives rise to a slightly more complex interrogation of the meaning of this identity (rather than the beliefs associated with it) in contemporary France, notwithstanding elements of comic caricature. The film's major source of humour is the contrast between veterinary scientist François' ostensible disinterest in his faith and the zeal of the converted Michèle, alongside humorous foregrounding of some of the more apparently arbitrary and anachronistic aspects of religious rituals, which renders them as being as much a masquerade as femininity becomes in the photo studio. Michèle's inability to distinguish outer ceremony from inner spirituality is crystallised in her obsession with ritualised detail, which appears another outlet for the kind of childish puerility that will later be associated with Amelie Poulain (see Moore 2006: 14). In this film, immaturity is rammed home by the excerpted phrases from Michèle's journal that divide the film into sections, executed in (pre-)pubescent 'bubble writing' peppered with exclamation marks, as well as by instances of her skipping, bouncing on a bed, pouting and generally being unreasonable. François' characterisation, by contrast, speaks more seriously of the conflicted identity of French Jews today. Thus while he feigns nonchalance about his background, his angry response when asked by police for his papers that 'this isn't the Gestapo', like his paranoid overreaction to Michèle's gesture of hanging a Mezuzah outside the door of his flat ('Do you want everyone in the building to think I'm Jewish?'), betrays a deep-seated insecurity about his racial makeup that has particular resonance in a country like France which was occupied, and 'cleansed', by the Nazis. Yet the strength of François' allegiance to his own heritage is reflected by the bitter argument – and ultimately break-up – he initiates after (falsely) accusing Michèle of failing to offer his mother a lift one day, when his Orthodox parents are visiting from Israel.

Despite a more complex and indeed conflicted relationship with his Jewish heritage, François meanwhile is as guilty as Michèle of confounding spirituality and corporeality, indeed carnality. Their relationship is presented as highly physical, including close-ups of their tongues kissing and numerous suggestive bedroom scenes, and François' final answer to Michèle's ongoing accusations of faithlessness is simply: 'I believe in you.' Leaving its couple nominally apart at the end, however, the narrative of *Dieu est grand* stops short of suggesting that faith in one other special person is sufficient to shore up the individual against the uncertainties of modern society.

II. The Mixed Couple and the Other

A number of films use couples of mixed races or ethnicities and/or religions to touch on similar issues of the relationship between religion, race and romance in more secondary ways than does *Dieu est grand*. These couples' construction reveals a variety of attitudes towards otherness within the films, while the viewing position addressed is most often a more 'enlightened' one, offering the idealised reconciliation in which the genre specialises.

At one end of the spectrum, blatant racism is satirised in *Je vais te manquer* and *Tellement proches* (Nakache and Toledano, 2009). In the first film, a macho immigration officer constructed as pathetic is prejudiced against Arabs because his wife left him for one. In the second, a running joke sees a black doctor repeatedly mistaken for a cleaner at the hospital where he works. The fact that this is set up as a source of humour suggests the extent to which low-level racism is a social norm.

The day-to-day complications of inter-ethnic unions are explored more prominently elsewhere. In *Ma Femme est une actrice/My Wife is an Actress* (Yvan Attal, 2001), a Christian-Jewish couple features in the shape of protagonist Yvan's sister Nathalie and her husband Vincent. In this case, the problems mixed religion partnerships can cause are brought to the fore by several scenes in which Nathalie and Vincent's continual and savage bickering focuses on the divisive issue of their child's potential circumcision. In *Mariage mixte* (Alexandre Arcady, 2004), a Jewish patriarch's resistance to his daughter's engagement to a gentile provides the central conflict, although the narrative focuses solely on the cultural trappings of Judaism, stereotyped to humorous ends, and moreover soon collapses the difference of faiths into straightforward paternal possessiveness. In both cases, the happy couple is finally united.

A more considered exploration of the possibility of inter-faith union is offered by *beur* actor-director Zem's 2006 rom-com *Mauvaise foi/Bad Faith*, in which he stars as Muslim Ismaël opposite de France's Ashkenazi Jewish Clara, mirroring his own real life union with his Jewish wife. Critics saw the film, which ends happily, as a plea for tolerance (Anon 2006c; Baudin 2006). In interview, Zem explicitly likens Clara and Ismaël's sudden impulse to embrace their respective faiths more fully following arguments between them – catalysed by her pregnancy – to young people's new tendency to take refuge in religion (Péron 2006).

It is significant that this film is less broadly comical than, say, *Dieu est grand*: a scene in which the couple fall out bitterly when Ismaël finds it difficult to accept Clara putting her career before family stands out for highlighting a serious cultural controversy around the place of women in Islam, and the difficulties of reconciling such attitudes with Western liberalism. Elsewhere, background extracts from the television news focus on the Israeli-Palestinian conflict. At one point in *Dieu est grand*, Michèle admits to being unsure whether it is acceptable for her to laugh at a humorous film set around the atrocities of World War II and François responds that it *is* a comedy. It is tempting to conclude that the events of 9/11 and its legacy had by 2006 made cultural issues with a link to race and religion something less of a laughing matter.

It is revealing to consider, too, the question of casting in mixed couple films. Neither Edouard Baer, Cécile de France nor Olivia Bonamy (of *Mariage mixte*) is known as Jewish, perhaps somewhat lessening the power of their on-screen union with non-Jews to persuade viewers of the acceptability of such pairings. An actor who *is* increasingly famed for his Judaism, though, is Jean-Pierre Cassel (not least through the prominence of his son Vincent personifying the Jewish character in global auteur hit *La Haine* [Mathieu Kassovitz, 1995]), who plays the father in both *Dieu est grand* and *Mauvaise foi*. The presence of parents is already noteworthy in underlining the importance of race and religion as markers of familial continuity, and in *Mauvaise foi* it is specifically Clara's father whom Ismaël fails at first to charm. At the same time, it is worth flagging up the newness of veteran Cassel's association with Judaism, absent from his roles and star persona for the many decades prior to the late 1990s in which he worked in cinema. This change is itself a barometer of the reification of ethnic-religious identities in a Western society like France in recent years.

Finally, some rom-coms do feature mixed race couples, without commenting on this aspect of difference, but rarely. Examples include *Belle maman/Beautiful Mother* (Gabriel Aghion, 1999), *L'Âge d'homme... maintenant ou jamais!* (Raphaël Fejtö, 2007) and *De vrais mensonges*. A typical attitude is displayed by teenpic/rom-com *LOL*

(*Laughing Out Loud*) (2008). Here the fact that the protagonist's best friend Stéphane (a girl) is dating an Arab, Mehdi, is not a source of conflict; however, the film still makes one circumlocutory reference to his racial makeup, when a friend jokes that he doesn't have the monopoly on being a victim of discrimination. In fact, the presence of Mehdi in *LOL*'s clique of sixteenth *arrondissement* schoolchildren smacks of the political correctness of a Benetton advertisement and ends up only highlighting the undeniable truth that the genre remains overwhelmingly white and middle class. Indeed, it is remarkable that racial and/or religious otherness in rom-com's mixed couples entirely bypasses related class issues.[6] Even *Mauvaise foi*, for all its commitment to tackling serious contemporary issues, does not bring class disparities into the equation (atypically for *beur* cinema). While making Ismaël an educated and urbane jazz music teacher may avoid clichés, it also avoids some inescapable realities. On the other hand, the presence of ethnic minorities in the bourgeois milieu of the rom-com also charts and has helped to legitimise the modest rise of a black and *beur* middle class in France.

Romances involving mixed couples also illustrate the tendency of the contemporary French rom-com, when it does choose to put romance in dialogue with questions of religion and race, to conceive these categories almost exclusively in terms of identity, as cultural markers – as opposed to engaging with issues of spirituality. This is partly because it is in their everyday social manifestations that race and religion bear most immediately on coupling culture; however, the secular approach is predisposed to skirt around more acute clashes between religions. Intervention in the most polemical ethnic-religious issues remains, for now at any rate, largely beyond the reconciliatory scope of national romantic comedy.

The confrontation staged in this section between the contemporary rom-com and the increasing visibility of religion and race in Western identities, moreover, epitomises the way in which this chapter has up to now sought to place the genre in the wider context of contemporary historical and cultural studies. This impulse recognises the changed status and nature of narratives about interpersonal unions in an era characterised by social fragmentation and endemic loneliness. In the remaining half of the chapter, my focus will narrow to consider the French rom-com's negotiation of recent changes specifically in the field of interpersonal and especially coupling relations.

Post-Romance

In Chapter 1, I argued that romance is a discourse, rooted in fiction. It would be more precise, though, to say that cultural ideas about romance in its broadest everyday sense, denoting love between two unrelated individuals who are usually but not always heterosexual, bring together a babbling polyphony of discourses. These discourses are differently inflected across both place and time and are in essence mercurial. Indeed, one of the difficulties underlying attempts to define romantic comedy is the multiplicity of meanings attached to the concept of romance itself as a kind of love. This version of love was promulgated most extensively through the literary form of medieval romance. In other words, romance in life as well as art always alludes to a fictionalised – and so unstable – narrative. In this way it points back to a chain of signification with no origin: it is a construct. Nonetheless, in this section my aim will be to try to pin down some significant features of cultural notions about love relationships of this kind as they pullulate in contemporary France via rom-coms. To this end, I borrow substantially from Shumway's (2003a) seminal study of *Romance, Intimacy and the Marriage Crisis* in latter-day North America and particularly his elucidation of what he calls the discourse of intimacy. While Shumway finds this discourse, which both overlaps with romance and exists in opposition to it, in full flower in the USA in the 1970s, it is a central argument of this study that the ideas associated with intimacy are more widespread in the past 20 years in France. However, given the variety of cultural notions jostling with one another in the rom-com during this period, while recognising the central importance of the concept of intimacy, I have preferred to summarise the contemporary situation under the rubric of 'post-romance'. This label acknowledges the way in which romance presupposes and entails its successors and rivals for cultural centrality, as well as its own ongoing pertinence. For this reason, I will start by analysing the relevance of the tradition of romance itself for French romantic comedy, in conjunction with the closely related national tradition of adultery. In the second and third parts of the section I will examine, in turn, two facets of the post-romantic contemporary landscape on display in rom-coms: the reach of the discourse of intimacy and the latter's relationship with a recent trend for a return to ostensibly highly romantic values.

Romance and Adultery

Despite the elusive character of romance, it is immediately associable with the extraordinary and the mysterious. Attempts to define it in its original literary manifestation focus on love outside marriage, wedlock being perceived as ordinary and familiar. In his study, Shumway suggests in this vein that narrative romance requires a triadic structure, which may involve a love triangle or another third character, 'enshrin[ing] the obstacle as the indispensable element' (Shumway 2003a: 14–5). Indeed, he argues that romance and marriage are incompatible (Shumway 2003b: 396–400) and even accuses romance of covertly sanctioning adultery (Shumway 2003a: 178).

However, Shumway also claims that, while the medieval and early modern context took for granted the incompatibility of love and marriage, first Shakespearean comedy and later the Romantic ideology of the nineteenth century wished to conflate the two. While this historical development considerably complicates the picture of attitudes to coupling, it is nonetheless not entirely dissociable from pre-existing ideas about marriage as alliance: Shumway notes most historians agree that there emerged in the seventeenth century a new form of union dubbed by Lawrence Stone 'the companionate marriage'. The significance of this development for the present discussion is down to its contrastive value with concurrent events in France, where there developed in aristocratic circles a convoluted social code for adulterous love labelled by German sociologist Niklas Luhmann (1986: 63) *amour passion*. This discourse, circulated by manuals, conceived seduction as a game wholly removed from marriage, as immortalised the following century by Choderlos de Laclos' epistolary novel *Les Liaisons dangereuses* and its various theatrical and filmic adaptations and spin-offs (Shumway 2003a: 16–21).

Notwithstanding the seismic ideological shifts that have taken place since the seventeenth century, the ongoing French adulterous tradition is reflected in classical national cinema by the frequent focus of the *comédie boulevardière* on how to sustain marriage in tandem with adulterous liaisons. This feature is cited by Rollet, in her discussion of the historical absence of rom-com in France, to support an argument that 'French culture does not place the same importance on, or view marriage as the USA traditionally does' (Rollet 2008: 93–4).[7] This is a complex issue and it might be more accurate to conjecture that marriage in France has been considered not so much as less important, but rather as less a question of romance, as within comedy adulterous narratives tend in fact to preserve the social institution of marriage intact. It is true, though, as this study will show, that the contemporary French rom-com fairly frequently rejects the classic post-Shakespearean 'Hollywood' happy ending focused on a newly united couple, preferably marrying. Considering that this is a change which Evans and Deleyto (1998: 2–9) have in fact picked out in the rom-com globally from the 1970s to the 1990s, it would be possible to make a case for French rom-com's rather limited embrace of this convention simply as a function of global influence's timing. But the legacy of *amour passion* via stage plays surely *is* an important factor in French romance narratives' relative eschewal of happy endings focused around marriage, given the frequency with which theatrical farces were directly transposed to film in the classical era (see Sellier 2010: 153).[8] Certainly a relatively high proportion of French rom-coms deal with the issue of adultery. In other words, in fact, Evans and Deleyto chart a shift that makes the format more compatible with the kind of narrative structures already favoured in France.

Unsurprisingly, however, given the multiple influences on contemporary French rom-coms it is possible to map both diachronically and exogenously (see also Chapter 5), far from simply celebrating adultery in the boulevard style, Gallic examples of the genre present such behaviour from varying perspectives. These encompass depictions of ongoing male infidelity, viewed with differing degrees of tolerance, and defiant visions of female promiscuity. In this section, after examining these two opposing poles in the adultery narrative, I attempt an overview of the spectrum of ostensibly old-fashioned and more modern attitudes towards romance and adultery on display, in order to argue that contemporary French rom-coms are frequently irreducible to the political status of merely either regressive or progressive narratives.

I. Libidinous Lotharios

Adulterous men feature in several rom-coms of the 1990s and 2000s, with some sense emerging of a shift from humorous acceptance towards dramatic questioning over the period. At least two hit rom-coms of the 1990s appear simply to accept the old binary of long-term love and passion as irreconcilable: *Le Zèbre* (Jean Poiret, 1992) and the Gérard Depardieu vehicle *Le Plus beau métier du monde/ The Best Job in the World* (Gérard Lauzier, 1996), both attracting just under 2 million theatrical spectators. The later film is the more frankly reactionary of the two, presenting womanising as one of the 'endearing' foibles of its loveable rogue protagonist, Laurent: a teacher exiled to a volatile *banlieue* school. Laurent's bravery, dedication and professionalism in the classroom and when faced with the local toughs on his estate play out shoulder-to-shoulder with a romantic plot that sees him courting the wife who has left him (following other infidelities) and a colleague, Radia, simultaneously. Adultery is treated, in fact, as a big joke, as Laurent muddles up conversations he has had with each woman, a detail that also suggests the women's interchangeability as sex objects for him. Despite a climactic revelation of his two-timing, Laurent and Radia are (re)united *deus ex machina* at the end of the film.

Although it was made four years earlier, *Le Zèbre*, based on a popular novel and blending high comedy with melodrama, treats in a more complex way discrepancies between passion and commitment. The film's protagonist is the archetypal comic eccentric, zany notary Hippolyte (Thierry Lhermitte), who constantly jokes and is described by one of his friends as *un drôle de zèbre*, or an oddball. Plagued by the romantic intimation that 'love is youth and fantasy', as his highly valued marriage to Camille approaches its fifteenth anniversary, he elaborates a complex plan to keep their flame alive. This involves feigning complacency and seducing her in the guise of a stranger (using anonymous notes and blindfolds). Thus Hippolyte is actually somewhat removed from the typical Lothario, as the only infidelity in his marriage proves fake. Nonetheless, in identifying himself positively with a romantic Casanova archetype, in his quest to lure his own wife, this character adheres to the belief that marriage is on its own second best. And this is true especially when it comes to the libido, since the scene in which he seduces his wife, who is blindfolded and clad in skimpy silk négligée, thanks to the camera's lingering play on Camille's skin, channels all the erotic charge shown to be absent from their home life. At the film's close, the apparent staging of Hippolyte's own death on a trip to the site of their honeymoon appears another measure designed to prevent her feelings from dampening into quotidian banality. However, the final twist reveals that he has in fact

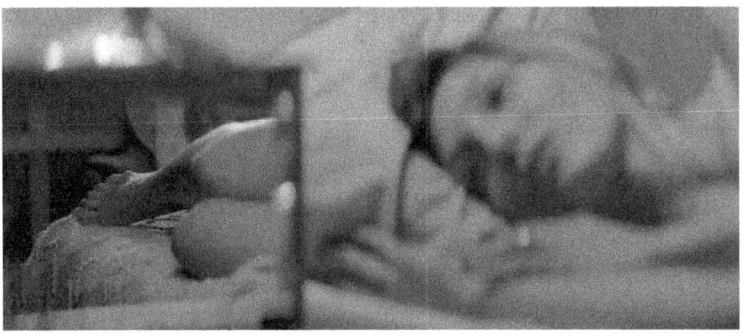

Figure 4. The mistress as object in *Ils se marièrent*. © Pathé

committed suicide in order to ensure that their love remains eternal, in a tragic ending that laments the incompatibility of the ideals of the companionate marriage and the drama of *l'amour passion*.

Nor are filmic legitimisations of this traditional opposition by any means absent from rom-coms post-2000. For example, in *Ils se marièrent et eurent beaucoup d'enfants/...And They Lived Happily Ever After* (Yvan Attal, 2004), wife Gabrielle (Charlotte Gainsbourg) chooses to put up with her husband Vincent's (Attal) affair because she loves him, despite his actions' apparent negative effect on her emotional state and their home life. This effect is potently underlined the morning after his first (within the narrative), ill-concealed indiscretion by jerky, close-range camerawork, isolating the couple in the domestic space, and a nervy percussion and piano score. In contrast, when Gabrielle is tempted herself to have a fling with a stranger played by totemic feminine idol Johnny Depp, she prefers to stick to fantasising. A comment in reference to her character by Vincent's friends in a late scene, that some guys have all the luck, endorses her long-suffering behaviour, as she clears the dinner table cheerily while Vincent telephones his mistress. Equally, an ultimately male viewpoint extends to the presentation of the secondary object of husband Vincent's affections, Chloé, who is initially filmed fragmented and out of focus [Figure 4] and gains only limited contours as a character later in the film: although she is in love with Vincent, she appears to have accepted at least on some level that he will not leave his wife, and the effects of his seemingly exploitative behaviour on her are given little exposure.

However, a critical counter-strain towards the wandering male emerges in the mid-1990s, particularly though not exclusively in female-authored films, epitomised by Sandrine Veysset's tragic semi-autobiographical family drama about a careworn mother-of-seven whose husband thinks nothing of leaving her to look after the farm while he attends to his second family, *Y'aura-t-il de la neige à Noël? Will it Snow for Christmas?* (1996). Rom-coms are no exception. Some early critiques of adultery achieved by showing its effects on the wives who are its victims are included in *Les Marmottes/The Groundhogs* (1992, directed by Élie Chouraqui – a man – but co-scripted with Danièle Thompson), where a rare jump cut betrays Frédérique's (Jacqueline Bisset's) anguish when she realises her husband has cheated; gay comedy *Pédale douce* (1996), which dedicates substantial narrative space to the distressing situation of jilted wife Marie (popular comedienne Michèle Laroque, also the wronged wife in *Le Plus beau métier*); and *On connaît la chanson/Same Old Song* (1997, directed by Alain Resnais but co-scripted with Agnès Jaoui and Jean-Pierre Bacri), where the same courtesy is extended to the plight of unsuspecting Odile (Sabine Azéma). It is significant that these roles are all played by well-established actresses.

While male adultery persists, then, in French rom-coms, it no longer benefits from the same level of social acceptability as in earlier eras. Even those rom-coms that tolerate it to some extent also present some opposition to it, while in several cases it is actively decried. As we will see in the next section, the same negative connotations do not apply when adultery is associated with women.

II. Contemporary Carnival and the Cuckold

The French adulterous tradition has not in fact been the preserve of men. Rather, David Grossvogel describes such narratives as generically concerned with mockery of men (2005: 83), while Mikhail Bakhtin (1984 [1941]: 243) in his writings on the medieval carnival alludes to a comic Gallic tradition of female violence against patriarchy. Today, too, alongside those rom-coms which simply frown on adulterers, another set of films prove at once more light-hearted in their presentation of the issue and more vituperative towards philanderers, by having wives administer to their husbands a dose of their own medicine. This trend echoes very clearly Kathleen Rowe's (1995) description of the Bakhtinian possibilities of comedy for reversing hierarchies and placing the laughing woman, symbolically, on top. It also reflects women's changed social status in an era where they no longer necessarily need – at least in economic terms – to grin and bear it when faced with male adultery.

Chronic adultery is the principal misdemeanour for which Alain Chabat's Laurent is punished in box-office smash *Gazon maudit/French Twist* (Josiane Balasko, 1995, 3.8 million tickets sold), by his wife having an affair with another woman. The fact that he considers his affairs unrelated to the true love he claims to feel for his wife, despite his deception of her, satirises the historical attitude separating marriage and adultery. His wife Loli's admission to her soon-to-be lover Marijo (Balasko) that she has already forgiven Laurent for one affair also suggests the way in which female compromise can facilitate male complacency. Similarly, cheating is one of the marks of disrespect extended by inconsiderate Bertrand (Vincent Pérez) towards his beautiful and saintly wife Marie-Dominique (popular star Sophie Marceau) in *Je Reste!/I'm Staying!* (Diane Kurys, 2003), for which he too is finally rewarded by her having an affair of her own. The same trajectory occurs, too, in comedienne Valérie Lemercier's spoof of the Charles and Diana story, *Palais Royal!* (2005) – in which she also stars – with the humiliation experienced by Prince Arnaud (Lambert Wilson) compounded by his wife's transformation from *housefrau* to gym-toned knockout and her love affair with the national media.

In the broadly mainstream comedies detailed above, adultery indulged in by women may be at least partly ascribable to an impulse for revenge. Two more 'artistically' positioned auteur films use the narrative device to reclaim female desire even more unequivocally for its own sake. There is a suggestion that César-winning *Quand la mer monte* (2004) reinvents the classically shady figure of the adulteress as a plump, gentle middle-aged performance artist [Figure 5]. Thus snippets of phone calls hint that Yolande Moreau's Irène has left a significant other at home, as she embarks on an affair with a puppet-maker while touring northern France with her one-man show. As with Lemercier's film, the fact that the possible adulteress is played by director Moreau herself speaks to Rowe's emphasis on auteur performers as triumphant joke-makers (indeed Moreau physically resembles Roseanne Barr, Rowe's preeminent example). One year later, Béatrix (Valeria Bruni Tedeschi) in musical comedy *Crustacés et coquillages/Cockles and Muscles* (Ducastel and Martineau, 2005) enjoys an affair without considering there is anything specifically wrong with her own, in this case sexually

Figure 5. An ordinary adulteress? Yolande Moreau of *Quand la mer monte*. © Pirates Distribution

active and healthy, marriage. As in *Quand la mer monte*, unlike with the traditionally needy female victims of adultery in rom-coms, it is Béatrix's lover who would like more from the relationship than the fun she seeks. While less apparent than with *Quand la mer*, carnival is still a relevant reference point for this story of transgression outside the everyday, in the liminal space of a holiday, in which celebratory song takes over the narrative for the grand finale.

The question of transgression in all these adulterous films is in fact not straightforward. In this section, I have first suggested that female adultery conceived solely as revenge *against patriarchy* remains a limited revolt in the sense of ceding the status of central reference point to the old guard. Secondly, I have posited some seemingly more radical alternatives where female desire is itself offered as a powerful libidinal and narrative drive. It remains to assess the overall politics of these latter and other comparable films from the point of view of gendered cultural assumptions about romance and adultery.

III. Transgression and Progression – or Regression?

Crustacés et coquillages retains a celebratory sense of sexual openness as positive not only through the fantasy elements of its musical space but also by having Béatrix's husband Marc busy with independent sexual pursuits. The fact that Marc's (Gilbert Melki, described by *France-soir* journalist Richard Gianorio [2005] as 'Melki-the-virile') own secret urges are inclined towards men suggests the need, in a society where divorce is rife and cheating therefore not only less tolerated but less alluring, to look beyond the simple adultery narrative to achieve a sense of transgression, with all its illicit appeal. This is a drive that has recurred throughout the genre in recent years.

La Vérité ou presque/ True Enough (Sam Karmann, 2007), *Détrompez-vous* (Bruno Dega, 2007) and Danièle Thompson's aptly named *Le Code a changé* (2009) present a third alternative to either the Lothario or the woman-on-top narratives, in depicting a mixed sex group where both genders indulge in adultery, which is neither presented as without emotional consequences nor as the blackest of sins. Karmann's film adds shock value by involving (offscreen) a nominally straight character in a hushed up gay encounter. Although it was released five years earlier *Embrassez qui vous voudrez/ Summer Things* (Michel Blanc, 2002) takes things further. In this ensemble piece, the couple given most narrative space, Elisabeth (Charlotte Rampling) and Bertrand, in their 60s with an adult daughter, are bored with one another. When he sends her on holiday alone, leaving him to enjoy some intimate time with a hermaphrodite colleague, she embarks on a journey of self-discovery, sharing a kiss with new acquaintance Lulu (Carole Bouquet) and a night of passion with a friend's 16-year-old son, Loïc. The latter is also shown (although not graphically) masturbating, and another couple in the ensemble enjoys recreational bondage. Like its title (literally, *Kiss Whoever You Want*) – and in contrast to the portrayals of freedom as loneliness and lack of meaningful connection detailed earlier in this chapter – *Embrassez* espouses a law of desire based on the individual, a discourse of pansexuality similar to that found in the ultra-'liberated' *Sex and the City* television show (see Henry 2004: 79).

However, despite their apparent nonchalance about diverse sexual matters and therefore potential surface shock value, these films adhere to an old-fashioned ideal of romance as outside socially recognised forms of coupling, in so doing ennobling the libido. Indeed, a character in *La Vérité ou presque* observes that 'love can last forever but not all the time, *that*'s the truth'. Seen in this light, they mediate a traditionally – in fact, medievally – romantic perception that extra-marital (like pre-marital) love may provide something which marriage cannot. This has great resonance in a French context: indeed, one way to understand the French adulterous tradition is in relation to an 'intensely individualistic' (Greenfield 1992: 523) view of human freedom in Gallic culture. Beyond the question of local mores, the adulterous sensibility moreover echoes sociological work which claims – grist to the mill for Freud's (1958: 183) arguments about the idealising tendencies of desire – that romance is unsustainable once the love object has been obtained (see Mitchell 1966).

Between libidinous Lotharios, carnivalesque women-on-top and agents of (ostensible) transgression, adultery proves an ongoing central reference point in contemporary French romantic comedy. Yet there is some movement away from the older acceptance of cheating as integral to marriage, with the damaging psychological effects of emotional treachery gaining narrative space. At the same time, at a moment when women in Western societies are estimated to account for around 30 per cent of adultery, with this figure on the rise (Taylor 2011), the adultery indulged in by both sexes in such films as *La Vérité ou presque* and *Détrompez-vous* may well resonate with audiences as redolent of real experience. Adultery may have been deglamourised to an extent by the rise of divorce but these films attest to the fact that it is very far from dead in France today.

The Trappings of Intimacy

If nineteenth-century thought wished to reconcile romance and marriage, in the wake of this attempt, according to Shumway, there grew up a different discourse that he dubs intimacy, which can be seen as one answer to the promotion of companionship in long-term relationships today. In this section I attempt to unpack this post-romantic discourse and to examine its importance for contemporary French romantic comedies.

Both an expression of post-nineteenth-century expectations of marriage and a response to the crisis they provoked, intimacy attempts to pick up where romance left off in 'provid[ing] a model for the continuing expression of emotion'. For Shumway the discourse burgeons in earnest after World War II and takes firm hold during and since the 1960s, as the women's movement and the doctrine of free love dealt further, definitively crippling blows to the already crisis-ridden institution of marriage and to traditional ideas of heterosexual romance as a whole (Shumway 2003a: 18–27). In film, he links it closely to what he calls 'relationship stories', emblematically in the films of Woody Allen and Paul Mazursky during the 1970s – by and large the same cycle of films referred to by Krutnik as 'nervous romances' – but also ongoing in rom-coms since then (ibid: 157–87).

The actual features of intimacy as it is circulated by discourse are only slightly more concrete than those of romance. In his discussion Shumway closely associates it with the popularisation of psychotherapy and psychoanalysis and therefore with self-disclosure, emotional openness, the substitution of friendship for passion as the Holy Grail of relationships and the idea that some individuals are better suited to one another than others (rather than being the romantic 'one and only' person for each other [see Giddens 1992: 61]). These moves away from romantic mystification frequently go hand in hand with stylistic tropes associable with a drive for greater naturalism – although the fact that these include framing devices foregrounds the unfixed nature of the concept of realism. Furthermore, in accordance with the discourse's blossoming during the 1960s and 1970s in particular, narratives of intimacy tend to offer more progressive roles for women. This frequently extends to exploring couples' sexual relations, and notably the issue of increasing female demands for fulfilment in this department, strictly banished from traditional romantic discourse (Shumway 2003a: 167–73). In other words, because sex is no longer mystified it is no longer the glue that binds the romantic couple. Extrapolating from this, intimacy might best be summed up as a conception of love in terms of compatibility and partnership transcending – that is, taking in its stride and going beyond – physical desire (see Neale 1992: 286).

One implication of this conception is that adultery narratives like those I have discussed above are informed by both romance (especially where bedroom scenes remain absent or merely titillating) and intimacy (especially when sex is more casually presented). 'Shocking' films like *Crustacés et coquillages* or *Embrassez qui vous voudrez*, for their part, alternate between formal adherence to a romantic paradigm, which needs to make congress less immediately available to lend it allure, and espousal of a highly contemporary move to demystify the physical aspect of coupling, including through more actively desiring female characters, which shifts the burden of meaningful relationships away from the erotic. I will now examine further means by which this dethroning of erotics is achieved in a number of films of the corpus.

I. *Screwball and Other Intimacies*

One apparently rather paradoxical means by which the contemporary French rom-com seeks to acknowledge and move beyond the banality of sex is by looking back to the pre-promiscuity days of the US screwball film, a 'sex comedy without the sex' (Sarris 1998). Such films as *Ils se marièrent* (2004), *Hors de prix*, *Quatre étoiles/Four Stars* (Christian Vincent) (both from 2006), *Ce soir, je dors chez toi/Tonight I'll Sleep at Yours* (Olivier Baroux, 2007) and others complement the inclusion of casual (non-graphic) sex scenes with the kind of screwball behaviours common in the earlier cycle, which now appear to stand in not for sexual tension at all, but for an inexpressible intimate connection. In the two films from 2006, both set in luxury hotels around Cannes and indebted to Ernst Lubitsch in their evocation of romance against an anachronistic luxurious backdrop, this is a question of fairly explicit pastiche, as mutually antagonistic male and female leads indulge in farcical capering, take on assumed identities and, in the case of *Quatre étoiles*, physically fight with one another. *Ils se marièrent* and *Ce soir* are more intermittently inflected by screwball sparring, in both cases in scenes that feature in their publicity materials [Figures 6 and 7]. The rebalancing of priorities in favour of intimate connection (rather than sexual attraction) is particularly clear in *Ils se marièrent*, where the sequence in question, in which married couple Vincent and Gabrielle's love is figured through a zany food and pillow fight, is accorded more than two minutes of screen time. Their subsequent sexual congress is contrastingly brief and muted as the camera fades out from a discreet long shot of their entwined bodies. It is worth noting that Shumway (2003a: 81–2) does point out that screwball films in some ways prefigure intimacy narratives, just as Lent (1995) has stressed their emphasis on the companionate nature of relationships. At the same time, their conception of romance as a battle of the sexes appears fitting in France, where there are reasons to suppose tensions between the genders run particularly high today. Additionally, sociologist Raymonde Carroll (1988: 63–9) has argued that the French in general value reciprocity in couple formation and often express intimacy through verbal negotiation and sparring (by contrast with

Figure 6. Screwball intimacy in *Ils se marièrent et eurent beaucoup d'enfants*. © Pathé and StudioCanal

Americans' preference for a relationship manifested as harmony and mutual encouragement).[9]

Elsewhere in the genre, further marks of intimacy are in evidence. Psychoanalysis and/or an interest in characters' childhoods as background to their psychological makeup feature prominently, for

Figure 7. Screwball intimacy in *Ce soir, je dors chez toi*. © Pathé and StudioCanal

example, in *Un divan à New York* (Chantal Akerman, 1996), *Décalage horaire* and *Clara et moi*, among others. Films too numerous to list incorporate sex into the main body of the narrative, with those that dwell on the act in a plainspoken fashion being most typical of intimacy. In *Irène*, for example, the heroine's first night with François, about halfway through the film, shows them having sex which is so awkward that he pauses to ask her if she is enjoying it. When she apologises for being somewhat tense he puts on a CD of ocean sounds, only to prompt a fit of giggles from her and the pronouncement that it sounds like a toilet flushing! After a good laugh together, however, the sex between the couple improves. In this way, sexual harmony depends upon a prior meeting of minds.

Irène also displays another trait connected to intimacy as opposed to romance: suspicion of the happy ending. Thus the heroine of this film and her new lover are shown in the same location at the end of the film, but nominally apart, following a row. Ensemble rom-coms, frequent in France, also disfavour the resolution of all storylines. Furthermore, this eschewal of uncomplicated resolutions goes beyond particular plots in multi-stranded narratives to include the central love stories of various dyadic (or triadic) French rom-coms, including those of

Gazon maudit, *Un grand cri d'amour* (Josiane Balasko, 1998), *Clara et moi*, *Si c'était lui/Perfect Match* (Anne-Marie Étienne, 2007) and *Mademoiselle Chambon* (Stéphane Brizé, 2009) among others. *Je reste!* is a case in point, closing with unexpected originality for an otherwise somewhat hackneyed triangular romance between a wife, her husband and her lover, making the fictional world of a character's novel merge with diegetic 'reality' to offer up a sequence of alternative endings.

A feature of many of these films' explorations of long-term commitment which relates closely to this discussion of 'intimacy' is pinpointed in Lynne Pearce and Jackie Stacey's suggestion that 'post-modern romance might be conceptualised as the condition in which romance itself has become *the obstacle* which the desirable love relationship must overcome' (1995: 37; original emphasis). *Mensonges et trahisons* is particularly clear in its treatment of this paradox, offering Raphaël two relationship options which equate broadly to intimacy and romance. While Muriel is characterised as open, loving and willing to commit to Raphaël, Claire is a bombshell who has come to symbolise the unattainable to him ever since she rejected him at university. The film resolves Raphaël's need to recognise the allure of romance as a mirage in order to embrace the real pleasures of intimacy. His remark that Muriel's best quality, her frankness, is also her worst, recalls Harry's declaration that he even loves several of Sally's irritating habits in *When Harry Met Sally*, a film analysed by Shumway as inflected by the discourse of intimacy (2003a: 182). As one of the central characters puts it in *Toutes les filles sont folles* (2003), a rom-com whose framing documentary-style interviews with couples again pay homage to Reiner's film, 'great love' is loving someone for all their faults.

In all these ways, then, the French rom-com is marked by the new intimate discourse's insistence on companionship and partnership, not as inferior to romance but rather as its grown-up successor. *Ils se marièrent* is especially overt but not un-typical in its idealisation of even an intimate relationship, paradoxically for its very quotidian joviality.

II. The Couple as Social Category

Those rom-coms depicting groups of acquaintances discussed earlier in this chapter formally accord friendship and love parallel status. Indeed, if intimacy is all about contradiction, it is obvious that the ensemble form in general, animated by a clamour of often discordant voices, is propitious for its staging. I have already referred to the frequency of this form in French rom-coms of the past two decades. To attempt now to concretise this claim, I have marked on my appended rom-com filmography with a *c* for *choral* (ensemble) all those films that focus significantly on more than one romantic plot line. The statistics I have extrapolated from this list should be prefaced by caveats. I have noted from the outset that my filmography is not – cannot be – exhaustive. Additionally, the issue of a film's 'multi-protagonism' is itself not straightforward. I have in this respect taken a broad sweep and viewed any films that present alternatives to a sole focus on the romantic couple or triangle as *choral*, including those that only examine in reasonably considerable depth two or three romantic plot-lines, as is common in family-focused rom-coms. On this basis, I have found more than one third (43 out of 115) of them have this structure. To compare with Hollywood, in a discussion of that cinema's targeting of varied audiences, Krutnik only briefly mentions 'films that approach heterosexual coupling as part of a broader network of family' – or in some cases, of surrogate familial-relations (2002: 137). More recently Mar Azcona has described this form as having 'started to mushroom within individual films' in rom-coms globally since the genre's reinvigoration in the 1980s (Mar Azcona 2010: 100; see Deleyto 2009b). However, even compared to her sample list of 17 films, the figure in France appears remarkably high. This trend coincides with the *choral* form's frequency in French popular cinema; however this in turn demonstrates that cinema's own commitment to a realist tradition that seeks to keep open contradictions, in this case about heterosexual partnerships in France.

While it has been suggested that French identity historically contains a strong strain of individualism, Carroll (1988: 61), comparing transatlantic conceptions of the couple, has proposed that, while America imagines the couple in individual terms, the French see it as an element within society. Certainly, discussions of most of the ensemble films analysed so far have shown how they exploit the structure to explore the tension between the allure of individualism and its possible impact on other people. Considering that romance, in the words of Rowe (1995: 111), traditionally 'affirms "life" [...] over "virtue"', or the individual over social order, as Mar Azcona (2010: 103) has also noted, the ensemble romance as a whole is self-evidently more compatible with the more pragmatic sensibility of intimacy. Ensemble rom-coms refuse the privileging of one couple by focusing on several. Moreover, they tend to present characters encoded as more ordinary by narrative detail (as well as, inherently, by the form), at different stages of relationships, some of which do not end happily. For example, *Mariages!* (Valérie Guignabodet, 2004) makes little distinction between marriage and the other, frequently adulterous and equally frequently dissatisfying, relationships in which the characters who come together for a family wedding are involved. It thus depicts and questions the human need for both romance and intimacy across the board, pointing up the tensions involved in such a negotiation between selfish needs and those of other people. By the end of the film, more couples have separated than been united and the ending substitutes the classic final image of a couple with an extended shot of recently emancipated former 'victim' wife Micky (Lio) walking into the distance alone. The fact that the film attracted just under 2 million spectators, while partly attributable to a recognisable cast including, as well as Lio, Miou-Miou and Mathilde Seigner, suggests that its unresolved contradictions resonated with French audiences.

Mariages! is thus a prime example of the way in which the preponderance of the *choral* in French rom-com means that the kind of films Shumway calls relationship stories are a particularly significant feature of the French rom-com panorama of the last two decades. The interest in desire's social construction that goes hand in hand with this structure is also at one point explicitly evoked in the narrative, when an allegation is levelled at bride Johanna that she may be marrying for the dress as much as anything. Revealingly, she is unable to deny the accusation. The power of social ideas about coupling is hinted at, too, in ensemble films *Le Goût des autres* (Agnès Jaoui, 2000) and *Vénus Beauté*, when female friend characters cause the heroine to reconsider a rejected lover by recounting their own missed or nearly missed opportunities and romantic dreams, and also in other rom-coms, through the attentions of a third party, which play an equivalent role in making one protagonist realise the other's 'worth', be it through the generic convention of the wrong partner (*Quatre étoiles*) or through a more secondary character (*Hors de Prix*). These instances demonstrate well, in other words, how the intimacy discourse in rom-com complements French cinema's pre-existing penchant for exploring the social.

Romance Reclaimed

The dominance by intimacy of the French rom-com landscape supports my argument that French society is negotiating some issues, about the changing nature of coupling relations in the face of women's greater emancipation and the decline of marriage, later than anglophone cultures. It is worth, though, clarifying that the long-term, committed relationships that continue to provide the ostensible goal of romantic films do not so much depart from marriage as simply replace it under a new, and only occasionally overtly provisional, guise – we are some way from the extremely casual, part-time relationships described for example by sociologist Zygmunt Bauman in his theorisation of postmodern 'liquid love' (2003). Indeed, intimate constructions of love might best be described as pragmatic partnerships from within whose shelter the overwhelming realities of the twenty-first century can more easily be faced. Not only that but this picture is not complete without acknowledgement of an apparently contradictory movement to resurrect traditionally romantic values.

Throughout my discussion of intimacy I have returned to the problematic question of its points of overlap with the very discourse it seeks to replace, romance. According to Shumway discussing US-led global cultural production, while the discourse of intimacy has not necessarily retreated, no new ground has been broken since the 1970s, and traditional rom-coms are far more popular (Shumway 2003a: 27; 187). This suggestion is borne out by theorisations of cycles within the genre. As indicated, the 'nervous romances' identified by Krutnik (1990) coincide roughly with Shumway's paradigmatic relationship stories. Two years later, Neale distinguishes these from the 'new romances' of the latter part of the 1980s described in terms of a reactionary return to traditional conceptions of romance and marriage. Specifically, he cites four key features of the new romance: the curing or marginalisation of any residual 'nervousness' or neurotic behaviour in (often) one character; a persistent endorsement and evocation of 'the signs and values of "old-fashioned" romance'; the triumph of conformity over deviance; and a narrative assertion of patriarchal values (Neale 1992: 294–8). More recently, Tamar Jeffers McDonald [2007: 91; 97–8] has added 'a de-emphasising of sex' as insignificant or even as immature to the list of attributes of her comparable, updated category of 'neo-traditional' Hollywood romances.

Adding nuance to this schema without contesting its broad categorisations, Krutnik (1998) shows how the new romance's emphasis on the miraculous nature of love via explicit reference to romantic texts, especially films and love songs, in fact evolves out of the nervous romance's simultaneous disavowal and signposting of the illusory nature of romantic love. Thus the new romance integrates, rather than throwing out, the complexities raised by the nervous romance. Krutnik's comparison of *Annie Hall* with *When Harry Met Sally* looks forward to Shumway's analysis of the later film as combining romantic tropes such as extended references to *Casablanca* (Michael Curtiz, USA 1942) with features typical of the relationship story, including the central message of friendship as the optimum basis for coupling and the use of narrative frames and other self-referential strategies (Shumway 2003a: 179–82).

If reflexivity characterises the relationship story, Krutnik's stress on the overt artifice typifying the 1990s proliferation of rom-coms, such as through scenarios of deception, certainly suggests a similar drive to denaturalise the stories they tell and embrace a romantic aesthetic of fantasy (Krutnik 1998: 30–31; see also Krutnik 2002: 140). It is suggestive that the parallels and distinctions between romance and intimacy should hinge here so pivotally on the question of self-referentiality, which is central to post-feminist (as all post-modernist) fiction and has proven a thorny issue for ideological critics of recent rom-coms. Particularly extreme examples of this tendency are provided by the spate of rom-coms produced in Hollywood since the mid-1990s telling stories of escape into either the past or imaginary worlds, which have been dubbed by Tasker and Negra 'retreatist', referring also to a regression to pre-feminist values.[10] Tasker and Negra's label indicates their critical attitude towards these films: for these critics, overt fantasy does not excuse the films' endorsement of reactionary gender stereotypes (Tasker and Negra 2007: 15). On the other hand, in line with the ambiguities of post-feminism, it is possible to argue, as commentators on the global super-franchise *Sex and the City* have done (Akass and McCabe 2004: 179), that the use of post-modern distancing strategies, which highlight romantic narratives' fictional status by including overtly fantastical, fairy-tale details, allows authors to foreground and explore contemporary women's persistent attraction to a myth that they recognize as such. Seen in this light, post-feminist romantic comedy can tolerate a playful nostalgia for the days of clearly delineated gender roles, which is in part aesthetic, without *necessarily* compromising ideologies that have moved on.[11] Indeed, the self-reflexivity of global new romances may have made the format more palatable in France, both in general and in particular with female directors negotiating the contradictions of post-feminist identities.

I will now turn to the French rom-com's intervention in this new romantic revival. My analysis will be organised around two categories that encompass the observations tracked by global scholars: firstly, films' construction of love as miracle and fantasy, partly through their parade of the signs of old-fashioned romance but also through more subtle details of mise-en-scène, and secondly how French films associable with new romance view marriage and commitment.

I. Mythical Romance

Quotations from pre-existing romantic texts, which act as a sign more through their familiar romantic ambiance than because of the specifics of their referents, are everywhere in the French genre. The prevalence of pre-existing love-songs is of particular note here, as films too numerous to list employ well-known love songs, often jazz classics, for their credit sequences and/or during scenes designed to elicit an emotional response. This strategy contains, too, a nod to transnational film culture, in the case of the numerous films which opt for American (or notionally American) songs. One richly allusive example is *Les Marmottes*, where a scene in which the family gathers around the piano to sing 'As Time Goes By' recalls both *When Harry Met Sally* and the keynote romantic text explicitly referenced by that film, *Casablanca*. In a hall-of-mirrors effect, *When Harry Met Sally* itself then takes the place occupied in its narrative by *Casablanca* as overt romantic reference point in self-ironising rom-com *Ma vie n'est pas une comédie romantique/It Had to be You* (Marc Gibaja, 2007).

Les Marmottes was co-written with Danièle Thompson, who would later become a rom-com director specialising in the exploitation of cultural myths. While her debut *La Bûche* delights in inverting stereotypes, her second film *Décalage horaire* makes humorous reference to both *It Happened One Night* (Frank Capra, USA 1934), by imprisoning its intolerant couple in a hotel room, and *Pretty Woman*, through its union of a wealthy but neurotic businessman with a lower-class beauty (this time a beautician rather than a prostitute) who teaches him to 'lighten up'. Equally, just as a character scaling a wall to reach his love in *Les Marmottes* recalls the Rapunzel story, in *Fauteuils d'orchestre* the character linking the film's multiple romances, Cécile de France's Jessica, a country girl come to Paris in search of fortune, is part latter-day Dick Whittington. The voiceover by Jessica's grandmother, recounting her own experiences of searching for glamour years earlier, foregrounds the folkloric dimension, while Jessica's ability to open the eyes of the spoilt bourgeois around her to her childlike joy at life is, like her union with wealthy playboy Fred, the stuff of fairy-tales.

Other films construct self-consciously artificial worlds either intermittently – as with musical numbers in *Clara et moi* and *Modern Love* – or throughout the main body of their narratives. Although rom-coms escaping explicitly into nostalgic or fantastic worlds or even rural idylls are for now much less common in France than the US – indeed *Il ne faut jurer de rien!* (Eric Civanyan, 2005) is the only recent French rom-com to adopt a pre-twentieth-century period setting – probably due to a combination of pro-realist bias and budget constraints, elements suggestive of a retreat into an unreal space where romance may flourish abound. Most obviously, staging is to the fore in a group of films that situate romance within theatrical settings. This is metaphorically true of the Parisian drag culture scene which provides a backdrop for the (primarily heterosexual) romance depicted in Gabriel Aghion's *Pédale douce*. More literally, professional associations with cinema link the heroines of *Au suivant!* (Jeanne Biras, 2005), *Ma femme est une actrice* and *Le Roman de Lulu* (Pierre-Olivier Scotto, 2001) to performance, while *Un grand cri d'amour*, *Fauteuils d'orchestre* and *Le Goût des autres* are all set around the theatre, each exploiting specific theatrical intertexts. As for *Vénus Beauté*, after humorously puncturing romantic discourse through a scene in which a stranger announcing his irrational love for protagonist Angèle is treated, with realism, as a potential stalker, the film's ending attempts tentatively to reinstate romance. While a revelation that Angèle accidentally disfigured her ex-partner in a moment of conflict associates romance with violence, a converse yearning for a more positive view of love as compromise of the ego is apparent in a subplot detail, which has an older man recount giving his wife a skin graft. At the close of the film, and despite being at her lowest ebb emotionally, Angèle is united with her previously spurned suitor. However, just as the beauty salon setting has foregrounded masks and performance throughout, here Angèle, (dressed for a New Year's Eve party) wears a fairy-tale princess costume for a climactic kiss. This moment is temporally elasticised by dissolves that uproot it from the flow of narrative to suggest transcendence, and additionally distanced by the intervening layer of the glass shopfront from outside which it is filmed, as well as a spray of sparks from a broken neon light. In other words any suggestion that the meaning of desire is love comes in this film with a clear warning of the illusory nature of such ideas.

In addition, the holiday (or festive period) settings of such films as *Les Marmottes*, *La Bûche*, *Venus Beauté*, *Hors de prix*, *Quatre étoiles*, *Embrassez qui vous voudrez*, *Coquillages et crustacés* and *Les Petits mouchoirs*, as well as the carnival space partly occupied by *Quand la mer monte* and *Laisse tes mains sur mes hanches*, also speak to a sense of liminal possibility associated with amorous encounters. In particular, the luxury elements of *Quatre étoiles* and *Hors de prix* not only echo the screwball film but in so doing further amp up the sense of pleasurable unfamiliarity that typifies romance. Indeed, in light of Cavell's (1981: 154) argument that wealth is particularly propitious for the expression of eroticism, it is striking in *Hors de prix* that Irène hijacks the 'one and only' romantic discourse in the context not of love but of money, when she remarks that a meal in an expensive restaurant makes her feel unique, while even her 'true' affinity with Jean is at first expressed through their shared love of an Italian cake. This blurring of romantic and materialist discourses, jointly expressed through consumerism, is visible, too, in those films featuring weddings centrally. As well as reflecting the current boom in the bridal industry, which can itself be linked to post-feminism (Tasker and Negra 2007: 11) and specifically to the ongoing investment in romance as staged construction, these potentially endorse the traditional patriarchal values associated by Neale with new romance. Exemplary here in the French genre are *Mariage mixte* (2004), *Belle Maman* (1999), *Mariages!* (2004) and *Pièce Montée/ The Wedding Cake* (Denys Granier-Deferre, 2010). However, just as *Mariages!* is, as I have indicated, in fact quite critical of the cultural power of the wedding narrative, the titular wedding cake of *Pièce Montée*, also translatable literally as 'staged play', underscores heavily the artifice surrounding the marriage ceremony.

II. Marriage and Commitment

Generic self-awareness notwithstanding, implicit in the preceding discussion is the relative conformism of films that promote marriage and often capitalism. Such narratives counterbalance intimacy's relativistic sense of relationships as contingent and unstable. It should be stressed, however, that marriage itself is less commonly an overt goal of French rom-com narratives – especially by comparison with the wedding-obsessed Hollywood genre – than is (more intimate) long- or at least medium-term commitment, reflecting the institution's demotion all over the Western world in recent decades.

Whether or not marriage is specified, a particularly interesting feature of such narratives tends to be the uneven positioning of female and male characters in relation to longer-term commitment. Female desperation for a 'serious' relationship is a cliché of the genre. The films of Stéphane Brizé *Je ne suis pas là pour être aimé* (2005) and *Mademoiselle Chambon* (2009) – both co-written with women – are particularly insidious on this point, making female desire for commitment an assumption that need not even be spelt out. In *Je ne suis pas là*, Françoise's sister mentions that she has waited 'so long' for her marriage. Given that she falls in love with someone else during the narrative, the suggestion is that she rushed into a partnership with an unsuitable man in order to marry someone. This is presented as understandable, since Françoise is an entirely sympathetic heroine, while her mother and sister's frantic planning of 'the big day' reflects social pressures to marry.

When it comes to men and commitment, however, the situation is rather different. Male unwillingness to commit is the plot motor in *Mensonges et trahisons* and, even more so, box-office hit *Prête-moi ta main* (3.6 million admissions), as Luis (popular comic Alain Chabat) devises a plan to stage a disastrous engagement in order to divert his sisters' and mother's entreaties for him to marry. In typical new romantic style, the deception scenario in which he and Emma (Gainsbourg) pretend to be courting leads to actual love. Luis' rebellious attitude contrasts with that of Irène, faced with similar pressure from her parents, in the film by the same name, where it is clear that the latters' comments are only adding to her sorrow and loneliness. While Shumway (2003a: 167) suggests that female characters in relationship stories often learn that they can survive on their own, by contrast Mar Azcona (2010: 107) argues that women are more often portrayed as commitment enthusiasts in ensemble films, and men as resistant. As Diana Holmes has noted, the inclination to equate sex with emotional commitment appears stronger in women. She cites female children's earlier emotional development as one possible explanation. More convincing, though, are the social factors she adduces: the persistence of the sexual double standard in contemporary Western culture, and the fact that women are still the main caregivers of children today (Holmes 2006: 125). This produces a paradoxical situation where women seek out the very roles that have subjugated them historically. Viewed from this angle the contortions of Luis and others appear, as it were, mere 'playing hard to get' – a reading which the happy endings based around union tend to support. In general, many French rom-coms endorse the female desire to settle down as normal, healthy and to be 'indulged', whether this involves marriage or other increasingly socially acceptable modes of long-term commitment. This is typical of the genre's overall address to an audience that continues to have faith in love relationships at the same time as recognising this faith may well prove misguided.

In thus pairing romantic tropes with the values of intimacy the genre gives the lie to its reputation as a form that simply overlooks the darker side of humanity. In general it reveals itself, in fact, to be far from immune to the anguishes associated with post-modernity's widely perceived status as a period defined by the scarcity of meaningful human connection. Indeed, such an apprehension is key to the primordial status enjoyed by romance in the rom-com and in Western culture as a whole today.

3
Gendered Identities in Love

If issues of gender frequently underpin all others in romantic comedy, in this chapter gender becomes the central object of scrutiny, as the structuring axis along which shifts in coupling culture work themselves out. Critically, while narratives about the 'right' love object and companion always involve gender, narratives about gender are by definition about more than the conventions for choosing a partner. As Judith Butler has famously argued, '[g]ender is a complexity whose totality is permanently deferred, never fully what it is at any given juncture in time' (Butler 1990: 22). That is, gender is constantly being reinvented, through multifarious discourses, including popular films. To attempt to unpack some of the implications of how the contemporary French rom-com constructs gender identities, the present chapter is organised into sections based on three major categories of these: femininity, masculinity and queer or alternative gender positions.

The New 'New Woman'

Cinema has a long history of reacting to increased demands for female emancipation with nervous laughter – going back at least as far as Alice Guy's *Les Résultats du féminisme/The Consequences of Feminism* (1906). Indeed, such demands on the part of French women are a key factor in rom-com's current proliferation in France. This is true in both a direct sense, through the rise of female directors in the genre, and a more contingent one, as directors of both genders use rom-com to take stock of and comment on the ways in which women's struggle for greater equality complicates relationship norms. The post-feminist backlash archetype of the lonely and vulnerable urban single girl seen in several films is consonant with observations about representations of femininity in popular culture globally made by Negra, who alleges that, '[w]idely acknowledged as a neoconservative era, the 1990s and early 2000s have been characterised by heightened pressure to define women's lives in terms of romance and marriage' (Negra 2004: 2). Although she does not say so explicitly, references elsewhere in her article confirm that her comments apply in point of fact to the USA. Whether or not she is telling the whole story about that particular (trans)national mediascape, the situation is different in France, where, despite some reactionary tropes, the overall sense is less of a concerted anti-feminist response than of France as simply, in the view of sociologist Dominique Méda writing in 2006 about women's move into public life since the 1950s, a society that does not appear to have got the measure of 'the silent revolution'.[1] Hence this chapter will explore a variety of comic new women to be found in the nation's cinema. Through this gallery of heroines, recent rom-coms certainly air fears about contemporary womanhood; but they also sometimes – almost always in films made by women – delight in the comic possibilities of female emancipation and its potential to subvert hierarchies. This section will therefore begin with a more detailed consideration of the faces of female insubordination towards patriarchy in rom-coms, principally those written or directed by women. I will then return to a more overall view of the genre, going beyond considering female characters' personality traits and idiosyncrasies and examining what social anthropologists have referred to as the 'economics' of coupling. By this is meant, in recognition of the cultural dominance of myths of female beauty and youth, an analysis of how women's aesthetic 'value', alongside and intertwined with their professional worth and indeed spending power, is viewed by the genre.

Feminine Rebellion

I. *Unruly* Femmes

The heading for this subsection is borrowed from Rowe's seminal study of 'unruly' women in popular American film and television, who use disruptive tactics including spectacle to reclaim space for female interests and desire (Rowe 1995: 8). While Rowe finds such figures requisitioning humour to transgressive ends in the personae of American comediennes like Mae West, screwball actress Katharine Hepburn and, more recently, Roseanne Barr, her work is openly indebted to Bakhtin's (1984 [1941]) theorisation of French Rabelaisian comedy. One instance of direct quotation from Bakhtin is his statement that: 'If on the high dramatic plane it is the son who kills and robs, it is the wife who plays this role on the plane of comic Gallic tradition' (1984: 243; Rowe 1995: 95). As recently as 2010, too, an audience study suggests that the theme of 'women rebelling' and/or strong female personalities are perceived as enduring features of French cinema as a whole today (for both French and British audiences) (Stigsdotter 2010: 177).

Rebellious heroines are plentiful in female-authored French rom-coms and several are particularly noteworthy thanks to the success or cultural prominence of the rom-coms in which they feature. The early precursor to the current cycle, *Romuald et Juliette*, sets the standard. Starring Daniel Auteuil and Firmine Richard, Serreau's fairy-tale unites an initially unscrupulous, bourgeois company director with an underprivileged black cleaning lady and mother-of-five, following his framing by colleagues for insider trading. Richard is notable for her considerable physical bulk, aligning her with the subversive comic tradition of the female grotesque, as well as her feisty performance. A scene in which Juliette berates Romuald for his continued selfishness casts her as the guardian of moral authority, adding force to Romuald's ultimate reform. It is also significant that she opts to keep her job, and relative independence, after their union.

Subsequent examples of female characters who refuse to be kept in their metaphorical place, at least during the central section of the narrative, are provided by two films starring Juliette Binoche: *Un divan à New York* (1996) and *Décalage horaire* (2002). These productions develop a bubbly star persona for Binoche at odds with her international 'mask-like and distant' (Vincendeau 2000b: 250) image, in a way that relies on building her characters out of various signifiers of femininity – and sometimes (feminine) corporeality – run riot. In *Un Divan*, as Béatrice, this occurs through her association with nature (her aviary and the house plants that burgeon into a 'forest' under her care) and messy vitality (the stain she makes on a shirt); in *Décalage*, her character Rose's excesses include frankness and emotional openness, such as when she spontaneously cries in front of a television programme in the presence of a man, Félix (Jean Reno), whom she barely knows, as well as a healthy appetite and the perfume and cosmetic smells that drive neurotic Félix to distraction. These latter traits, and the notion of physical appetites in particular, also hark back to the grotesque carnival tradition (even if the accoutrements of performing femininity complicate this redolence). This association makes apparent the connection, in turn, with a more recent example: in *Où avais-je la tête?* (Nathalie Donnini, 2007), Agnès (Judith Rémy) participates in one of carnival's modern-day successors, a burlesque cabaret. Childlike in their enthusiasm but womanly in physique, these women eclipse the wan silhouettes of Audrey Tautou, Cécile de France or Julie Gayet, coming closer to the 'combination of post-feminist sophistication, romantic aspirations, and embarrassing physicality that has become a regular convention of twenty-first century [Hollywood] rom-coms' (Deleyto 2011). 'Embarrassing' these excesses may be, but these narratives tend to align the viewer with their loveably excessive comic heroines – even though, at times, these positive portraits are infected with reactionary elements. Thus often – such as when she says psychoanalysis is 'beyond her grasp' – Béatrice seems not so much an *ingénue* as an *imbécile*; Rose's childlike lack of inhibition can also be linked to her position at the start of the narrative as a victim of abuse by a violent boyfriend and as a woman of low professional status and Agnès' self-proclaimed excessive promiscuity, despite earlier being a source of unapologetic amusement, leads to her falling pregnant by the 'wrong' man. Once again, even female directors' visions of new womanhood are usually coloured by older prejudices.

A less physically embarrassing or kooky variant of feminine unruliness is offered by the more naturalistic, wry persona of auteur writer-director and performer Agnès Jaoui. In such films as *Un air de famille/Family Resemblances* (Cédric Klapisch, 1996, co-written with Jaoui), *On connaît la chanson* (Resnais, co-written with Jaoui) and *Le Goût des autres* (Jaoui), time and again the characters played by the filmmaker are a law unto themselves. In *Un air*, as Betty, she irritates her backward family by indulging in the 'unfeminine' activities of smoking, drinking and riding a motorbike, representing for Sellier (1998: 122) an example of contemporary gender non-differentiation in behaviour and dress. In *On connaît*, her character Camille is a 'frumpy' and reclusive historian who has just completed a thesis on a topic whose obscurity provides a running joke, and who apparently cares little for others' opinion. In *Le Goût*, meanwhile, Manie is, like Betty, a tough, independent woman, who engages in two traditionally masculine activities: managing a bar and – in defiance of the law – selling cannabis. Her relationship with macho bodyguard Moreno (Gérard Lanvin) crystallises many of the conflicts faced by the post-feminist woman. She is physically attracted to Moreno's unapologetic Latin masculinity – the film's title in fact comments on the inherent conventionality of taste as a cultural construct based on inherited ideas – but she cannot accept his disapproval of and attempts to curtail her lifestyle. The only way they can get along is through either sex or semi-ironic role-playing, as Manie goes from one moment playfully suggesting Moreno become a house-husband to the next herself assuming an uxorial role as she offers to cook him dinner. The fact that they joke about getting married in front of the mirror underlines the extent to which their negotiation of roles is a struggle to understand their own identities within their couple formation. This narrative thread is left unresolved as Manie watches passively, if a little ruefully, as Moreno finally leaves her house to go his own way, at least for now. Although Jaoui's next film *Parlez-moi de la pluie/Let's Talk About the Rain* (2008) takes a small step away from imagining female experience in autonomous fullness without heterosexual love, her persona is all the same an example of feminist rebellion amid a sea of traditional and often less complex representations. Moreover, it complements the more excessive, occasionally grotesque unruly variants of Binoche and Rémy with a version of feminism that is both more intelligent and more likely to be reconcilable with spectators' lived reality.

II. Female Desire

Like Agnès of *Où avais-je la tête*, the character of Manie in *Le Goût des autres* addresses the specific question of female libido. While no longer new or shocking, cinematic representations of this issue have a sufficiently short and patchy history for the question to warrant detailed attention here, in a genre that has itself elicited divided responses about the centrality or marginalisation of sexuality (see Deleyto 2011). As Deleyto concludes, however graphically or otherwise sex is presented it is in fact at the core of romantic comedy. Since the 1960s, this has extended at times to sustained representations of active female desire. In contemporary France, such a move dovetails with exploration of the same theme in recent French auteur and especially so-called extreme cinema, for example in the work of Catherine Breillat and Virginie Despentes.

Films featuring 'the single but sexually active "Cosmo girl" of popular culture' (Handyside 2007: 221) are reasonably common in the French rom-com. Two prominent films that treat the rise of this figure ambivalently, both directed by well-established female auteurs in 1999, are *Venus Beauté (Institut)* (Tonie Marshall) and *La Nouvelle Eve/The New Eve* (Catherine Corsini). Marshall's film portrays promiscuity as an antidote to chronic loneliness. Thus Angèle offers up minute personal details to the first man she finds in a self-service restaurant who will listen, in implied exchange for the sex she then offers him. The cheapness of the act is underlined by her insistence that it take place in his car. Although Angèle professes to enjoy short-term flings, an early scene in which she pursues and insults a 'conquest' who wants no more to do with her, along with her own admissions about being wary of love thanks to the pain it has caused her, belie her bravado. There is moreover a parallel between the way in which the contours of Angèle's face blur at the end of the anonymous *rencontre* sequence described, as they head for the stranger's car, and her later description of herself beginning to fall for a potentially unsuitable man: 'It was a blur. I let myself go.' This fluidity of self recalls psychoanalytic notions of love and congress representing a loss of self through a return to a state approaching the wholeness of infancy. This interpretation casts forty-something Angèle not, as she would have it, as a world-weary cynic and sexual predator, but instead as a lost little girl.

In *La Nouvelle Eve*, sexually experimental Camille (Karin Viard, in an energetic performance prompting comparison with Katharine Hepburn [Anon 1999]), appears as a figure both of liberation and of sleazy egotism. An early scene appears to criticise 'conventional' relationships as based on the patriarchal coercion of woman into a position of constraint through the denial of education, when Camille's married brother reveals that he prefers to keep his wife ignorant about contraception. By contrast, Camille is independent and dynamic; she seduces men for her own pleasure. On the other hand, a scene in which she refuses the gift of a sex toy from her ardent lover Ben in order to avoid obligation to him sounds a parodic note, bringing to mind a marriage proposal or comparable offer of symbolic commitment. Replacing wedding rings with cock rings and dildos is humorous but the implied contrast also underlines the squalidly hedonistic, empty dimension of this exchange. Camille's alleged interest in socialism proves equally vacuous, apparently nothing more than a pretext for spending time with a (married) man to whom she is attracted. Her destructive obsession with the latter moreover suggests a desire for intense involvement as opposed to casual intercourse and thus conveys her dissatisfaction with her life of drink, drugs, meaningless sex and depressing mornings after. Despite Camille's unruliness, Vincendeau (2000a) therefore rightly pinpoints the film's embrace of a conventional Bridget Jones ideal – contrasting with Rollet's (2008: 96) reading of a subversion of the same model. The text ultimately adopts a position of pseudo-Christian morality and reproduces this religion's drive to imprison women in the strictures of a double standard that casts them as sinning 'Eves' who must be hidden away from public life and the freedoms enjoyed by men, at a time when these are available to them.

Two years later, *Reines d'un jour* also features Viard, amongst an ensemble cast, in a similar role. Here she plays Hortense, who is married but acts as if she were single, hell-bent on multiple affairs, seemingly to offset her insecurities about whether she is still attractive – a common theme in films by women. Here unruliness manifests itself as mania, telephoning men repeatedly and throwing herself at them, and becomes indistinguishable from neediness. Such traits align Viard's character in this film with hysterical female lovers in contemporaneous dramas by women *Post coïtum, animal triste/After Sex* (Brigitte Roüan, 1997) and *Si je t'aime, prends garde à toi/Beware of my Love* (Jeanne Labrune, 2002). Hortense's unhappy trajectory is also complemented by the fate of a more central character, impecunious singleton Marie, for whom a moment of reckless passion (with a groom at his own wedding) results in unplanned pregnancy. Vernoux's film thus privileges the negative aspects and repercussions of sexual openness by women, questioning the extent to which such behaviour is liberating as opposed to merely playing into the hands of the philandering male, for whom meaningless sex cannot have the same consequences.

Even in these films by women, then, promiscuity leads to emotional emptiness, if not mental unbalance, and may be punishable by unwanted pregnancy (while in retro male-authored *Clara et moi* it leads to contracting HIV). This can certainly be read in terms of a fearful backlash against increased liberty that has taken hold of French women from within. However, this is not the full picture. A key champion of female desire without punishment is auteur comedienne

Josiane Balasko, a French female star originally from the Splendid *café théâtre* troupe, whose persona has also been compared to Rowe's unruly woman (see Tarr with Rollet 2001: 185–6). The films of playwright, actress and director Balasko, the most popular French director after Claude Lelouch in the mid-1990s (Vincendeau 1996: 24), are frequently but not exclusively vehicles for Balasko's larger-than-life characters. Nowhere is this persona's disruptive status more obvious than in the opening credit sequence of *Gazon maudit/French Twist* (1995). Here the van belonging to Balasko's character Marijo passes through a tunnel, appropriating the now standard visual metaphor for *male* penetration, to what Waldron (2001: 69) has rightly described as a gentle, 'feminine' landscape of blissful peace, evoked by Procul Harum's 'A Whiter Shade of Pale' on the soundtrack. At the same time, this long shot evokes proleptically lesbian Marijo's attraction to married Loli (Victoria Abril) and her consequent penetration and detonation of the bourgeois family, and the chauvinistic values of southern France, in favour of women claiming pleasure for themselves.

More recently, Balasko has explored heterosexual female desire in a non-judgemental way. In *Cliente* (2008), she casts Nathalie Baye as the desiring – and, more unusually, older (Baye was a very youthful 60 in 2008) – heroine, Judith, through the tale of a divorcee who pays for sex from 'escorts'. Relevant here is the well-documented and widely publicised struggle Balasko had in raising finance for a narrative that attempts to lift some of the taboos around mature female desire, despite her star status (she plays a secondary role). Significantly, escort Marco (Eric Caravaca, then aged 42) describes sex with Irène as 'pure pleasure', while it is implied, such as through a sequence intercutting between Marco's parallel relationships with his wife and with Judith, that their climactic break-up is precipitated by their becoming too attached to one another. On the other hand, enriched by the intertext with *Vénus Beauté*'s vision of Baye amid urban solitude, a penultimate scene in which Judith reacts to Marco's departure by dissolving into anguished tears subscribes to the conventional view that women find it more difficult than men to separate sexual and emotional desire.

Also deserving of a mention here is Julie Delpy's *2 Days in Paris* (2007), in which revelations about her alter ego Marion's (Delpy) torrid sexual past are the main source of comedy in a narrative about bringing her American boyfriend home to meet her French family and friends. Delpy's trajectory from muse of male auteur films like *Trois couleurs:*

Blanc/ Three Colours: White (Krysztof Kieslowski, 1994) to author of her own roles is itself impressive, while her emphasis on her (admittedly few) physical 'imperfections' as she ages, from body fat to snorting, owes a small debt to the female grotesque – even as such a stress is tempered by being typically conveyed by dialogue as opposed to performance. The fact that Marion's active sexuality proves threatening to her neurotic, Allenesque partner (Adam Goldberg), although he is sometimes witty and likeable, is meanwhile ultimately presented more as his problem than hers, not least due to the imbrication of her personae as the narrative's star and orchestrator of its humour. In general, however, there is a slight decline in narratives about female desire in the 2000s. This may be partly attributable to the genre's increasing globalisation – via American 'prudery', especially in the new romance – and also its increasing masculinisation. It represents in any case an unwelcome edging out of space in which femininity may exist unbound in all its facets.

III. Female Friendship

The masculinisation of the global rom-com in the 2000s has been acknowledged within both academia and popular culture, through terms like 'homme-com' (Jeffers McDonald 2009) and the increasingly common 'bromance' (see Patterson 2009). I will argue in the next section that a similar progression is perceptible in the French rom-com. In light of this, it is important to highlight a modicum of feminine retaliation to the development, in rom-coms that privilege female friendship.

Female friendship provides a secondary plot to the central romance in *Laisse tes mains*, a film whose debt to Pedro Almodóvar is visible in its celebration of wacky femininity (through a group of friends who regularly gather to get drunk and dance wildly to the hit Adamo song that lends the film its title), as well as in the casting of the Spanish director's erstwhile 'muse' Rossy de Palma. However, Karen Hollinger (1998: 238) has critiqued a dominant model in American female friendship films, involving an identificatory system in which women's shared experience of social constraints makes the latter appear inevitable or even rewarding. There is something of this system at work here, as for example one friend visibly revels in complaining about having to cook dinner for her family before being allowed out with her girlfriends. Furthermore, even seemingly self-sufficient, extrovert international businesswoman Myriam (de Palma) is overcome by loneliness following a failed internet date.

The rom-com that depicts female friendship on a roughly equal footing with romance in a mode most superficially akin to everyday reality is *Tout pour plaire/Thirty-Five Something* (Cécile Telerman, 2005). This film picks up on a shift noted in the (already relatively recently consolidated) genre of the female friendship film identified by Hollinger, from dyadic to group films, where three or more female characters embody different life choices, as also prominent in global television series such as *The Golden Girls*, *Desperate Housewives* and (also on film) *Sex and the City*, points of contact with the latter being much remarked upon by critics. As in *Laisse tes mains*, the friendship group in *Tout pour plaire* comprising Marie (Judith Godrèche), Juliette (Mathilde Seigner) and Florence (Anne Parillaud) offers a forum for telling bitter truths about the imperfections of each character's romantic situation – as well as for letting the decorous feminine mask slip, as when the women dance to classic feminist anthem 'I Will Survive' by Gloria Gaynor, decrying men and, in the case of newly separated former model wife Florence, swigging wine from the bottle. The fact that Florence actually leaves the husband who has abandoned all childcare duties and become emotionally distant makes this a more rebellious text than *Laisse tes mains*. So does the fact that she simultaneously quits her advertising job working for a despotic male boss, as well as ultimately rejecting romance in favour of sorority by standing up a date to spend time with her friends. For this reason the usual closing rom-com image of heterosexual union is strikingly ousted by a vision of the three friends.[2]

Regarding the other two protagonists, while Godrèche's Marie is a successful doctor who does rebel against her layabout artist husband to the extent of forcing him to increase his contribution to the household budget (although not domestic duties), it is in single lawyer Seigner's Juliette that Telerman offers perhaps the most complex vision of modern empowered femininity, no doubt partially based on her own experiences as a media lawyer. Seigner, who is square-jawed and solidly built, but toned and generally well turned out with lustrous long hair and piercingly blue eyes, often plays feisty women who combine 'feminine' traits, including female desires, with relatively 'masculine' features: women who, as one review of *Tout pour plaire* puts it, search for happiness while refusing to be doormats (Carrière 2003).

Not only is Juliette a formidable businesswoman who learns in the film to manage a corporate (i.e. patriarchal) client who has been trying to take advantage of her status as a lone (female) lawyer to postpone paying her, she also performs other traditionally masculine tasks, such as scooping up a drill following the departure of a flaky ex. Here she looks a far cry from the embarrassing physicality Deleyto associates with contemporary Hollywood rom-com heroines, as she sets about taking charge of the DIY in her new apartment herself with a confident, aggressive stance. Although she does end up in a nascent relationship with her bank manager, this is symbolically only after achieving financial independence and he is forced to accept the privileging of Juliette's friendships, when Florence interrupts their first date in need of moral support.

However, at times Juliette does blame herself for her ex's departure – when in fact his characterisation as an eternal student encodes an inability to see anything through – and she is on many occasions troubled by fears of her lack of appeal to men. This reflects some of the real difficulties that successful and extrovert women may face when it comes to heterosexual courtship – according to one of Juliette's dates, 'women today demand a lot'.[3] One issue about which this character does feel insecure is her physical appearance, a topic also referenced by the film's title. Literally translated as 'everything to please', this phrase refers to the efforts made by women to keep men happy (although the fact that it is frequently used ironically in common parlance underlines the film's subversive stance on female subordination). Such anguish seems particularly unjust in the case of a character like Juliette who is a high achiever in so many other arenas, over which she has more control. This is an appropriate place to begin considering explicitly the economics of looks and partner 'worth' that underlie the game of courting in romantic comedy and beyond.

Sexual and Other Economies

According to anthropologist Kingsley Davies (1941: 376): 'A cardinal principle of every stratified social order is that the majority of those marrying shall marry equals.' However, this 'equality' is often measured on value scales that differ for the two genders. Specifically, women have traditionally been prized for their looks in a way that does not apply to the same extent to their male counterparts even today. Stacey summarises the situation with regard to contemporary global culture and cinema acutely, arguing that while the increasing commodification of masculinity today extends to cinema – reflected by illustrations of the potent possibilities of the male body on screen as object of an erotic gaze by such theorists as Richard Dyer, Steve Neale and Miriam Hansen (as well as Tasker [1993]) – a chasm remains between 'the discursive inscriptions of femininity and of masculinity'. Unlike with feminine ideals, physical appearance is for constructions of masculinity merely one in a list of possible ideal features, and not the most important one (Stacey 1994: 225).

The ways in which the myth of feminine beauty oppresses women have been discussed by such cultural theorists as Sandra Lee Bartky (1982) and Naomi Wolf (1991), in the latter case in a polemical bestseller that brought its author a degree of international celebrity. The issue is not only the one-dimensionality – and glaring injustice – of physical appearance as a criterion for judging people. As Wolf (1991: 59) rightly points out: 'A beautiful heroine is a contradiction in terms, since heroism is about individuality, interesting and ever-changing, while "beauty" is generic, boring and inert.'

The cultural hold of the myth of feminine beauty is in evidence at every turn in France – one only has to think of the fact that the models for Marianne, a national symbol of the Republic, have included such world-renowned beauties as the actresses/models Brigitte Bardot, Catherine Deneuve and Laetitia Casta. Not only that but France has a particular history of cultivating female seduction specifically (see Bard 1999b: 31–2). Femininity's frequent congruence with both the aesthetic and the erotic in France is in fact surely a factor in many female directors' choice to publicly deny the importance of gender to their work – even when that work betrays a feminist bent, as notoriously with Akerman, Kurys and Balasko, amongst others. In any case, as we will see, the rom-com reflects and contributes substantially to the tradition of idolising the female body, as opposed to females' achievements, notably in the world of work.

The tensions between femininity and professionalism are complicated by the issue of wealth. Cinderella narratives, pairing beautiful women with rich men, are an archetype of Western culture. They are also flourishing in global rom-coms of recent decades, from *Pretty Woman* to *Maid in Manhattan* (Wayne Wang, USA 2002) or *Music and Lyrics* (Marc Lawrence, USA 2007), where low-status women are 'rescued' from their jobs by powerful patriarchs. It is important to note here that pairings of lower-income or lower-class women with affluent men represent only a minimal deviation from the resolutely middle-class setting of romantic comedies. This feature of the genre reflects the historical fact that it is this privileged class that in fact leads changes in intimate culture (see Shumway 2003a: 7). This is largely because such changes have been driven principally by women's acquisition of power, which is considerably greater for those who can afford such luxuries as, for example, childcare. In other words, the 'economy' of rom-com is a fairly elite one. In this, the genre mirrors feminist movements themselves, in France even more than in anglophone nations (see Duchen 1986: 148).

In this section I will argue that double standards about gendered appearance and seductiveness are the norm in French romantic comedy and that the beauty myth, alongside its close cousin the cult of youth, is both a structuring framework and at times an overt theme. Bearing in mind the paradigm of commodity exchange set up in this introduction, this will lead in turn to a consideration of how women's work is constructed across the genre as a whole, interrogating the extent to which women's 'value' as a coupling prospect has been updated in the post-feminist era.

I. *Seductresses – and Clowns*

In focusing on disparities in the presentation of male and female characters in relation to the aforementioned cultural notions about what makes men and women attractive, it is important to bear in mind that the question of what is seductive depends on a number of filmic (and profilmic) elements. These comprise, in the first place, quite simply the physical appearance of actors and, in the second, how their characters are constructed, especially through performance style, mise-en-scène and more generally cinematography.

Beginning with the issue of actors' looks, although my discussion of *Romuald et Juliette* highlighted Firmine Richard's departure from today's conventional norms of physical attractiveness (including, crucially, slimness), in contemporary French rom-coms in general – as in cinema as a whole – the myth of feminine beauty is still generally in force or at best tentatively questioned. As in so many aspects of her fictional trajectories, contradiction thus characterises the status of the typical rom-com heroine, both endowed with a degree of subjectivity within the narrative – indeed often as much or more than her male counterpart – and struggling with the negotiation of her place in society, but at the same time neither ordinary nor average when it comes to her powers of attraction, as a list of the actresses who embody such heroines illustrates. Salient examples include Juliette Binoche, Audrey Tautou, Cécile de France, Emmanuelle Béart, Carole Bouquet, Fanny Ardant, Charlotte Gainsbourg, Valeria Bruni Tedeschi and Sophie Marceau, among many others. The fact that such actresses' 'extra-curricular' work has very often involved modelling for the same corporations that are the architects and guardians of the myth of seductive femininity is also important. Although there is no French equivalent to the significant strand of Hollywood 'shopping' rom-coms, including *Pretty Woman* (see Brunsdon 2000), that unapologetically celebrate female consumerism, the same age-old alliance of capitalism and sexism (see Hennessy and Ingraham 1997: 68, citing feminist Barbara Ehrenreich as early as 1976) is more insidiously at work in such actresses' part in naturalising women's desire to look good.[4] This underscores the problematic status of their success and celebrity for feminism. Needless to say, fabulous (and often skimpy) dresses are still very often part of the spectatorial pleasure offered by the French rom-coms themselves, too, with texts conscripting wealth in the service of seduction. This is particularly obvious in those set in luxurious milieus like *Hors de prix*, *Quatre étoiles* or *L'Arnacœur*, all set on the Côte d'Azur, notwithstanding all three films' overt final rejection of opulence.

As might be expected, the men who play opposite these leading ladies vary in their conformity to received standards of attractivenes, as does the degree to which the costumes, narrative and in particular cinematography objectify them by comparison with the actresses starring with them. Comic stars like Jean Reno (*Décalage horaire*, playing opposite Binoche), Alain Chabat (in *Gazon maudit*, opposite the pertly pretty Victoria Abril, and in *Prête-moi ta main*, opposite Gainsbourg) and Michel Blanc (in *Embrassez qui vous voudrez*, opposite Carole Bouquet, and *Je vous trouve très beau*, opposite attractive and much younger Romanian actress Medeea Marinescu) and others not only incorporate some physical features tending towards the grotesque (for instance Reno's and Chabat's prominent noses or Blanc's shortness), but in rom-coms their performances actually underline physical imperfection and awkwardness. In *Gazon maudit*, Chabat's Laurent is catapulted into

Figure 8. A figure of fun: Alain Chabat in *Prête-moi ta main*. © Optimum Releasing

ungainly farce mode, leaving Balasko's lesbian Marijo to supplant him in the role of the gallant romantic hero. In *Prête-moi ta main*, a montage sequence ridicules his character Luis as he is poured into over-the-top bondage gear, posing in a subservient position with the sinuous Gainsbourg [Figure 8]. In *Embrassez*, the significant height difference between statuesque Bouquet and diminutive Blanc is only the most obvious in a list of features contributing to the asymmetry between her as classical beauty and him as bald clown. A manic performance style *à la* Woody Allen, interspersing nervous chatter and paranoid speculation about being cuckolded with the frenetic and farcical capers dictated by the plot, further stresses Blanc's character Jean-Pierre's physical gaucheness.

By contrast, female leads less often partake of this comic presentational mode and are more likely to be made static objects of desire. A clear example is Yvan Attal's autobiographical debut feature, *Ma femme est une actrice*, starring himself (another fairly short actor with irregular features, but also 'sexy' brooding dark eyes and floppy hair) opposite his real life partner Charlotte Gainsbourg and told in the main from his point of view, including through wry voiceover. The first shot of this film about the anxieties of an ordinary man (if one whose masculinity is somewhat 'mischievously over-determined' through his job as a football journalist [Smith 2011: 186]) married to a glamorous star heralds the camera's fetishistic stance towards its female protagonist, by lingering over a silent, smoking Gainsbourg, viewed from a three-quarter rear angle to show off her strong jaw line and distinctive profile [Figure 9]. Several reviewers commented on Gainsbourg's beauty in this film and one critiqued it for making of this talented actress an 'inanimate cypher' (Harris 2002). From the same year, another debut by an even better-known actor, Richard Berry's *L'Art (délicat) de la séduction*, covers similar ground in a register whose extreme vulgarity is likely to partially explain its rejection by the French public at the box office despite its star cast. The film follows car designer and confirmed bachelor Etienne (Patrick Timsit) in his struggle to seduce the alluring Laure (Cécile de France), who is difficult to see as a character with any inner life of her own at all. She toys with Etienne, promising him sex in several months' time and in the meantime meeting him only in public places to plan the big event, for which she says she wishes to be an object. Playing opposite the short and wholly physically unremarkable Timsit – whose character Laure at one point informs that men do not have to be as physically in shape as do women – de France is insistently fetishised, notably through cutaway shots of her long legs sheathed in mini-skirts. In one scene, when the promised congress is drawing near and Etienne's frustration palpable, she sits provocatively astride a phallic column talking to another man [Figure 10].

Rare exceptions to this necessarily schematic overview tend to deviate from the most conventional dyadic rom-com narrative structure. The preeminent example of female 'clown' is Balasko, whose short, sturdy physique does not conform to ideals of feminine beauty. In *Ma vie est un enfer/My Life is Hell* (1991), her portrayal of Leah, a secretary made so unhappy by her plain appearance that she sells her soul to the devil, uses humour to criticise the beauty myth. Thus Leah's lascivious boss Xavier (the handsome Richard Berry), representing the pinnacle of sexism, is punished in a striking scene in which Leah, having lured him into sex by appearing in a Barbie-like body, grows a penis and rapes him. Another candidate is auteur comedienne Valérie Lemercier, whose unglamorous roles and highly mannered performance style, including fast speech and clumsy movements, generally downplay feminine allure (see Tarr with Rollet 2001: 189–92). Exemplary are her farcical rom-com *Palais royal!*, where she plays a rebellious French Princess Diana, and the satirical *Agathe Cléry* (Étienne Chatiliez, 2008), where she 'blacks up' to make a point about racism. Karin Viard of *La Nouvelle Eve*, *Reines d'un jour* and other films, who is also relatively unusual-looking with a characteristic, prominent nose, has meanwhile

Figures 9 and 10. Fetishistic views in *Ma femme est une actrice* and *L'Art (délicat) de la séduction*. © Pathé and CTV International

developed an association with verbal comedy and trenchant one-liners. Finally, less comical but equally far removed from beauty conventions is the persona developed by the voluptuous Yolande Moreau in *Quand la mer monte* (2004). This film is daring in mobilising a highly romantic (less humorous) discourse to describe the experience of a female protagonist whose age and physique might once have consigned her to a comic older spinster/shrew role. Particularly remarkable is a lyrical scene in which her character Irène makes love and her 'imperfect' breasts are bedecked with a garland of flowers. In this way, the film finds beauty in a lived-in female body. But here again fantasy is signalled, by her puppet-maker lover's occupation, in the realm of carnival, and by the film's surrealist aesthetics, including distorted landscapes created using irregular length lenses and intended to mimic the look of Ensor and other Flemish Expressionists (Welcomme 2004). While

Leah of *Ma vie est un enfer* ends up with a jovial demon from the Underworld played by Daniel Auteuil, Irène and Dries' relationship does not outlive the duration of her tour, emphasising its status as a utopian interlude rather than a viable paradigm for contemporary couples.

Equally, more classically good-looking actors do feature in rom-com, from William Hurt (*Un divan à New York*) and Thierry Lhermitte (*Le Zèbre*) to younger candidates like Samuel Le Bihan (*Vénus Beauté*) and Gad Elmaleh (*Hors de prix*). Indeed, the latter film makes much of objectifying Elmaleh's Jean, in his role as gigolo to an older woman who, for example, buys him shirts to complement his strikingly blue eyes. On the other hand, this is a marked or unusual element in this film linked to one of its central comic threads: the idea of a man playing a part – i.e. paid sexual slave and trophy partner – that is traditionally feminine. Not only that but Jean's aestheticisation in some scenes does not stand in the way of mining his physical imperfections for comedy in others, notably when his benefactress buys him dumb bells to encourage her willow-framed beau to beef up. Jean regards his gift as a monkey might a mobile phone and uses the accessories only in an ostentatious, excessive fashion for his lover's benefit. This is much more typical of French comedy's general drive to disguise actors' good looks in order to promote humour, as also with Elmaleh as a transvestite in *Chouchou* (Merzak Allouache, 2003) or Jean Dujardin, who alongside appearances as one of the characters in melodramatic rom-com *Mariages!* has continued to deploy his comic persona with the high comedy of *Brice de Nice*, where he plays an air-headed surfer, and the spoof series *OSS117* (Michel Hazanavicius, 2005 and 2009), send-ups of an eponymous French Bond-esque series from the 1960s which mock his polished appearance as an arrogant, macho spy.[5]

As so often, there is some correlation between the gender of filmmakers and how male and female characters are presented. It is certainly not the case that female directors are above selling their films on actresses' beauty. Pertinent here is Stacey's (1994: 125) illustration of the close association between femininity and utopian images, including cinematic ones, and therefore of the way in which ideals embodied by stars may be even more important to female spectators. However, most female directors avoid fixing the female body as an object for admiration frozen in time in rom-com – unlike, say, in the female-directed films of the New Extremism, which tend to feature full frontal nudity and/or graphic sex. There is also, arguably, a difference between objectification and frank eroticisation, which is even less likely to feature in rom-coms by women, despite French cinema's generally relaxed attitude about explicit material. By way of contrast, there is no doubt that Laure of Richard Berry's *L'Art (délicat)* represents a sexual fantasy primarily addressed at men. As well as her legs, during the climactic sex scene of this film we are shown much of the rest of her body, in the usual fragmented way that has been associated with Hollywood (although the inclusion of protracted medium close-ups of her breasts is more typical of French 'raunchiness', at least as far as rom-coms are concerned).

While it is in female auteur pieces by the likes of Balasko, Lemercier and Moreau that I have argued ideals of feminine beauty in romance are most clearly rejected, another female-authored film, box-office hit *Je vous trouve très beau* (2006), warrants mention for a degree of self-awareness on the issue of looks as currency, although this is finally papered over. The narrative creates cringe-making comedy by making overt a system of sexual exchange that is generally latent, when Blanc's farmer Aymé buys a Romanian young woman, through an agency, to replace his wife following her sudden death. Aymé is initially portrayed as a misogynist, who asks only for a woman who is healthy enough to work the farm and knows how to use a washing machine. However, the financial aspect of the courtship is in the end minimised, by having Aymé – morally redeemed through love – symbolically free Elena with a gift of money he pretends she won herself on the horses. It is only when Elena later realises by chance what Aymé has done that she returns to him, convinced of his true feelings for her. Yet her own feelings are glossed over at best, along with the relationship's sexual dimension as a whole: during the central section of the narrative, Aymé twice refuses Elena's invitations to sleep with her. The second time, she makes the offering of her body on bended knee, underlining the uneven power dynamic between them; but he merely kisses her forehead in a chaste and fatherly way. Even for their final coming together, they embrace rather than kiss. This total desexualisation of the union obfuscates the typical realities of such arrangements. Female director Mergault does introduce a feminine perspective on Elena's experience as an economic migrant forced to leave behind a young daughter, an event presented as tragic. However, other aspects of the film bespeak backward misogyny, including the portrayal of three 'plain' middle-aged local spinsters as an irrelevant comic background noise. The nadir of the second act 'low' section comes when one of these characters attempts to chat Aymé up: a mature woman approaching a man of her own age is here a source of (risible) horror indeed.

II. Age Matters

The age difference in *Je vous trouve* exemplifies the persistence of the 'incestuous' model of French comedy, where older male stars historically partnered young women – another facet of inequality. The model is not the dominant one in the contemporary rom-com but it certainly remains a significant paradigm, in particularly extreme evidence, for instance, in the pairings of Jean-Hugues Anglade and Julia Maraval (26 years younger) in *Dis-moi oui* (Alexandre Arcady, 1995), Robert Hossein and Tautou (49 years younger) in *Vénus Beauté*, Thierry Lhermitte and Claire Keim (23 years younger) in *Le Roman de Lulu* and Gérard Darmon and Zoé Félix (29 years younger) in *Le Coeur des hommes/Frenchmen* and *Le Coeur des hommes 2/Frenchmen 2* (Marc Esposito, 2003; 2007).

To counter narratives like these, a number of rom-coms directed by women, or more unusually men, reverse the pattern, by matching up older women and younger men. This chimes with the global visibility of the 'cougar' and may also be influenced by the growing sense in the Hollywood industry that, in contrast to earlier views on the matter, older women can be a profitable audience, exploited, for example, by the recent 'older bird' chick flicks of Nancy Meyers (2003; 2009) (see Tally 2008: 119; 127–9).[6] Examples of actresses who have reversed the incestuous paradigm in France include Chantal Lauby (in her late 40s) in *Laisse tes mains*, Carole Bouquet (aged 50) in *Si c'était lui*, Catherine Deneuve (56) in *Belle maman* and Nathalie Baye, who has had a second wave of success as an older romantic lead (she was 60 in 2008), in several films: *Vénus Beauté*, *Une vie à t'attendre* (Thierry Klifa, 2004), *Passe-passe/Off and Running* (Tonie Marshall, 2008), *Cliente* and *De vrais mensonges*. In the majority of these narratives, however, the usual economy of looks is compensated by the heroines' superior economic status by comparison with their male partners: in *Laisse tes mains* middle-class actress Odile enjoys a liaison with a funfair worker, in *Si c'était lui* best-selling academic writer Hélène takes up with the down-and-out Valentin and in *Cliente*, most extremely of all, Baye's successful television executive Irène begins to fall for the penniless male escort whom she loves to treat to expensive nights out. Not only that, but the heroines in question all continue to conform to classical norms of female beauty, potentially endorsing the view that within this de-individualising, anti-romantic economy of exchange their 'worth' may be extended beyond the average lifespan of the woman 'on the market'.

It is pertinent to recall here, too, Susan Sontag's observation about Gallic culture: 'French conventions of sexual feeling make a quasi-official place for the woman between 35 and 45. Her role is to initiate an inexperienced or timid young man, after which she is, of course, replaced by a young girl' (1997: 21). This appears to be the pattern in Blanc's *Embrassez qui vous voudrez*, where Elisabeth (Charlotte Rampling) enjoys a one-night-stand with a friend's teenaged son. At the time of the film's production in 2002 Rampling was 56, suggesting – like earlier examples – how 50 and even 60 have today become 'the new 40'. It is significant that, rather than simply objectifying Elisabeth, this narrative is concerned with the benefits of the coupling for her, ushering in a renewed self-confidence and serenity that allows her to look on with a beatific smile as her husband spends time with his lover. On the other hand, Rampling's star persona is associated with a certain reserve that is constructed as tantalising, a veil behind which sexual secrets lie (see Slater 2012). This is also true of Deneuve, with her impassive acting style and relatively immutable face (Austin 2003: 42). This actress has in fact visibly undergone plastic surgery – not to mention referring in interview to ageing as a 'problem' about which any woman who claims to be insouciant is lying (Anon 1994). Bouquet's persona, too, has been set up in male-authored texts as a vision of 'inaccessible' beauty, for example in Luis Buñuel's *Cet obscur objet du désir/ That Obscure Object of Desire* (1977) and Blier's *Trop belle pour toi/ Too Beautiful For You* (1989). In *Embrassez*, an appalling act of violence by her character Lulu's husband Jean-Pierre, who attempts to penetrate the beautiful wife he never feels he can truly control with a bottle, similarly suggests blatant misogyny and in this case, specifically, fear of the empowered older woman who can no longer be banished from cultural visibility. However, this visibility

Figure 11. Enslaved to the beauty myth forever in *Laisse tes mains sur mes hanches*. © *ARP Sélection*

is conditional, simultaneously and paradoxically, on keeping hidden from public view 'the grotesque, laughable, and fearful' signs of female ageing (Wearing 2007: 290). A contrast might be drawn between these actresses' mystique and the fate of Brigitte Bardot, whose eschewing of plastic surgery and therefore 'natural' ageing means she is cruelly mocked for her looks, in the British popular press and on the internet. Consequently, older actresses' reasonably strong presence in the French rom-com does not signal a modification of the importance placed on good looks; it is merely a symptom of a culture in which adherence to the beauty myth is demanded for longer, as borne out by soaring plastic surgery figures in France and globally.

An image from *Laisse tes mains* of a gym in which even women who look to be in their seventies sweat miserably makes this very point sardonically [Figure 11].[7] Indeed, the fear of female ageing is frequently thematised in rom-coms by women featuring older heroines – unlike those examples discussed above by men. Most directly concerned with this issue is *Vénus Beauté*. Here Baye's character Angèle is both sympathetic and occasionally pathetic in her attempts to stay young, such as when her boss suggests she has resisted promotion to try to remain forever 'one of the girls'. Typically for a female-directed 'older bird' rom-com, then, while the cult of youth is critiqued and women are presented as its victims, they are also recognised to be complicit in maintaining its stranglehold.

III. Working Girls

While the preceding discussion made reference to a number of rom-coms whose older heroines enjoyed higher economic status than did their partners, female characters' professional status in the genre as a whole represents a key topic in its own right. In fact, almost all the women in French rom-coms are employed – perhaps unsurprisingly, given that women made up 46 per cent of the French work force in 2005.[8] This group is heavily dominated, moreover, by women between 25 and 49.[9] In other words, settling down with a partner and even having children is no longer likely to keep French women at home.

The most common tendency in the construction of women's work in the French rom-com is for the female characters to have medium- to low-status jobs, or else jobs – notably in the media – constructed as superfluous, that do not interfere with their romantic story arcs. Female workers' overall lower status in the genre conforms broadly to social reality. Claire Duchen (1994: 164) has described the way in which certain jobs became dominated by women, and thus denigrated, in postwar France. More recently, in 2013, despite the high number of women workers there, wages were still 16.3 per cent lower for French women than men.[10] Representative jobs for women in the rom-com include cleaner (*Romuald et Juliette, Ensemble, c'est tout*), concierge (*Le Bison [et sa voisine Dorine]* [Isabelle Nanty, 2002]), beautician (*Vénus beauté, Décalage horaire*), hairdresser (*De vrais mensonges*), model (*Dieu est grand, je suis toute petite*), agony aunt (*Ma vie en l'air*), midwife (*Fauteuils d'orchestre*), waitress (*Amélie, Fauteuils d'orchestre*), care-worker (*Mauvaise foi*), teacher (*Quatre étoiles, Mademoiselle Chambon*) and writer of lowbrow romantic *romans-photos* ('photo novels') (*Toi et moi*). The significant sub-trend for films featuring women in 'frivolous' media-related jobs includes *La Bûche, Au suivant!, Au secours, j'ai trente ans/Last Chance Saloon* (Marie-Anne Chazel, 2004), *Ce soir, je dors chez toi, Tout pour plaire* and *Cliente*. Additionally, actresses (and other types of performer) are also common, for instance in *Le Goût des autres, Ma Femme est une actrice, Le Roman de Lulu* and *Laisse tes mains sur mes hanches*. Since well over half of these films are directed by women (including actress-directors Jaoui and Lauby for the films about actresses), there appears to be an autobiographical-narcissistic element to this tendency. This does not detract from the relevance of Lucy Fischer's (1989:

64) claim that actress characters are ubiquitous in Hollywood films as they emblematise the role-playing in which women are condemned to participate in a patriarchal system where their principal function is to please men. Similarly, Tasker's (1998) study of working girls in popular cinema suggests Hollywood frequently constructs women's work as sexual display – which in this case would obviously apply to the job of model and potentially to those of beautician and hairdresser, too.

Ma Femme est une actrice provides exceptionally revealing insight into male anxiety about the second sex's increased presence in the work space. In this film, director Yvan Attal's character, a sports journalist also called Yvan, is made insecure by the success of his film star wife Charlotte (Gainsbourg, Attal's real life partner, with obvious autobiographical resonances). This manifests itself in paranoid anxiety about her participation in love scenes, which reaches a climax at the comic moment when he visits her on set to find the entire crew naked (in an improbable act of solidarity with Charlotte, who has protested at doing a nude scene) and reacts by vomiting and fainting. Rarely has there been such a clear illustration of the argument that male discourses seeking to associate women's work with adulterous temptation displace real anxiety about the threat to their position of power in the world (see Leonard 2001: 110). It is equally difficult to disentangle the sexually-expressed spousal anxieties of Jean-Pierre of *Embrassez* from his insecurities about the dwindling revenues of his journalistic career by comparison with those brought in by his wife's job as a lawyer. Indeed, several French rom-coms from the 2000s (*Irène, Au-suivant, Tricheuse*) embody the negative story archetype identified by Negra (2004: 3) in global rom-coms in recent years, which 'stress[es] the need to school women to scale back their professionalism lest they lose their femininity', and which she logically interprets in terms of male desire to protect men's dominance of capital flows. Remarkably, the newspaper *Les Echos*' review of the exemplary *Irène* reinforces this pernicious model, revealing the difficulties women with demanding jobs may have reconciling work and their other needs, by affirming that the majority of single women in France belong in the top socio-professional category (Anon 2006).

However, a few films dedicate a degree of narrative interest to women's careers, and related – often gendered – challenges. In *Fauteuils d'orchestre*, sex discrimination is overt in the *Bar des théâtres*' policy of hiring only men – although the fact that they make an exception for heroine Jessica brushes the issue under the carpet (and the hospitality industry is not the most obvious potential culprit for rejecting women). In *Au suivant!*, casting director Jo has to overlook the over-familiarity and wandering hands of a famous film director, who also abuses his position in order to seduce beautiful women. Dealing with the same problem, the background detail that Jessica of *Fauteuils* has been chased from her job as a midwife following unwelcome sexual harassment raises an issue that, according to Marie-Victoire Louis (1999), may be particularly grave for women in France, where in 1983 the number of cases reported was 33 per cent higher than the European average.

The specific challenges of juggling a romantic relationship with the demands of a serious career also feature in rom-coms. In *Mauvaise foi*, for instance, Clara's (de France again) partner Ismaël is incandescent when she is made late for a meal with his (Muslim) relatives by her evidently highly worthwhile job as a care-worker for the disabled. Interesting in itself, too, is the fact that, as in *Fauteuils*, de France's character works in healthcare but not as a high-status doctor. In fact, women make up well over one third of French doctors – a reality more closely reflected by female doctors' contrasting presence in television (mini-)series including *Une femme en blanc* (1997) starring the high profile actress Sandrine Bonnaire or the less 'quality' soap opera *Sous le soleil* (1996–2008).[11]

The balancing act of career and romance is one of the principal themes of Jaoui's latest comedy, *Parlez-moi de la pluie* (2008). Jaoui's character politician Agathe airs contemporary concerns about women's difficulties carving out a space in certain spheres, for instance by defending the need for positive discrimination for women in politics. The hostility faced by a female in a traditionally 'masculine' role provides much of the film's comedy. A sequence in which Agathe is forced to take shelter in a rural farmhouse after a storm comments on the way in which identity-related challenges are multiplied for a woman who complements femininity with responsibility for public affairs, as one of her hosts sits with his eyes glued to her 'pretty little white arms' and another berates her for the problems of French farmers. Agathe's job no doubt responds to the considerable press attention women's relatively recent move into positions of political power has attracted of late. Furthermore, the well-known cases of Ségolène Royal, who led the Socialist Party to be narrowly defeated by Nicolas Sarkozy in France's 2007 elections, and more recently Eva

Joly, the 2012 Green party candidate whose first round results were disastrous, attest explicitly to the problems faced by women in male-dominated professions, given that both women made public allegations about the sexism (and in Joly's case ageism) faced even within their own parties.[12] In the end, the tensions provoked in Agathe's romantic relationship by her busy schedule appear resolved in favour of love, as she seeks out neglected boyfriend Antoine for a reconciliation. This film's stance therefore tallies with the broader move in feminism since the 1970s for finding a space in even highly successful women's lives to admit romantic relationships with men.

Even if work by definition takes second place in the rom-com's generic value scale, the normalisation of female professionalism across this body of contemporary texts is significant. It should however be noted that not only are rom-coms a middle-class genre *par excellence*, but Alison Light (1984) has argued that the tendency to actually sublimate class issues has been a staple of the literary genre for centuries. A similar drive has been repeatedly remarked on in filmed rom-com (Schatz 1981: 155; King 2002: 55–6; Krutnik 2002: 142). Of the films examined in any depth in this section, only *Fauteuils d'orchestre* suggests its female lead must work to survive. By the close of the narrative, however, the accent is no longer on Jessica's professional development: rather, it is through association with a playboy that she looks set to be absorbed into the film's resolutely *grand bourgeois* Avenue Montaigne milieu. Moreover, the majority of rom-coms are even more disingenuous about women's need to engage in difficult and potentially unrewarding forms of labour, from *Je vous trouve*, with its downplaying of the realities of prostitution, to *Décalage horaire*, whose finale sees beautician Rose simply abandon a job in Mexico to be with wealthy Félix. After all, work, and women's work in particular, can only have so much importance in a genre whose *raison d'être* is the union of the two sexes.

Melodramatised Masculinity

If both rebellious and regressive female characters in French romantic comedy can be seen as translating women's increasing demands for more equal role-division in social relations (the latter as backlash stereotypes produced by social panic), the impact of these demands on men is also a subject of negotiation by the genre. This section examines how the depiction of male characters in a spread of recent rom-coms explores men's need to adapt to women's new, relatively emancipated place in society.

An important critical paradigm for this analysis is the figure of the 'melodramatized male', postulated by Rowe as a counterpart to the unruly woman in Hollywood comedy and also featuring, classically, in films by Woody Allen, whose influence on the French rom-com is substantial. In this, Rowe coincides with the view put forward throughout this study, that many films are informed by both comedy and melodrama. It is useful to cite here a distinction between the two structures proposed by Deborah Thomas, for whom 'melodramatic characters are far more likely than comedic characters to experience the mood or "feel" of their world in ways that match viewers' experience of it' (2000: 13). In other words, conceiving masculinity as 'melodramatized' rests on the suggestion that male characters are being offered as worthy of the audience's sympathy – at least to a degree, since they still exist within (romantic) comedy's intermittently more distanced, objectifying narrative mode. Specifically the presentation of male romantic heroes attached to backward notions of gender roles frequently blends mockery with some sympathy and the proportions in which these attitudes are discernible vary considerably, correlating at times with the gender of the director.

In accordance with the substantial genealogy of the Western perception of masculinity as in crisis, 'the intense, suffering male hero has a long history in French culture and cinema', including such distinguished comic antecedents as Fernandel, de Funès, Bourvil and Depardieu (Vincendeau 2000b: 223–30). Indeed, Mazdon (2000: 100) has argued that the crisis of masculinity is thematically more popular in French comedy as a whole than it is in Hollywood. In rom-com, the melodramatised male appears with such frequency across various strands of the genre as to have become a stock character. He is, however, a slippery figure. Just as Modleski (1991) and, in France, Christine Bard (1999a: 324–5) have associated the notion of the crisis of masculinity with anti-feminism, Rowe (1995: 193–7) is critical of the melodramatised male's appropriation of the traits traditionally associated with female suffering and his concomitant vilification of women. Certainly depicting men's position as worthy of sympathy takes the focus off the ongoing inequalities still confronting women. Some feminists have further suggested that male appropriation of 'feminine' characteristics – such as suffering – 'represent[s] an expansion of the concept of legitimate masculinity, and thus an extension of its power over women' (Chapman 1988: 247). However, analyses of Allen's attitude towards male and female characters have been marked by division. Evans and Deleyto (1998: 22–3), by contrast with Rowe, argue that the director's self-critique can avoid the straightforward scapegoating of women. Indeed, as the following discussion will illustrate, the manifestation of melodrama within comedy implies particular ambiguities.

Melodrama and Mockery

The examples Rowe cites locate the melodramatic elements of character construction on the whole in narrative and to some extent performative, as opposed to stylistic, details, the latter remaining consonant with an overall comic perspective. Context can in fact make the suffering male ultimately as much a figure of fun, including mockery, as of tragedy. Several rom-coms limit themselves to the more superficial features of male melodrama, making of them ingredients in comedy that 'mock[s] the masculinity that tragedy ennobles' (Rowe 1995: 103–4).

This is often the case with the the work of those female directors who make films about rebellious women, notably in the 1990s and early 200s. Generally in a broadly comic, and only gently mocking, mode, Serreau's *Romuald et Juliette* never portrays its hero with anything less than benignancy, with a degree of compassion for him facilitated by the narrative detail of his unjust framing by his colleagues and the casting of highly popular and 'respectable' actor Auteuil. In Balasko's films, too, unreconstructed male characters tend to be foci of contumely more than tragedy. Chabat's Laurent of *Gazon maudit* suffers the ultimate humiliation when wife Loli discovers his multiple affairs and his place in the homestead is threatened by her lesbian lover, sending him into paroxysms of frequently slapstick fury. An episode of theatrical weeping is undercut by his drunken inability to ride his bicycle, as well as the fact that the aim of his journey is to visit other women for sex. Having said that, Laurent's predicament is not only ridiculed. A scene in which he repents of his previous mistreatment of women and commiserates on life's disappointments with an ageing prostitute, an obvious maternal figure, introduces a melodramatic tone in earnest. It is this more sensitive side that allows him to be rehabilitated to form a happy trio with Loli and Marijo at the end of the film. In line with the physical unremarkability I have highlighted in rom-com actors in the last section, it is worth pointing out here that excessive handsomeness may be ill-suited not only to comedy but also to melodrama (as opposed to tragedy). In these examples, the actors' 'ordinariness' contributes to the impression that their worst misdemeanours represent only everyday selfishness and thoughtlessness.

It would, however, be inaccurate to suggest that all female directors portray particular characters critically and all male directors eulogise them, as *Embrassez qui vous voudrez* illustrates. Director Michel Blanc here establishes a distance from his male characters that makes the narrative at times more critical of them than it is of female counterparts – although he combines this with an in-depth exploration of male psychology. Blanc's character Jean-Pierre finds it difficult to handle his wife Lulu's (Bouquet) better looks and higher salary, despite her obvious devotion to him. This aspect of the character is enriched by the perennial association of the actor-director's star persona with incompetence, submission and failure, sexual or otherwise, notably in his roles with 1970s troupe *Le Splendid*, in *Les Bronzés/French Fried Vacation* (Patrice Chéreau, 1978) and its sequels and in *Tenue de soirée/Ménage* (Blier, 1986), where his character is seduced by Depardieu's macho stud in drag. This aspect of his persona partly accounts for explicit comparisons with Allen (for example Valens 2002). Crucially, it is Jean-Pierre's excesses that convey the director's critical distance. These are at first comical, as he capers round a hotel in pursuit of innocent strangers whom he imagines to be his wife's lovers. At the same time, his absurd behaviour is recuperated by details eliciting sympathy, such as patent adoration of his wife and explicitly aired insecurity. As the narrative progresses, however, increasingly his actions move beyond the pale. The climactic violent act of trying to force the bottle into Lulu's vagina exposes in no uncertain terms the misogyny at the core of his psychological difficulties, which finally see him institutionalised. No wonder numerous critics commented on the film's extreme tonal mixing.

More sympathetic is Blanc's depiction of another melodramatised male, Jérôme (Denis Podalydès, usually seen in dramas): a harried husband whose financial woes prompt him to attempt suicide. Viard plays his nagging, parasitic wife Véro, yet she is also blessed with wit (when a female friend wonders it would be like to experience a male orgasm, she smartly ripostes that she would like to try a female one), while the film's scenes of sisterhood radiate an atmosphere of feminine vitality reminiscent of Almodóvar. Véro's claim that men are more fragile than women in particular echoes the Spanish director, while it also belittles Jérôme's failed suicide attempt. So too does Elisabeth's observation that men make a performance of things (*font leur cinéma*), simultaneously suggesting the extent to which melodrama has become a key mode for social configurations of contemporary masculinity. Both of these charges are more traditionally levelled against women. The audience is primed to be receptive to Lulu's wistful observation, following one of Jean-Pierre's paranoid episodes, that women might be better off without men. On the other hand, the issue remains rhetorical, given the frequent focus of the women's conversation on romantic relationships. This detail foregrounds the number one limitation of rom-com as a genre for radical feminists of earlier decades, perhaps best summed up by a strapline from George Cukor's 1939 *The Women* (USA): 'It's all about the women – and their men.'

Post-Modern Narratives and the Recidivist Male

While backward masculinity must either reform or be punished in the previous stories, some films directed by men use melodrama to explore the issue in a more ambivalent way. If Henri Bergson (1911: 87) has identified mechanical rigidity in living creatures as comedy's cornerstone, the inadaptability and awkwardness of the regressive male always leaves him open to elements of ridicule. However, several films go beyond Blanc's blurring of the boundaries of male filmmaker and character through self-casting, to ally narrative point of view so unambiguously with the director's own, often self-deprecating, perspective that little angle remains for judgement. The result is to locate the authorial and implied audience position closer to straight allegiance with the character than to the critical distance towards him often invited by his actions. An observation by Tasker and Negra (2007: 15), that in global popular culture of the late 1990s and early 2000s irony has frequently allowed retrograde masculinity to resurface, is germane; indeed, the multiplication of representations adhering to this mould in the French rom-com gathers force in the 2000s.

Mensonges et trahisons offers such a divided perspective on male failure and romantic unease. While in previous examples the story was split between characters, here it belongs exclusively to stand-up comedian Edouard Baer's beleaguered protagonist Raphaël, thanks to both narrative focus and the formal privileging of his point of view. The film opens on an extreme close-up of Raphaël's face and introduces his voiceover, designed here to align the viewer with a strikingly sexist point of view. As the camera moves out, it becomes apparent that Raphaël is listening to a woman sitting opposite him, while his voice informs us in a bored tone that she has been recounting her life to him 'in detail' for the last hour, and that he switched his attention some time ago to the conversation of two men seated at the next door table in the café where the scene is taking place. These two are discussing a new relationship with a woman in which one is involved, analysing whether or not the lady in question has 'given the right signals'. Raphaël expresses amazement that men have gone from 'that', followed by an inserted scene of a caveman forcing himself on a woman after beating her, to 'this', in other words modern day courtship with all its complications and uncertainties. An audible snippet of the conversation in which his interlocutor, in a caricature of vacuous femininity, discusses her (typically for the genre, 'superfluous') job in fashion, dispels any doubt that it is the primitive scene that Raphaël prefers.

This is not to say that Raphaël's character is simply a brute. In fact, another character, Kevin (popular comedian Clovis Cornillac), a footballer who employs him to write his biography, is a parody of bestial masculinity. Priding himself on promiscuity and openly discussing his sex life – including an occasion when he 'took [a girl] a bit violently' – he provides a foil for Raphaël's more nuanced position. For, like the male characters of US 'relationship' films since the 1970s examined by Shumway (2003a: 167), Raphaël finds he needs a partner. Hence the rest of the film dramatises his struggle to overcome his atavistic urges and behave reasonably, including embracing the positive aspects of a modern, assertive femininity that, while terrifying, is not without its positive aspects.

Attal's romantic comedies deploy voiceover and narrative perspective in an equivalent fashion to cue audiences to find sexism funny and male anxiety endearing. *Ma femme est une actrice* (2001) objectifies

Charlotte Gainsbourg and twists fear about female professional success into the spectre of female infidelity, which the narrative never wholly dismisses. *Ils se marièrent* (2004) adopts an equally narcissistic perspective and an even more ambivalent stance towards contemporary femininity, and towards the range of male behaviour that is acceptable in heterosexual partnerships. Filmed in an Allen-esque naturalistic mode, this film eschews the use of self-reflexive address found in both *Mensonges* and *Ma femme*; however, the filmmaker does (again) star. Moreover, while the title and opening suggest a focus on the relationship between his character Vincent and the latter's wife Gabrielle (Gainsbourg), feminine subjectivity is soon relegated to make room for scenes between Attal and male friends, described by Communist paper *L'Humanité* as 'joint-smoking, poker-playing, neo-primitives, obsessed with cars and bimbos, amongst whom one is cheating on his wife and another fancies himself a Don Juan' (Anon 2004a). Their activities also include note-comparing on their various romances, in particular complaining on the part of Vincent's friend Georges (Chabat) about his wife Nathalie. A clue as to the interpenetration of Vincent's and Attal's attitudes is provided by this character. Played by Emmanuelle Seigner as an avowed and belligerent feminist and an 'unruly' – with the negative connotations originally traced to the word by Rowe (1995: 400) – hysteric, Nathalie constitutes an unsubtle anti-feminist caricature. By contrast, saintly Gabrielle's final decision to say nothing about the affair which she has guessed her husband is having reads as a male wish fulfilment fantasy.

By the mid-2000s, numerous features of these films become recognisable tropes within the subgenre of the male-oriented rom-com. In *Ma Vie en l'air* (Rémi Bezançon, 2005), Yann's (Vincent Elbaz, another popular, *jolie laide* actor, with a long, hooked and asymmetrical nose) neurosis is channelled into a fear of flying. Dispensing even with much of the usual couching of misogyny within self-deprecation, Bezançon has the nagging girlfriend Charlotte, with whom Yann settles down, throw away his beloved comic collection, symbolising masculine culture. She demands children and marriage, taking control of his apartment to invite her best friend over for conversation restricted to the topics of childbirth and dieting. The camera positions us to occupy Yann's point of view in the face of this extreme stereotype of female self-absorption, in such a way that we are primed to delight in his taboo-busting but aggressive response: that swallowing sperm is the best diet. Undemanding, tracksuit-clad 'ladette' Alice (Marion Cotillard), the girl next door, for whom Yann ditches Charlotte at the altar, inhabits the role of idealised male fantasy. Even more extreme is *Ce soir, je dors chez toi* (2007). This film stars well-known television comedian Jean-Paul Rouve, who resembles a young Woody Allen, a likeness underlined here through his character Alex's status as a writer. Paired with the extremely feminine-looking, doe-eyed, slim but curvaceous Mélanie Doutey, Alex's stance towards his partner is one of openly expressed fear. The title refers to his reluctance to move in with his girlfriend, whom he dreams about morphed into a military figure giving him orders, or before whose naked body in the shower he is struck dumb, in a scene which then conveys his desire for her by lingering on her naked torso and adding music composed of moans. However, such 'effeminate' traits as nervousness and passivity are counterbalanced by the character's linkage elsewhere with behaviours coded as masculine: where Yann of *Ma vie en l'air* hoarded vintage comics, Alex is protective of his record collection. These details signify both a desire to cling to rational order in the face of the more 'intuitive' realm of the feminine and also nostalgia, including for a time of greater gender differentiation.

The Buddy Film as Rom-Com

Friends frequently play an important role as sounding board or point of comparison in rom-com, while adding elements of the buddy narrative, as in *Ils se marièrent*, may increase commercial potential for directors globally with their eye on the 'date movie' market. However, Moine (2007b: 165–7) has argued that a particularly marked focus on male friendships even in rom-com is nonetheless typically French. It is also the case that the global rom-com has witnessed a progressive masculinisation over at least the last two decades (Deleyto 2003: 172; Jeffers McDonald 2009: 147). Recently, the enormous success of Judd Apatow's buddy film rom-com hybrids, starting with *The 40-Year-Old Virgin* (USA 2005), has lent the cycle renewed vigour. With roots, then, in both national tradition and transnational developments, a final subgroup of recent French comedies explores the question of romantic suffering within a more exclusively male context.[13]

In *Le Coeur des hommes* and *Le Coeur des hommes 2* (2003; 2007, not to mention a third instalment in 2013), which featured in the box-office top 20 for their respective years, men's escape from their wives to an idyllic holiday setting explicitly represents freedom from a feminine influence perceived as representing restraint and routine, against which they frequently rail. Esposito even has one of the men's much younger girlfriends pronounce beatifically that she does not need any female companionship, as she has him. However, films presenting buddy duos often even more clearly replace heterosexual relations with homosocial, and often the spectre of homoerotic, ones. Although similar observations have been made with regard to Hollywood cinema (Deleyto 2003: 173), in this case the substitution of man for woman can be understood in the context of a French tradition in which the male has often incorporated the feminine (Vincendeau 1993: 22; 2000b: 228; see also Sarde 1983: 11).

Early example *Les Apprentis* (1995), for instance, constructs homosocial bonds as highly intimate within a comic exploration of male anxiety and dysfunction. The film laments the shortcomings of contemporary masculinity while simultaneously extending its exponents' comprehension, both by aligning the perspective exclusively with them and occasionally using humour to celebrate masculinity. The heroes, Antoine (François Cluzet) and Fred (Guillaume Depardieu), exist at the periphery of society, mostly unemployed and living for free in a borrowed apartment. Antoine conforms to the Allen archetype, plagued by anxiety and hypochondria and told by ex-girlfriend Sylvie that if they had remained together, she would still be poor, badly dressed and hungry and would never have had an orgasm. His hangdog attitude is comically extreme, as when he fails to secure a job writing crosswords because he has only chosen words like *loneliness*, *suicide* and *renunciation*. Consonant with the late Depardieu's reputation as a wild child, Fred, in contrast, is the irrepressible comic eccentric, his physical excesses (pulling off his shirt in the street and putting his arm round a stranger) coupled with a childlike innocence, including ignorance of all practical matters. He is also effeminate, with his long blonde hair and the slender, hairless torso he often displays. More suggestively, he and Antoine spend a considerable amount of narrative time semi-clad in their flat, often lounging together on the bed. On one occasion, as they lie together chatting about sex, the camerawork and lighting underline intimacy, firstly by shooting the pair from outside the room, showing only their feet, as though not wishing to intrude, then shrouding their exchange in darkness. After Antoine tells an erotic story, Fred admits he has an erection, before they fall asleep together.

Les Apprentis is ambiguous in its construction of femininity through a masculine lens. Both Antoine and Fred are fascinated, as well as intimidated, by women. Sylvie's indictment of her relationship with Antoine may be harsh, but his ineptitude and self-obsession suggest it is warranted. In other respects, she is a friend and support to him. Fred's difficulties with women relate even more explicitly to their increased sexual confidence and freedom. His idealised image of the actress on whom he becomes fixated, Agnès, is destroyed when she reveals she has a boyfriend but is happy for them to have sex in front of the latter, expressed by the comically literal shattering of a pane of glass behind Fred as the news is delivered. Fred cannot, though, be said to be a much better romantic prospect than Antoine, his love declaration consisting of the revelation that the sight of his darling makes him think he should take a bath, presumably in a parody of cultural discourses around pure femininity. The film thus situates the bulk of the blame for masculinity's woes with men themselves. This does not preclude a wistful celebration of Antoine and Fred's nonconformity and childlike masculine vitality, as in a utopian final scene – which is narratively unmotivated (since Antoine has suffered a breakdown and even his relationship with Fred is on shaky ground) – in which the pair play football with children in the street to the strains of rousing Italian music, the final shot fading to black on an image of Antoine's smiling face.

An updated take on the model of rom-coms in which women barely feature is provided a decade later by *Je préfère qu'on reste amis*, this time starring Depardieu senior (Gérard) opposite Jean-Paul Rouve, as Serge and Claude, two ordinary and lonely single men who become friends while struggling to find a woman. The film is clearly indebted to buddy rom-com *Wedding Crashers* (David Dobkin, USA 2005), borrowing the Hollywood hit's device of having the heroes sneak into weddings to chat up female guests, at the suggestion of older and more worldly divorcee Serge. The men lack, however, the relative good looks of American stars Vince Vaughan and Owen Wilson. While Depardieu is just within the bounds of healthy size in this film, he makes an undeniably craggy, if charming, 59-year-old. As for Rouve, his physical 'plainness' is magnified here even more than in *Ce soir*, through his succession of drab grey suits and in particular the playful fact that his dating agency has all its members adopt the pseudonym of a celebrity. Rouve's is Johnny Depp, locating his mediocrity in a negative comparison with ideals of physical perfection but also, interestingly, implying that troubled masculinity goes hand in hand with being French (rather than American). Once again we are presented with a highly feminised persona, too, notably through Claude's hypochondria: a scene in which he takes the place previously occupied by Serge's young daughter in a doctor's consultation room uses a graphic match to make a humorous comparison.

In this film it is above all dialogue and language that underscore the status of Serge and Claude's friendship as a substitute for heterosexual romance. Early in the film their interaction mimics the rites of courtship, as Claude leaves the more independent Serge various messages, then asks, 'Why didn't you call?'. When Claude falls ill, Serge abandons a date in order to tend to 'my Claude', putting him to bed to gentle piano strains in the score. The low point at the end of the second act consists of a rift not between Claude and a woman but Claude and Serge, over a woman, prompting Claude to pronounce with all the petulance of a wronged lover that 'your behaviour has not given me much appetite for continuing our relationship'. The film's ending, after thwarting Claude's union with a woman with whom he has fallen in love, reconciles Claude and Serge against the romantic backdrop of the Manhattan skyline, accompanied by a song called 'The One To Love', with the latter admitting: 'I've spent 15 years looking for a woman and since meeting you, I feel a bit less alone and stupid.' Like *Les Apprentis*, then, *Je préfère* mobilises the utopian and transformative codes of romance in the domain of male friendship. It is pertinent to note in this context that Deleyto, in his work on friendship in global rom-coms, gives only one equivalent example, *I Love You, Man* (John Hamburg, USA 2009) (although it might be argued that at least one more is offered by teen buddy rom-com *Superbad* [Greg Mottola, USA 2007]). As he observes, the conflation of friendship with the 'uncanny intensity' and 'magic space' usually reserved for desire 'puzzles even as it fascinates' (Deleyto 2011; see also Deleyto 2003).

Like *Les Apprentis, Je préfère qu'on reste amis* demonstrates clearly the inadequacy of any interpretation of a film, especially a comedy, based exclusively on narrative details. The two films' heroes could be described as dysfunctional, semi-criminal egomaniacs and dull, socially inept skirt-chasers respectively; yet they are made loveable by humour and performance. In general, the tragic qualities of the melodramatised males of this chapter and the associated 'redemptive function of damage' (Powrie et al. 2004: 13) for contemporary masculinities are tempered to varying degrees by featuring in comedy, which can render even the surface trappings of melodrama themselves laughable. Nonetheless, melodrama is a key register for French comedy's exploration of the demands for man to adapt in order to be successful in heterosexual coupling today, whether this is construed as a workable challenge, an unnecessary exigency or, in an increasingly prominent trend at the close of the 2000s, a hopeless struggle. Just as Modleski (1991) has famously alluded to the possibility of 'feminism without women' in the sense of excluding female perspectives, so this latest development gives us the paradox of a rom-com, figuratively, without women.

Alternative Sexualities

As several film scholars (Ince 2002; Johnston 2002; Swamy 2006) have noted, in the years up to and following the passing in 1999 of French laws grouped under the umbrella term Pacte Civil de Solidarité (PaCS), which allowed couples who are not heterosexual partners access to some of the rights enjoyed by married couples, the on-screen visibility of alternative (non-heterosexual) sexuality in mainstream cinema has ballooned. A handful of these depictions occur in films roughly fitting the rom-com profile, often exploring the challenges of [reconciling] gayness with heteronormative social desires linked to family structures.

Of course, the increasing prominence of gay, lesbian, bisexual and transgender communities and individuals forms part of a wider cultural phenomenon in France (and elsewhere). As well as the attention 'gay' issues, especially arising from the PaCS and related questions – such as gay marriage and legal sanctions for gay parenting in France, which only came in in 2013 – have attracted in mainstream newspapers, *Canal Plus* broadcasts an annual 'Gay Night' to coincide with Gay Pride and signs of the 'increasing visibility of homosexuals in the media' (Anon 2000: 25) are everywhere. The election in 2001 of the openly gay Bertrand Delanoë as mayor of Paris represented a milestone in French tolerance of homesexuality – although in 2012 a failed attempt by openly homophobic Muslim immigrant Azedine Berkane to stab him suggests that tolerance is still far from universal.[14] In this section I begin by examining rom-coms that simply reflect the prominence of [...] gayness today in a relatively tokenistic way, before looking in more detail at how the genre feeds into more complex debates about queer or alternative identities and sexualities. Finally, I examine how it seeks to reorient the traditional family to accommodate these new configurations.

Token Gayness

Gay friends were already so familiar in Hollywood rom-coms by the mid-1990s that *My Best Friend's Wedding* (P.J. Hogan, USA 1997) was able to use this recognisable feature to create a new twist on the genre. They are much less common in France, although one features in *Laisse tes mains*, whose debt to the Spanish queer cinema of Almodóvar I have already mentioned; this is itself a rather token allusion, however, since queerness features as a means to make central character Odile, and the whole film, appear edgy, youthful and alternative. The gay character in question is clearly marked as gayness by his effete performance style and high voice but his life is not explored. Similarly, a gay nightclub features in *Au suivant!* simply as a marker of 'cool', associated with the media world of youthful casting director Jo.

These examples foreground the interpenetration of sexuality and class in the rom-com: the fact that a broadly middle-class genre – especially one disproportionately peopled by 'media types' – is well placed to include gay characters. They also suggest how a dose of queerness can sometimes form part of a film's positioning and therefore marketing strategy. This idea can be applied more obviously, for example, to the work of 'on-trend' gay auteur François Ozon. One specific possible instance is a kiss between stars Fanny Ardant and Catherine Deneuve in Ozon's hit film *8 Femmes/ 8 Women* (2002), which Lucille Cairns (2006: 96) has dismissed as no more than a 'lesboerotic dalliance', no sooner initiated than 'liquidated and disavowed'. These remarks are to be taken in the context of the imbalance in French cinema's – and indeed in all French cultural production's (Heathcote, Hughes and Williams 1998: 15–17) – historical portrayal of gay men and of lesbians, the latter group being considerably underrepresented (see Ince 2002: 90).[15] A similar accusation of gimmickiness could be levelled at a lesbian kiss between Rampling and Bouquet in *Embrassez*, although it is less sexualised than in *8 Women* and contributes to the yearning for a feminine utopia discernible in the film.

Slightly more considered in its inclusion of a secondary lesbian thread is female director Amanda Sthers' *Je vais te manquer* (2009), in which Anna (Cécile Cassel), one of the daughters of terminally ill central character Julia, is a lesbian. A mark of the film's greater openness is that Anna's sexuality is neither suppressed nor caricatured. We learn that she is gay through an early sequence in which we see her pick up a woman in a club, then leave her conquest in bed with a cursory goodbye the next morning. This detail avoids the stereotype of the clingy lesbian/woman (although Anna's partner, displeased to be abandoned, might fit this bill) and instead forms part of Anna's broader characterisation as acerbic and introverted, particularly in response to her mother's illness. Lesbianism is an important but not all-encompassing feature of her identity and it is not desexualised.

Returning to queer male identities, the reverse is true of the gay character in another ensemble film from the previous year, *Modern Love*. Here the gayness of Jérôme, best friend of protagonist Elsa, is so token as to be neutralised by falling for Elsa during the narrative. Embodying all the clichés of [feminised] gay male identity as sensitive, attentive and house-proud, Jérôme proves the perfect boyfriend. However, despite him having abandoned his gay sexuality for her, Elsa ultimately decides that he is not 'my man': an obvious slur on his 'ersatz' masculinity. Put differently, the film unwittingly brings into relief the threat [posed by] queerness, an increasingly troublesome fly in the ointment for the traditional heterosexual romance plot, precisely by disavowing and then punishing that sexuality. It can thus be situated in the context of the homophobic backlash that has inevitably accompanied the official recognition of gay couples and the growing presence of gay of gay life in France (see Johnston 2002: 23). Nor, it should be noted, are open expressions of homophobia absent from French comedy. Alain Brassart (2007: 238–9) discusses the obvious ambivalence of Veber's hit satire on political correctness *Le Placard/The Closet* (2001) on this question, encapsulated by the remark of the openly 'tolerant' company director: 'That poof is a drag.' A negatively constructed wrong partner in ensemble piece *Au secours, j'ai trente ans* (2004), selfish patriarch Thomas, is repulsed by his wife's gay friend's public displays of affection towards his partner (and suggests that gayness may be the cause of a cancer the character develops). More subtly – and recalling the same actor's embodiment of a straight character's gay transgression 'despite himself' in *La Vérité ou presque* – in *Les Petits mouchoirs* Max (François Cluzet) reacts with revulsion when a male friend communicates his (in fact supposedly platonic) 'love' for him. Attal's embodiment of backward masculinity in *Ils se marièrent* also includes feelings of disgust at the idea of two men kissing in his list of attributes. As I have argued in discussing melodramatised masculinity in this film, the difference is that in this case the audience is generally invited to identify with the homophobic character. In this way it is the worst offender within this group of films that tends to extend limited attention or hostility to gay [identities], while nonetheless resgistering their existence as a mainstream cultural development.

Queer Identities and Gay Sexuality

The presence of gay characters as one minimal element of otherwise pro-heterosexual narratives in the films detailed so far clearly falls a long way short of any self-consciously queer filmmaking practice. In fact, Bill Marshall (1998: 262) has argued that this limitation applies to French cinema more generally. This situation appears unchanged in the 2010s; certainly the French rom-com has only occasionally been queered.

It is important here to make a distinction between identity positions and sexuality itself. Any sustained attempt to evoke gay desire is absent from most of the films detailed so far (although *Je vais te manquer* does at least make a lesbian pick-up look relatively 'sexy', by suggesting the chemistry between two attractive young women through an exchange of gazes and flirtatious remarks). This distinction goes right to the heart of some of the differences between the Anglo-American tendency to celebrate gay [desire] and a French one to sublimate it. A comparison between the French PaCS and the British civil partnership is telling. While the PaCS makes no distinction between same sex and other unmarried couples, such as co-habiting siblings, the civil partnership is available to gay couples only. However the PaCS is also considerably inferior to marriage by comparison with the civil partnership – although same-sex marriage and adoption have been made legal in France in 2013, soon after Britain and Wales. All the same, having historically been deprived of a collective (unassimilated) voice, French people identifying themselves with alternative sexualities have had less means to make their desire for equal rights heard.[16]

A rom-com that illustrates well the distinction between identity and sexuality is *Chouchou* (2003). The film stars Elmaleh as the eponymous Chouchou, a cross-dressing illegal Moroccan immigrant whose character originated in the performer's cult comic stage shows. It certainly celebrates difference, as the gentle and helpless Chouchou, whose goals comprise a job and preferably the chance to wear women's clothes, gradually wins the hearts of all those around her and gains the confidence to defy those who seek to obstruct her modest desires. A scene in which she tells a policeman that his gun is a phallic symbol and his authoritarian career choice the symptom of a repressed libido epitomises the narrative's intoxicating disregard for social legitimacy. The film also contributes to the strong strand of mockery of bourgeois heteronormalcy focalised through the figure of Chabat in *Gazon Maudit* and later *Prête-moi*. Here he plays, against type, the bombastically named Stanislas de la Tour-Maubourg, a an Eastern European who falls falls for Chouchou in a transvestite club and is finally united with her in a mock wedding ceremony. The extent to which this reconfigures the classic rom-com wedding, using actors who have both starred in highly successful examples of the genre (although Elmaleh's *Hors de prix* came later in 2006), is apparent. On the other hand, Chouchou is a collection of caricatural features of feminised gay masculinity, a scatterbrain who is obsessed with the colour pink and Princess Diana. It could be argued that this reflects the highly overdetermined nature of transvestite and transgender femininity itself, which involves an imitation that by nature tends towards caricature. More problematic is the total absence of any real sense of homosexual desire between Chouchou and Stanislas, whose courtship is conveniently rendered highly 'proper' by both characters' humorous association with old-fashioned gender ideals, of feminine chastity and masculine chivalry respectively. While Rollet (2011) cites the absence of specific behaviour associated with gayness as one aspect of the film's queering of the audience's expectations, for Brassart cross-dressing becomes here merely a gag (2007: 234).[17]

The particular variant of the separation between identity and sexuality effected by *Chouchou* reverses a more common one: the trope of illicit his homosexual desire ascribed to a character who identifies themselves as heterosexual. As well as *La Vérité ou presque*, *Le Placard* is salient, as Depardieu's hyper-masculine cipher suffers a breakdown when he realises his homosexual desire for his colleague – and his character is never redeemed. A more obviously romantic example comes in a musical comedy by gay directing partnership Olivier Ducastel and Jacques Martineau, *Crustacés et coquillages* (2005). While the auteur filmmakers – who agree that 'in France the concept of gay cinema is not well defined' (Anon 2005b) – reject the interpretation of this as a gay film (unlike their more arthouse piece *Drôle de Félix/Adventures of Felix* [2000]) because it also deals with heterosexual libido, the film sanitises neither form of desire. In an alternative take on the classic narrative of the family holiday, in addition to the extra-marital antics of the parents, their son Charly is secretly desired by his visiting friend Martin. One humorous scene, refusing to shy away from the earthier aspects of gay male sexuality, features Charly searching for Martin in what is, unbeknown to him, a local cruising area and being approached fairly aggressively by predatory men. The real shock comes, though, when he encounters his father Marc there. There are also several shots of the male body, included to show Charly and Martin's uninhibited friendship and to display the toned physique of Marc's love interest.

While at the end of *Crustacés*, Marc recognises that he is in fact gay, he explains that he was unable to accept the possibility of fatherhood being foreclosed to him. This raises the important question of the relationship between alternative sexualities and traditional family structures in the rom-com. Indeed, this is the question with which the rom-com genre of reconciliation and renewal is most concerned when it comes to its portrayal of such sexualities.

Homosexuality and the Family

In her 2002 article on 'queering the family' through 'fantasy and the performance of sexuality and gay relations' in rom-coms *Gazon maudit* and *Pourquoi pas moi?* (Stéphane Giusti, 1999), Kate Ince argues that in these texts the paradigm of the bourgeois family shifts to accommodate queer identities. At the end of *Gazon*, lesbian Marijo has joined married couple Laurent and Loli as the triumvirate sets about raising the baby who is the product of a one-time liaison between Laurent and Marijo. Not only that but 'difference proliferates' as there is a hint that staunchly heterosexual Laurent may be starting an affair with another man. In *Pourquoi pas moi?*, several families come together in a Catalan country house for their children – including, unusually, three lesbians (and one gay man) – to break to them the news that [they are] gay. Thanks to the couple-swapping antics of the older generation, by the end of the film, '[a] wholesale "queering" of the family has occurred, which is reinforced by the new relationships forged' (Ince 2002: 95–6). As Ince notes, the role of performance in constructing gender and identity (not to mention the Spanish setting echoing Almodóvar's work) in the film feeds into its queer aesthetic, as for example when two mothers Diane and Sara's feelings for each other are reawakened by singing a song together for the group. While these women – and Diane's husband Tony – are both singers, Eva's father is a world-famous torero, played by Johnny Hallyday. Even more excessive is the film's finale, which – like visions of the Virgin Mary appearing before Chouchou – uses kitsch to create a 'camp and sentimental' decor and atmosphere, as 'a spangle-attired cabaret singer atop an illuminated podium draped with semi-naked dancers clad as angels/cherubs performs a love song called "Crazy"' (ibid: 95).

Pédale douce and also *Crustacés* adhere to Ince's model. The 1996 film, as already mentioned, is set in the colourfully excessive world of Parisian drag, which – echoing Kath Weston's (1991) description of the networks formed by some queer groups in San Francisco – operates in the film as an alternative kinship structure. Brassart rightly attributes *Pédale douce*'s huge success (3.9 million spectators) to changing attitudes [about] gayness in France. Hence gay Adrien's assumption of paternity of another man's child can be presented as positive – although biological father Alexandre does show up at the christening, prompting a 'liberating' final image of the parental trio and the baby driving around Paris in a car singing the highly camp 'Sans contrefaçon' by Mylène Farmer. Interestingly, in contrast to Tarr with Rollet's (2001: 189) argument that the film's 'outrageous drag queens function primarily as an exotic backdrop to the development of a conventional, heterosexual romance', for Brassart the film's strength lies in the parallels it draws between gay and straight identities. Thus Adrien's paternal desire echoes Alexandre's wife's fear of being separated from her husband, both of these being socially constructed – as feminist Elisabeth Badinter has observed in relation to parental care in *L'Amour en plus* (1980) (Brassart 2007: 234).

Where mainstream hit *Pédale douce* foregoes realism in favour of high melodrama and the humour of grotesque caricature, especially through the presentation of resolutely comic actor Timsit [Figure 12], but also in details like transvestite godparents at the christening, *Crustacés* places

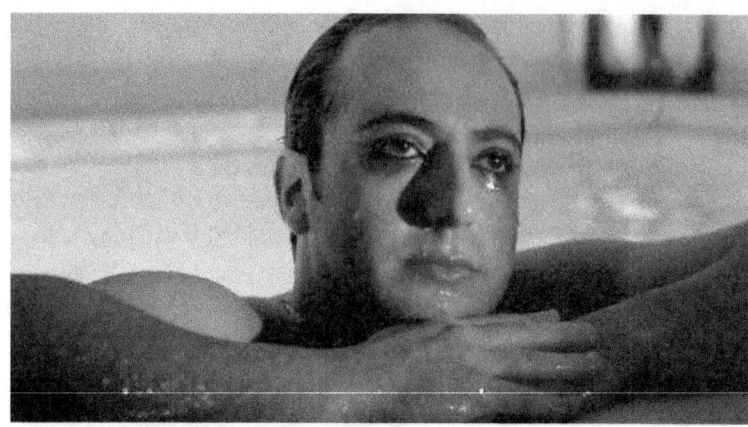

Figures 12 and 13. Caricatural gay melodrama versus a 'serious' consideration of queerness in *Pédale douce* and *Crustacés et coquillages*. © Pathé and Peccadillo Pictures

its auteur favourites Melki and Bruni Tedeschi in a world characterised generally by a naturalistic look and acting style [Figure 13], with gentle comedy here a function of the upbeat tone within an idyllic holiday setting. This aesthetic expresses formally the film's conception of queer not as a markedly different identity – a conception relying on a binaristic inversion of heteronormative values – but rather as an everyday, universal possibility existing within the heart of the 'heterosexual' family (see Coste 2011). Thus Béatrix's discovery of Marc's queerness prompts not histrionics but a considered reflection on their life together, in which she points out some of the positives of having had a husband with a 'feminine' disposition. In this case the ending stands stylistically apart from the main narrative, as an epilogue returns the central family to their holiday home one year on, now reconfigured so that, while both the children have invited along a heterosexual partner, mother Béatrix's lover Mathieu is on site and so is father Marc's plumber boyfriend. Here the group, all dressed in yellows and oranges, give a mannered, frenzied song and dance performance of the original title song composed by director Martineau with Philippe Miller (echoing in reverse lines from 'La Madrague', famously rendered by Bardot), in which lists of shellfish are reeled off jubilantly in an obvious metaphor for the beauty of nature's diversity.

These two endings from otherwise very different films present queer takes on the French family at least as heavily marked by fantasy as those of *Gazon maudit* and *Pourquoi pas moi?*. However, my interpretation of their resolutions differs slightly from that of Ince, for whom the fantasy dimension of such endings 'may have a politically performative force', and who closes by asking whether, in the wake of the PaCS, a traditional model of patriarchal familial identity is likely to give way to one closer to these idealistic endings. While tying new familial configurations to sequences of happiness and liberation, often associated with motion, excitement and perhaps uplifting song and dance, does demand to be read politically, the fantasy elements of these sequences still locate them at some distance from everyday French reality. These familial reconfigurations remain, for now, coded as utopian mirages.

Fantasy also colours in a different way, through its generic allegiances, queer musical rom-com/drama by popular auteur Christophe Honoré *Les Chansons d'amour*, in which the heterosexual couple is replaced by a threesome composed of a young man and two young women, all of whom are sexually involved – until the untimely death of one of the girls prompts this to give way to an uncertain relationship between the male protagonist and a gay acquaintance. Although Iris Brey (2014) has argued that the film marginalises queer identities to the Parisian *faubourgs* or outer districts, it does offer up a matter-of-fact (singing notwithstanding) depiction of mobile sexuality. Such a conception of sexual identity contributes to the sense of the frailty of human bonds in evidence in the contemporary rom-com as a whole. It is also significant to find such a daring portrayal in a film whose international cultural prominence was facilitated by Honoré's self-conscious auteur positioning and the branding of his film as an alternative Parisian love-story. The former impulse is exemplified most obviously by the casting of Louis Garrel, godson of Truffaut's 'alter ago' actor Jean-Pierre Léaud, in the central role, as well as by an explicit homage to – or subversion of – the dyadic couple featured in Truffaut's *Baisers volés/Stolen Kisses* (1968) in a scene which shows the threesome in bed together in a composition similar to one of those featuring just the man and woman in the earlier film. This detail recalls my earlier claim that some New Wave films can in fact be seen as rom-coms. Indeed, Jill Forbes (1992b) has shown that in French cinema going back to the New Wave, the triangular relationship itself undermines traditional family structures – an observation that might well be applied to several other auteurist rom-coms of the contemporary period, such as Marion Vernoux's *Love, Etc.* (1996, another film starring Charlotte Gainsbourg and Yvan Attal and focused on adultery, based on a novel by the British writer Julian Barnes and released in the UK).

Further rom-coms that interrogate overtly the question of reconciling familial identities and gay sexuality are *L'Homme est une femme comme les autres/Man is a Woman* (Jean-Jacques Zilbermann, 1998), *Belle maman* (1999) and, most recently, *Comme les autres/Baby Love* (Vincent Garenq, 2008). In the first of these comic elements largely give way to melodrama by the end of a tale in which gay Orthodox Jew Simon Eskanazy (Antoine de Caunes) attempts to 'go straight' by marrying in order to secure his inheritance. At the close of the narrative, he stands alone in the rain watching his pregnant wife Elsa walk away and close off the possibility of him taking a role in their child's upbringing. Just as its sex scenes make a feminised caricature of Simon's body (virgin Elsa, with Sapphic overtones, likes his rounded buttocks – prominent on the DVD cover and film posters – but is afraid of his 'big thing'), the English title of *Man is a Woman* spells out the suggestion that 'men ultimately deal with the threat of female power by incorporating it' (Modleski 1991: 7). Interestingly, in an article published to accompany the film's release in popular paper *L'Evènement du jeudi* (Bernard 1998), two young Jewish gay men asked about the film attested to its premise's status as extremely true to life, mirroring a trend they recognised within their communities. It would seem queer identities were was, at the end of the1990s (and probably still today), very far from being accepted in those social and religious and/or racial groups where the family still holds greatest sway.

In *Belle maman*, Aghion simply assumes the untroubled existence of *familles homoparentales*, or families with two parents of the same sex, by having Léa's (Deneuve) mother (played by veteran actress Line Renaud) live with her long-term lesbian partner. Léa, we learn, was the product of sperm donation. The 'rose-coloured view of gay parenting' (Johnston 2002: 28) to which this gives rise, through the close and respectful relationship between Léa and her mother(s), is in its own way as utopian as the fantasy families described earlier in this section. Interestingly, Johnston further suggests that this idealisation is linked to the femininity of mother(s) and daughter and draws out a potential double standard in the text with respect to a secondary character, married father Pascal, whose revelation of gayness is received as somewhat more shocking.

By 2008 in *Comme les autres*, gay *male* parenting is allowed to take centre stage, in a film about paediatrician Manu's (Lambert Wilson) compulsive desire to be a father. The clichés normally associated with maternal desire are in full force, as Manu finds himself surrounded by adorable children, in particular his niece, and the strength of his longing is sealed when he sacrifices his loving relationship with chiselled judge Philippe (Pascal Elbé) – who has no desire for children – in order to pursue his goal alone. Resulting scenes in which Manu poses as a single straight man when the adoption agent visits speak to the reality that in 2008 not only did PaCSed couples not have the right to adopt, but being PaCSed to someone of the same sex might hinder an application (Gross 2001: 250). In fact, Manu fails to convince the agent in the scene in question, because he has forgotten to hide a sexually suggestive portrait of a nude man on his apartment wall. This detail is not trivial. While over-sexualisation in portrayals of gay people reduces their identity to one dimension, I have suggested that avoiding the issue completely excludes that sexuality itself from representation *as a sexuality*. In general, Manu and Philippe could not be more reassuringly characterised, as a doctor and a judge, while Wilson in particular is an actor typically cast as successful, patriarchal characters. Moreover, Manu's exceptional bedside manner with his child patients singles him out as a much more caring potential parent than, for example, his heterosexual sister and her husband, who like to unceremoniously dump their (on one occasion ill) baby daughter on him. In this context, the nude image at the adoption interview acts as an important reminder of the couple's sexual identity.

More generally, films like this one have reflected and contributed to the cultural and eventually legal change that has seen same-sex couples given the right to adopt in France in 2013. This constitutes an important endorsement of alternative forms of social organisation - albeit within the parameters of so-called homonormativity, rather than embracing a radical rejection of mainstream culture's "reproductive futurism" in the way proposed by queer theorists such as Lee Edelman (2004). Conversely, the rom-com is surely an accurate social barometer in suggesting that the persistence of family values in France is still the biggest obstacle to social acceptance of newer identities in general, be they queer, feminine, masculine or a combination of the above.

4
Family Affairs

The French family has always occupied a position of ambivalent status and cultural prestige, and this is much in evidence today. This chapter will examine romantic comedy's exploration of new configurations of the Gallic family in a contemporary climate where, as partner choice is less determined by material and dynastic interests and more by individual choice, 'so the love story has become the essential basis, the *raison d'être* and the *sine qua non* of the family unit' (Holmes 2006: 115). This will encompass, on the one hand, the genre's often celebratory depiction of the nuclear family's march towards its long prophesied death and, on the other, its more frequently visible role in translating a corollary trend for pro-familial discourses.

The historical background to these counterpoised moves is that which underpins this analysis in its entirety and has been well documented in Western society. Woman's move in the twentieth century into the public sphere has caused unprecedented change to societal organisation and placed her, the traditional family-maker, at a nexus of several life 'choices', amongst which motherhood is – at least ostensibly – only one. Capitalist society's contrivance to mobilise the female workforce looks from the perspective of the early twenty-first century to have created the single most formidable threat to the propagation of those societies from within, with birth rates declining in the vast majority of Western countries. However, postwar French politics have been pro-natalist and family-oriented (Duchen 1994: 96–127) and in 2010 France represents a demographic curiosity, with the second highest birth rate in Europe (Badinter 2010: 34).[1] Despite soaring divorce rates, then, in its most straightforward sense denoting procreation, the French family appears in this light to be an institution in rude health.

What is clearly undergoing considerable flux is the nature of the family as a social unit. Most obviously, the dethroning of marriage has led to the rise of broken families as well as *la famille recomposée*: strictly, families where one (or both) of the parents already has children from a previous union, although the phrase loosely evokes sprawling and structurally unconventional families in general. Other changes are more convoluted but all can be rooted in the destabilisation of patriarchy and the greater fluidity of roles occupied by each of the genders. Since second wave feminism's liberation of women from automatic responsibility for the domestic sphere, there is some evidence of a rise to prominence of the nurturing father, as famously depicted in French film comedy by Serreau in her 1985 hit *Trois hommes et un couffin/ Three Men and a Cradle*. However, sociologist Catherine Hakim (2000: 10) argues that in the twenty-first century still very few men in fact take on the raising and education of children as their principal activity, even in Scandinavian countries where generous offers of paternity leave invite them to do so. Accordingly, after a flurry of activity around him in (global) US cultural discourses in the 1980s and early 1990s (see Kaplan 1992: 184–8) and 1990s films (Mazdon 2000: 64), the nurturing father appears to fade somewhat from public consciousness. He is not, in any case, a central figure in the French romantic comedies of 1990s and 2000s and will only appear in a secondary way in this chapter. All the same, motherhood is today certainly less often an exclusive life-goal for women, who are leaving it until later and more often combining less children with a career. The latter is particularly true in France where, relative to other European countries, high numbers of women return to work after having children (Badinter 2010: 234).

The mise-en-scène of what well-known French psychoanalyst Elisabeth Roudinesco (2002) has called *la famille en désordre* is fast becoming a cliché of studies of French cinema. Prédal (1998: 19) has noted its thematic prevalence in the work of *jeune cinéma français* directors – Ozon, Klapisch and Dominick Moll are obvious examples. The recent move away from the cinematic representation of actual family to the portrayal of surrogate or tribal community groups identified by Powrie (2007) constitutes one of several reactions to the decline of the traditional family. Vincendeau (2008) has further pointed to an opposed counter-reaction to the same phenomenon, especially since the 1990s, as the family becomes more disarrayed, through films focusing on relatively stable family groups.

The Ensemble Family Rom-Com

Ensemble rom-coms are markedly frequent in France. In particular, echoing the historical Gallic predilection for mixing comedy with 'serious' themes, rom-com here frequently hybridises with family melodrama, typically focusing on two or more romantic plot-lines across the generations. In a US context, the cultivation of cross-generational family audiences has been linked to the advent of home video consumption in the late 1980s and early 1990s (Allen 1999: 113–6). Such films in any case have a wide target audience and provide a platform for a gallery of bankable stars. Given theorisations of melodrama as the woman's film *par excellence*, as well as French female filmmakers' documented interest in interrogating the status of the modern family, it follows logically that a small majority of these hybrid ensemble rom-coms released in France in the past 20 years have been made by women. In the context of a French genre where women's participation is already strikingly high (44 out of 115 films, or 38 per cent, rising to 47 per cent if including the ten films on which a woman received a writing credit, as marked on the filmography), within the ensembles women directed 19 out of 43 films (44 per cent), but including women with writing credits – since narrative structure is born in the screenplay – raises the figure to 26 out of 43 or 60 per cent.[2]

Ensemble romances refuse to view romance as a cure-all, or legitimate one-dimensional identities, which have in the past been culturally prescribed to women in particular. This feature helps to explain the appeal of the *choral* film for female filmmakers. Discourses of individualism have been understood as a fundamentally masculine take on the world. From a psychoanalytic perspective, Chodorow and Jessica Benjamin have argued that the Oedipal imperative to separate from the mother is less powerful for women, with the result that their sense of identity is more entwined with that of others (see Holmes 2006: 142). At the same time, more socially-oriented feminists have seized on Foucauldian ideas of *general*, as opposed to *total* history, returning women to the framework by insisting on the insignificance of the individual life (see Kaplan 1996: 3).[3] The ensemble narrative conveys a similarly relativistic conception of the world that is inherently resistant to romance's pigeonholing of the genders in familial roles.

This stands in direct contrast to the logic of strict causality, progress and resolution informing the traditional rom-com. While feminists have accused the 'seamless' linear style of the classical Hollywood romance of essentialising the roles presented, the ensemble narrative remains episodic, with different stories – and characters – jostling for investment, often displaying a degree of tonal discord, and the seams more readily apparent. For Tröhler, in fact, multi-protagonist films of the 1990s 'constitute chronicles of reality today and their many characters are offered as multiple facets of a socio-political portrait. In this respect, *French* films are perhaps rather specific [...]' (2000: 86; original emphasis). Tröhler's arguments echo my own linkage between the ensemble focus and an interest in social reality that has been seen as prevalent in French cinema, romantic and otherwise, both historically (see for example Grossvogel 2005: 2–3) and today (Moine 2007b: 144). There is a tension here with romance's ostensible rejection of realism. Although I have argued that romance can play a key role in imaginative identity-construction in the real world, the most formulaic manifestations of the romantic genre are associated with contrived plotting and instances of the miraculous. In the ensemble, however, this is framed by a relatively realist aesthetic, especially when it comes to the topos of the universal, so potentially humdrum, family. Such an aesthetic has repercussions for the films' style. Namely, in the ensemble films formal details generally conform to a more recognisably 'French' mould, with longer takes, fewer close-ups, longer shots and tableaux compositions, and fewer meretricious stylistic flourishes altogether. This contrasts with the tendency of US ensembles of the 1990s and 2000s to adopt what David Bordwell has dubbed intensified continuity style, characterised by fast editing, 'extreme' focal lengths, a predominance of close-ups and wide-ranging camera movements (Mar Azcona 2010: 39), highlighting the French ensemble form's autochthonous roots. In the family ensemble the romantic tropes of magic and fantasy are often distilled in details of narrative and mise-en-scène, from a holiday setting (*Les Marmottes, Embrassez qui vous voudrez*) to romantic intertextual allusion (*Les Marmottes*) or a focus on a wedding (*Mariages!*); but romance is generally more diluted than with dyadic or triangular rom-coms.

It should also be noted that such narratives' preoccupation with groups of people and governance by a degree of verisimilitude is no guarantor of their ideological commitment to a broad 'socio-political portrait'. Far from it, one by-product of family stories' potential for incorporating autobiographical details is their frequently (upper) middle-class focus (Vincendeau 2008: 16) – and a concomitant relative absence of career women. Middle-class credentials also mirror not only French feminism's association with the bourgeoisie, but the transnational phenomenon of post-feminism, as manifested in the media since around the same time as the global rom-com's renaissance in the 1980s. In France, meanwhile, the middle class has been growing thanks to the slow migration into it of the former skilled working class. At the same time, a middle-class focus is in any case a feature of both the French rom-com and indeed French cinema generally.

Bourgeois settings do not in any case detract from the significance of the ensemble film's reconfiguration of the binary approach to role-assignment that typifies mainstream US romance.[4] In fact, the episodic structure of these films is closer to television series than to Hollywood, and in particular soap opera, whose own debt to the melodramatic 'woman's film' is overt in its domestic settings and quotidian dramas. Indeed, soap opera's female address can be linked to its roots in serialised literature, which was often of the romantic variety and, as in the case of France's *feuilleton*, aimed at a female readership (see Thiesse 1984). This address has been discussed by, amongst others, Modleski (1990 [1982]: 90–103) in ways that resonate with the ensemble romance. According to Modleski, the soap illustrates human interconnectedness and contingency, dispelling the myth of total individual agency. By dispersing audience investment among different characters, whose stories do not usually all end with romantic union, multi-protagonist films refuse predictability and keep open a sense of uncertain futurity. They also show how one man's gain is another man's loss. This is implicit in my discussion of the French rom-com's foregrounding of the complications of adultery: it is a *choral* focus which asks the viewer to engage with the pain suffered by betrayed women in *Pédale douce*, *Les Marmottes* and *On connaît la chanson*.

Whether employed by a male or female director (or writer), then, the ensemble rom-com can in this sense be dubbed anti-romance, or formally anti-familial. The high number of women directors who opt for the family romance *choral* thus suggests their typically ambivalent attitude towards both romance and the family, reconfiguring the latter at one remove from patriarchy. With regard specifically to rom-com, it is interesting to note that research by Sharon Thompson suggests that, where for men romance often ends with conquest, women see it more in terms of an ongoing narrative (see Pearce and Stacey 1995: 20). It is highly appropriate that explicit recognition of this difference by Jaoui's surrogate family ensemble *Le Goût des autres* (2000) comes in the context of women's penchant for watching soap operas, as protagonist Castella is berated by his wife for changing channels at the moment when the on-screen couple come together for a kiss, at which point his interest evaporates.

In other words, the ensemble form may bear structural affinities with women's particular experiences, which include romance and family life, as well as the cultural narratives associated with them. Modleski attempts to link her argument to (different) aspects of women's physiological and social being, by proposing that the soap opera's multi-climaxing, interrupted rhythms mimic the structures of both female sexual pleasure and housework. She also compares the ideal soap opera spectator to the mother invested in several childlike egos and, referring to Mulvey's work on classical film narrative's suturing of woman into a position of powerlessness, claims that the idealised female spectator is frequently paralleled by disempowered mother characters in the narrative itself (Modleski 1990 [1982]: 92). In the French ensemble rom-com, maternal impotence in the face of adolescent rebellion is a central theme in several films I consider as *choraux* to one extent or another, including *Les Marmottes*, *LOL* and *Une semaine sur deux*. In *Les Marmottes*, it is further invoked through the device of a recipe for happiness in a letter left by the dead family matriarch to one of her sons, read at the end of the narrative by the wife from whom he has separated.

More importantly, Modleski's point highlights the fact that the instability of identities already inherent in the ensemble structure can be even more evident in familial formations, where the boundaries of individual identity become indistinct. Significantly, another of Tröhler's arguments, that in multi-protagonist films 'the narrative construction of an audience shuffles between proximity and distance' (2010: 470), extends this familial model of interaction to include the viewer, further helping to explain the popularity of several recent French ensemble rom-coms.

'Familles: je vous hais'

Given the French rom-com's position at the juncture of domestic and global film cultures, it is pertinent to seek out local as well as US antcedents to or catalysts for the contemporary trend. A strong candidate is Klapisch's 1996 adaptation of Jaoui and Bacri's play *Un air de famille*. Dramatising a family's wait for the arrival of one member for their weekly dinner ritual in a dimly-lit bar, the film openly satirises the French family. Themes of stultification and genericity are captured by an early view of the exterior of the matriarch's residence, a modern block characterised by uniform geometric repetitions, which are bifurcated by straight slats reminiscent of prison bars and shot from below to tower oppressively over the camera. Such themes are reinforced by subtle details of costume – the mother, Madame Ménard (Claire Maurier, familiar as the flawed mother from Truffaut's 1959 *Les Quatre cents coups/The 400 Blows*), has the same haircut and drab beige coat as her daughter-in-law – and composition – inside the bar, the use of deep focus facilitates the evocation of characters' confinement by their encasement within architectural frames, while reflective surfaces recalling the sets of Sirk and Fassbinder suggest both incommunicability and resemblance between the family members. The discomfiting presence of a paralysed dog, on one occasion shot to the enervating buzz of a fly, provides another visual metaphor for family in its most negative incarnation.

The narrative tends to literalise the battle of the sexes, notably through brothers Henri (Bacri) and Philippe's (Wladimir Yordanoff) reactionary attitudes and their interactions with the female characters. If the views aired by Henri and his failure to listen to and respect his wife Arlette – hence her lateness and finally non-appearance for the dinner – are openly bigoted, second brother Philippe's attitude towards his own wife Yolande is more insidious. In short, by feigning niceness only to encourage her into submissive weakness, he casts her in the role of inconsequential airhead who must be humoured. The resemblance between a studded choker bought by Philippe for Yolande's birthday and the dog collar for which it is first mistaken leaves little room for doubt about power relations between husband and wife. It is a measure of the film's feminist bent that at its close Henri and Arlette are not finally reconciled, while Yolande has ignored Philippe's attempts to keep her 'in her place', got drunk and enjoyed a dance with waiter

Denis (popular actor Jean-Pierre Darrousin). The narrative is also book-ended by its focus on another romantic relationship, between Betty (Jaoui) and Denis. Betty's initial annoyance at Denis' failure to call her because she has her own life, 'like you do', is incontrovertibly reasonable, placing women on an equal footing with men. That she and Denis finally together escape the oppressive space of the bar on a motorbike allows the rom-com mode to trump that of family drama. It also looks at first glance like a classic naive-cum-regressive finale in which problems melt away. But Denis' characterisation throughout as kind and unassuming, a foil to the bickering family, along with the fact that the woman occupies the driving seat (unlike, in the final sequences of *Amelie* and *Hors de prix*) appears to suggest the possibility of a future for their relationship based on compromise.

Un air also exemplifies the model remarked on by Vincendeau (2008: 16) in post-1960s French cinema of the absent (or otherwise weakened) patriarch.[5] Here Monsieur Ménard is dead and his memory ambivalently invoked, with fondness but also negatively through comparisons with Henri as outmoded, like the bar as a whole – and by contrast with Philippe, a stereotype of (post)modernity (Sellier 1998: 122). The promotion of the matriarch resulting from this deposing of her masculine counterpart in French cinema further chimes paradoxically with Modleski's stress on female disempowerment, by lending itself to portrayals of (vain) maternal struggles to shore up the family against social convulsions. Certainly, in this film, impotence is strongly associated with Madame Ménard, who favours paralysed dogs (having given Henri an animal of the same breed as her own erstwhile paraplegic pet), whose attempts to influence her children fall on deaf ears and who is at one point physically incapacitated by a fall down a staircase. In this case, in view of the character's resolutely negative presentation, her disempowerment reads as a punishment for her attempts to hold the family together.

A significant number of other films in the corpus figure family life in this vein, as stagnation or misery. This is often linked to the question of adultery, as in *Embrassez qui vous voudrez* and *Mariages!*, or to the issue of freedom more generally – for instance in *La Nouvelle Eve*. However, two ensemble rom-com/family drama hybrids by male directors from later in the period of study, *Le Premier jour du reste de ta vie* (Rémi Bezançon, 2008) and *Tellement proches* (Nakache and Toledano, 2009) temper the unflattering presentation of family life with positive details and consensual endings that recuperate the unit. Often melodramatic in tone, *Le Premier jour* enacts five key days in the life of a couple and their three teenage or twenty-something children. One of these, which has the father diagnosed with cancer, at the same time as it leaves another matriarch paralysed to prevent the splintering of her family, illustrates a further observation made by Vincendeau (2008: 17) with regard to French cinema's destabilisation of the patriarchal family: the rise of the so-called medical theme.[6] The father's illness and subsequent death in this narrative, however, is offset by the roughly simultaneous resolution of many of the problems afflicting both parents' relations with their three children: a petty grudge between the father and the oldest son, the middle son's disinterest in a finding a career and leaving home and the youngest daughter's histrionic teenage rebellions. Strikingly, it is particularly the daughter's (unplanned) pregnancy that appears to seal her restored relations with her mother, echoing sentimental flashback scenes of the latter's own pregnancy. Generational continuity and heritage are further underscored by a storyline in which the middle son learns his grandfather's trade. That this involves wine connoisseurship implicitly evokes the linkage between familial and national continuity.

While *Un air de famille* and *Le Premier jour* depict provincial middle-class families, *Tellement proches* is set for the most part in the archetypally negatively constructed familial space of the Parisian suburbs – specifically around a huge modern Créteil block – and makes much of arduous journeys back and forth across the *périphérique* ring-road encircling the central metropolis. The film delights in humorous depiction of the awful chaos of life with young children. Reminiscent of hit Hollywood comedy *Parenthood* (Ron Howard, USA 1989), it is perhaps most noteworthy for extending the tropes of melodramatised masculinity to the terrain of fatherhood. In particular, despite its focus on several characters of both genders, it is Vincent Elbaz's Alain who appropriates the narrative through voiceover, which aligns audiences with him at the same time that his actions (ignoring long-suffering wife Nathalie when she tries to discuss their son's problems at school, flirting with a teenage babysitter and showing little impetus to find regular employment) are hard to endorse. It is interesting that despite his other failings Alain does maintain a relatively close relationship with his own father in this film. Indeed, Kaplan's comment that *Parenthood* explores different kinds of fathering and begs the question of why no equivalent film constructing various different constructions of motherhood exists also applies to the contemporary French context (1992: 199–200). Within *Tellement proches* itself the desire for motherhood – as well as female desire for romantic union itself – is instead belittled through the character of Nathalie's sister Roxane, a hysteric who chases men and steals babies. The end of this film, however, elides such difficulties to find all its couples some years on and Alain's bad son 'come good': having inherited his father's *métier* as an entertainer, he is putting on a show, watched by his parents with lachrymose pride.

Dissecting Divorce: familles cassées et recomposées

Several rom-coms deal too with a major destabiliser of the nuclear family listed by Vincendeau (2008) in a discussion of dramatic devices deployed in family-focused films: divorce.[7] *Les Marmottes* is one of these, through the inclusion of the narrative strand focusing on Max's (Gérard Lanvin) strained interaction with his ex-wife and the value he places on his relationship with his daughter. Indeed, Vincendeau here highlights the national cinema's increasing tendency to integrate children as part of its family groups and the paramount importance of children's welfare in depictions of *la famille recomposée*. This would appear to bear out Badinter's recent argument that the global move to elevate children to sacrosanct status is now slowly beginning to make its mark in France (Badinter 2010). The amplification of this focus in two very recent Paris-set comedies about divorce, *LOL* (2008) and *Une semaine sur deux* (2009), suggests the intensification of the trend year on year. Both these films – *LOL* especially – explore the relationship between a mother and her (pre-)teenage daughter (in the latter case she is 12). This is significant in view of the general absence of complex representations of the mother-daughter bond in dominant (male-oriented) representations of the family in global culture. Tarr and Rollet (2001:112–3) have noted the contrastingly recurrent probing of this relationship in films by French women directors in the 1980s and 1990s. Thus the family rom-com continues French women filmmakers' important contribution to the on-screen portrayal of females' homosocial relationships – as well as allowing for some additions to this trend by male directors.

These divorce films also coincide in splitting the narrative focus between parental and teenage romances, further widening their target audience – a strategy that paid dividends for *LOL*, which attracted over 3.5 million viewers. Such an approach contrasts, for example, with the privileging of adult needs in Nicole Garcia's 1990 divorce drama *Un week-end sur deux/Every Other Weekend*. It therefore mirrors the wider increase in French films focusing on children discernible since 1990 and identifiable with concern for their fate following the perceived failure of the traditional family, as popularised by Roudinesco's writings (see Powrie 2010: 60).[8]

Une semaine announces its interest in the effects of family rupture particularly clearly with an opening that subverts the rom-com's common representation of the marriage ritual by presenting, instead, that of divorce. Shortly afterwards, a comic moment in which a schoolteacher tells pupils they now provide two reports for those with divorced parents, asks who needs two, and is faced with a sea of hands encompassing almost the entire class, extends the film's exploration of a social reality beyond the individual story. It is also noteworthy that divorce is now so commonplace as to have migrated from the more dramatic territory of *Un week-end sur deux* – or *Kramer vs. Kramer* (Robert Benton, 1979) in the US – to become the stuff of comedy, as also in conversations between young protagonist Léa and a classmate whose parents are planning to remarry . . . each other! This is not to say that the film does not refract key issues about the effect of divorce upon children, as well as its significance for adults. While both Léa and her younger brother are constantly moving between residences, the focus on her experiences is signalled by her voiceover, connected frequently to internet chat forums or to a word-processed diary or blog. As the older child, Léa is able to exploit her parents' divorce for her own ends (she asks to spend more time with her father when her mother has punished her for sneaking out late at night); and it might be argued that her excessive investment in a romantic relationship is related to the absence of a stable home life.

Léa's parents are presented in a conflicted way. Psychotherapist François exemplifies the French trend for 'sensitive' but still insidiously sexist rom-com anti-heroes. Despite his benign appearance, his adultery broke up the marriage and during the narrative he indulges in a secret affair with Léa's (young) piano teacher. Where François is associated with openness and physical affection, his ex-wife Marjorie (Mathilde Seigner) is presented as tough. Introductory shots show her at boxing practice and Léa's voiceover description of her here as 'a woman who's got it in for men' suggests the metonymic function of the punch-bag to which she administers an aggressive pounding. By contrast with François' romance, Marjorie's liaison with neighbour Jérôme fails, seemingly as he finds her too challenging – when he complains that men now have to cook if they want to eat well, she ripostes smartly that 'women have developed other skills'. Marjorie's refusal to conform to old-fashioned stereotypes of femininity, while constructed as problematic for her, is also championed in the film. A telling melodramatic scene where François and Jérôme, united in their failure to subjugate her, get drunk, weep and rail against her, casts them as pathetic, thanks to the comedy of François' drunken inability to pronounce properly the misogynist insult he attempts to level against her as a 'ballbreaker' (*castratrice*). Moreover, Marjorie's failed romance is posited as a consequence of the increased priority she accords to both her career in property and to motherhood. A celebration of her relationship with the children substitutes for a romantic climax, through shots of the three of them happily on holiday and a final image of Léa's and her mother's faces together, as also on the DVD cover and posters. Such a focus illustrates Shumway's (2003a: 227) suggestion that the increased value placed on relationships with children in recent years coincides with the breakdown of other social relations, including romantic ones. This kind of ending is common in the French rom-com. Here the pro-familial subtext is further conveyed by Léa's voiceover, reflecting that she used to feel she was in the wrong family but now feels lucky to have this one: a clear affirmation of the value of even Roudinesco's 'disarrayed' family.

While it is less explicitly predicated on the effects of divorce, focuses on a slightly older mother and daughter and excludes male perspectives altogether, Lisa Azuelos' *LOL* shares many features with *Une semaine*. This film's romantic focus is hinted at in its title. While Lol is the daughter character Lola's (Christa Theret) nickname, a subtitle reveals that it is also acronymic for the English phrase *laughing out loud*; but the latter in turn stems from a parodic twist on an abbreviation for the common English correspondence sign-off *lots of love*. An ostentatious style, including both rapid editing and an expressionistic approach to Lola's individual experience (at one point she nostalgically 'watches' herself with her ex-boyfriend Arthur) is well suited to a highly romantic discourse. Notably, the film neutralises any subversive suggestion that male-female friendships may provide an alternative to romance by converting Lola's best friend Maël rapidly to her love object. When this desire is finally satisfied, the event takes place one night in bed on a school trip to England, removed from the banality of ordinary life, and is discreetly presented and couched – as Lola's 'first time' – in terms of love. As in *Une semaine*, however, romances across the generations run side by side, inherently undermining the specialness of both. Thus, as Lola abandons last year's dalliance and falls in love for the first time, her mother Anne (Marceau) finally breaks it off with her ex-husband and embarks on a new relationship. The extreme parallelism is here highlighted by the concurrency between Anne's first night with another man and the loss of Lola's virginity. Also as in *Une semaine*, and in harmony with the new preoccupation with children's experience, the daughter character in fact appropriates the voiceover. Yet we are also privy to Anne's concerns, through conversation discussing the challenges of parenting and her own conflicted attitude towards female sexual liberation, which she finds to be a good idea in principle but more troubling in practice.

Interestingly, these conflicts of attitude are borne out in Lola's interactions with her schoolfriends, who form another surrogate family. When the teenager fraudulently claims to have been as sexually active as her (soon to be former) boyfriend Arthur, she is repeatedly labelled a 'slut' (*pétasse*) by him, emphasising the persistence of a sexual double standard. Similarly, while Lola and her friends are portrayed as budding *séductrices* who sneak into sexy underwear unbeknown to parents – and best friend Charlotte in particular displays a rampant and perversely-oriented libido, as in a humorous scene she inserts a webcam into a chicken to pretend to masturbate for strangers online (also invoking the US 'gross-out' tradition) – their schoolyard enemy and Lola's possible competitor for Maël's affection, Isabelle de Peyrefitte, is referred to by them as a slut. While the portrayal of young women as active agents of desire is a welcome departure from traditions within both France and especially the global teenpic historically, the girls' attitude towards their peer speaks to a popular view of the powerfully divisive force of romantic rivalry between women, as well as suggesting female internalisation of misogynistic discourses. However, later in the film, female solidarity takes precedence over romance – contrasting with the male group's dynamic. Notably, Lola and her friends defend de Peyrefitte when she is attacked by Arthur for wearing makeup whose production may have involved cruelty to animals. Female friendship is moreover a source of joy, laughter and comfort throughout the narrative (another rarity in the global teenpic, unlike with male buddy groups [Mar Azcona 2010: 91–4]).

Even more exuberantly championed, as in *Une semaine*, is the mother-daughter bond. Neither film shirks representing the difficulties this relationship can entail. In *Une semaine*, Léa's blaming of Marjorie for her parents' divorce, on the grounds that she failed to forgive her father's cheating, displays a warped logic speaking of both the internalisation of unequal gendered models and also, perhaps, of straightforward Freudian mother-hatred. Certainly, the plot development that sees Marjorie put a stop to Léa's night-time socialising and thus obstruct her progress towards adult womanhood through the relationship with schoolboy Hugo is a source of violent resentment. The boundaries of individual identities are made even more porous in *LOL* by the close parallelism of the mother's and daughter's sexual relationships and especially Lola's habit of borrowing Anne's clothes, signalling her encroachment onto her mother's role of seductress. Maternal interference in her sexual development is also the first characteristic of Lola's relationship with her mother depicted, as Anne disputes her daughter's claim that shaving her pubic hair is nobody's business but her own. Later, it is such unwanted interference that prompts Lola to opt to live temporarily with her father. At the end of this film, though, once again the mother-daughter union takes the place of any romantic one, as the pair lie gossiping together in bed. Moreover, the narrative's cyclical teenage time, marked by a final act which returns to the same moment as the start of the film, the beginning of the school term, and echoing the opening sequence's break-up between Lola and Arthur by showing imperfections creeping into the relationship with Maël, illustrates by contrast the endurance of the maternal relationship.

As indicated, Anne's character presents contradictions from a feminist perspective. The first image of her is one of idealised 'natural' motherhood, as she baths unhurriedly with her younger daughter. This is borne out in the rest of the film through her prioritisation of relationships with her children and her success, for the most part, in maintaining good relations even with the volatile Lola, through a liberal style of parenting. Casting is again crucial to Marceau's role here as the archetypal 'cool Mum'. The actress' recent work has been something of a return to her grass roots in popular national cinema, where *La Boum/Ready For Love* (Claude Pinoteau, 1980) made her a child star.

Lately she has appeared in the sympathetic roles of nurse (*Nelly* [Laure Duthilleul, 2004]), invalid (*L'Homme de chevet* [Alain Monne, 2007]) and frequently in that of 'sexy' and youthful mother (also in romcoms *Je Reste!* and *De l'autre côté du lit* [Pascale Pouzadoux, 2008]). In this latter role, she appears, too, on the cover of *Elle* magazine's May 2010 special edition dedicated to exploring the current social condition of women. The interview with real-life divorcee Marceau – photographed in a simple white T-shirt and trousers, with short hair and minimal makeup – focuses on juggling work and child-rearing (Anon 2010c: 134–7). While this struggle is negotiated in *De l'autre côté du lit*, discussed later in this chapter, this raises a salient point with regard to the image of motherhood Anne offers in *LOL*, i.e. her lack of career. Indeed, despite a glancing reference to the fact she has an architecture degree, the same introductory bath scene appears if anything to promote her frivolity, as when her daughter asks her what her favourite subject is, using the French word *matière*, also meaning *material*, and her answer is the charmingly insouciant: 'Cashmere, darling.' With her three children, Anne conforms to the schema elaborated by Neil Gilbert for the USA, according to which even highly educated women rarely combine even part-time work with more than two children (2008: 31–2). In this case, of course, Anne's situation is further complicated by her status as a single mother. While the practical challenges of mothering itself (as when Anne has no time to shower before driving Lola to school) and especially of balancing this with time for a new relationship (she turns up unwashed for a date after losing track of time reading Lola's diary) are reflected in the film, this is not complemented by any suggestion of a desire for a career. In this respect, the film shows no progress away from from the model of pre-millennial US cinema, indicted by Kaplan for failing to depict women who combine motherhood with both sexual and professional fulfilment. In view of Marjorie's failed relationship in *Une semaine*, the same might be said of that film. The difference, though, is that Calbérac's film makes the issue a subject of conflict rather than skirting it. A reference in Léa's closing voiceover to her mother's view that she may be ready for a relationship next year at least keeps alive the possibility of a reconciliation of all three of these spheres of feminine experience – something of a Holy Grail for feminist thinkers. As Kaplan remarked in response to the absence of such representations globally from her study two decades earlier: '"Sex, Work, and Motherhood" is evidently [a] threatening [...] combination on a number of levels' (1992: 183).

These analyses show, then, how an ensemble architecture in rom-com lends itself at once to prescription and description of familial instability. This is borne out thematically by a number of films of the period, whether they critique the nuclear family from within or depict families post-divorce. Films by women directors in particular question the benefits of familial structures, although this genre by its nature also highlights positives in the family as basic social cell – albeit one that finds itself subject to new configurations in the post-modern age. For divorce, in these narratives, is not constructed as wholly inimical to romance, familial or otherwise; rather, the genre mirrors society itself in finding ways to reconcile the latter's widespread advent with its other overarching discourses, while to greater or lesser degrees acknowledging the difficulties this implies. It is also worth flagging up the extent to which the post-divorce rom-coms end up being films which deal substantially with parenthood and, above all, motherhood – the vast majority of children from broken homes in France, as elsewhere, still live with their mothers. This is an appropriate point at which to turn to the maternal question and its treatment across French rom-com as a whole.

The Mummy Myth

The motherhood position may have been more fetishised than any other in human history. Its elevation in the service of patriarchy is well known at least since *The Second Sex* (Beauvoir 2004 [1949]) and has become a commonplace of cultural studies since Foucault's (1984) work on the subject. For film studies, the definitive text is Kaplan's already cited 1992 study, in which the writer analyses a century of American (almost always male-authored) representations of motherhood collapsed into the dichotomy of idealised self-sacrificing angel versus unnatural 'witch'. These two images, erected with the clear goal of keeping the mother at home, are for Kaplan identifiable with a 'modern motherhood discourse' born in eighteenth-century France with the philosophy of Jean-Jacques Rousseau. However, in her final chapter dealing with the post-modern era, Kaplan notes the impact of the disassociation of the maternal process from the female body, through cultural developments around surrogacy and in particular major advances in reproductive technologies. For her, such developments had, by the 1980s, made the female body a site of contestation, with women rediscovering the pleasures of motherhood because the latter is no longer 'viewed as an automatic, natural part of [their] life-cycle' (1992: 180–219; 181).

Interestingly, much of the impetus for this discursive shift can be located in French philosophy, in the works of feminist philosophers Cixous, Irigaray and Kristeva, all of whom attempt to appropriate motherhood away from (patriarchal) society and re-inscribe it as a personal experience that in some way defines the feminine.[9] It should be emphasised that these writers' theories represent only one current within third wave feminism – and one which is particularly visible from the outside perspective of anglophone writers, given its lack of equivalent in British and American culture. Equally important to bear in mind are the obvious changes to the status of motherhood brought about by the mass availability of contraception from after the 1960s. Badinter (2010: 83–4) is perhaps overstating the issue when she alleges that in the space of less than a decade between the late 1970s and the early 1980s feminist theory did a 180° turn away from Beauvoir's culturalist approach. Nonetheless, the existence of this strand of thought is highly significant and surely an important factor in France's high birth rate and pro-natalism. Feminists' championing of motherhood also highlights its conflicted ideological status, as resumed by Kaplan with the incisive question: 'Since patriarchy wants women to want children [...] how can a woman distinguish her desire for the child from that imposed on her?' (1992: 4). Badinter herself has argued convincingly that, in the French press in the early 2000s, motherhood is idealised in a way that is beneficial to patriarchy (2003: 200) and that a major neo-Rousseauist move to re-naturalise maternity today is closing off women's choices, in particular the possibility of combining motherhood and work (2010).

Eternal Mothers

Given their availability for exploitation to both feminist and patriarchal ends, it is unsurprising that discourses idealising maternity arise frequently in French cinema across the board. Specifically, the maternal resolution is a staple of the national cinema. On this subject, Tarr and Rollet observed in 2001 that '[in] the last year of the millennium a number of films by women end with pregnancy or childbirth, as if to affirm women's commitment to an unknown and uncertain future' (120). This explanation leaves room for further interpretation in light of the frenzied mythologising of motherhood set out above.

Deferring for a moment the question of the ending, maternal desire arises fairly frequently in the genre. In addition to the example of *Tellement proches*, *Les Marmottes* and *Ce soir, je dors chez toi* both depict female characters who are largely defined by the desire to procreate. In *Les Marmottes*, this borders on the pathological, as one character, Marie-Claire, does nothing but badger her husband Stéphane to impregnate her and feigns suicide by jumping out of a window naked into the snow in order to reinforce her demands. In *Tellement proches*, attempts by a young woman, Roxane, to steal a baby arguably fall more in line with a narrative pattern discussed by Tarr and Rollet in two films by women, Danièle Dubroux's *Border Line* (1992) and Claire Simon's *Sinon, oui* (1997), which 'expose and problematize the ideological pressures on women to consider motherhood as women's destiny by presenting childless women who resort to crime in order to preserve the fiction of their assumed, false identities as mothers' (2001: 124). *Tellement proches* is not, though, concerned to the same extent with any problematisation of these pressures – rather, Roxane is largely a madcap figure of humour. Both she and Marie-Claire in *Les Marmottes* in fact suggest that the stereotype of the hysterical proto-mother has become a target of mockery.

My analyses of *Les Marmottes* and *Tellement proches* suggest that this caricatural figure can be read in a Jamesonian fashion, as revealing in ways that surpass authorial intention. Indeed, it is not trivial that the directors of these two films conveying the pressure on women to become mothers – a pressure that spans the two decades covered by this research, as the films were released in 1993 and 2008 – are men. The unsympathetic attitude is achieved through a lack of alignment of the point of view with the female characters in question. This is striking in *Les Marmottes*, where we are formally positioned with Marie-Claire's partner Stéphane inside their bedroom when he is momentarily terrified by her apparently jumping to her death out of a window (although the ground outside the window turns out actually to be only a couple of metres down). In *Tellement proches*, Roxane's unreasonable behaviour is simply not explained. By contrast, the divorce narratives *LOL* and *Une semaine* (as well as, in a more secondary way, *Laisse tes mains sur mes hanches* and *Je vais te manquer*) depict mother-daughter relationships from the inside, thus avoiding what Leahy, paraphrasing Kaplan, has recently described as the traditional 'othering' of the mother. As Leahy comments, '[w]hile representations of maternal subjectivity may now be more common than when Kaplan was writing, they are still far from frequent'. The examples she offers are films by auteurs, both male and female (Philippe Claudel, Régis Wargnier, Krzysztof Kieslowski and Sandrine Veysset) (2010: 163). Taking romantic comedy into consideration suggests a stronger link between female authorship and interest in the experience of motherhood.

However, the fact that *Une semaine sur deux* is directed by a man, Ivan Calbérac, reflects the pitfalls of an essentialist approach to authorship. I am particularly wary of tying arguments too closely to directors' gender, given the collaborative nature of filmmaking; indeed, I have stressed the possible significance of women's input as screenwriters – including Thompson on *Les Marmottes*. Nonetheless, it appears significant that time and again male authors depict women's desire to reproduce – especially when this is pathologised.

Despite the acknowledged limitations of films' resolutions as a criterion for assessing all their ideological affiliations, these nonetheless obviously stake a certain claim to the status of narratives' goals, at the least in a temporal sense, and in French rom-com they often include children. It should perhaps be recalled that babies do appear from time to time at the end of rom-coms globally. However, this feature is much more common in France. More importantly, a tendency for making reproduction pivotal to the plot resolution is discernible in the French genre. It is one thing for a film like *Notting Hill* (Roger Michell, UK/USA 1999) to simply include a baby in its flash-forward idyllic final vision of the couple united. This also occurs in such French exemplars as *Au suivant!* and *Ce soir, je dors chez toi*. Similarly, pregnancies or children feature in the endings of *Romuald et Juliette, L'Art (délicat) de la séduction, Mariage mixte, Ensemble, c'est tout, Celle que j'aime* and *Je vais te manquer*. More remarkable, though, is the fact that in several French rom-coms it is the prospect or arrival of a baby that binds a previously nonexistent or antagonistic couple. In *Célibataires*, for example, it is when his friend Nelly mentions being artificially inseminated by one of her male friends that protagonist Ben decides to seduce her. The fact that Nelly accepts Ben's advances, in the absence of earlier hints that she may harbour romantic feelings for him, presents coupling as a means to avoid 'unnatural' single parenthood. In *Mensonges et trahisons*, although Raphaël's decision to return to Muriel precedes his realisation that she is pregnant, the labour ward setting of the reunion cements their newfound intimacy, as does the scene from the epilogue which shows them sleeping with the baby at their side.

Another subgroup of rom-coms effects a similar move, with the slight variation that the baby in question is not the direct progeny of the couple. Thus *Gazon maudit* and *Pédale douce* queer the French family around the arrival of a new baby. In *L'Ex-femme de ma vie/The Ex-Wife of My Life* (Balasko, 2005), Nina is reconciled with her ex-husband Tom while pregnant (by another man) and the dialogue hints that their divorce stemmed from their failure to have children. One storyline in *Je vais te manquer* presents a woman suffering from infertility, which is constructed as deeply distressing, before 'healing the wound' by pairing her off with a man who already has a child. More recently, *Prête-moi ta main* (2006) is the only film in the corpus which goes one step further, by representing dislocations in the maternal process, a trend discussed by Kaplan in an American context. In this case it does so through the transnational theme of adoption, a phenomenon that has led to the globalisation of the 'most private and local social unit' of the family (Brysk 2004: 167). However, its inclusion appears more a function of plot expediency than a reflection of profound interest in the social or psychological impact of adopting children: Emma agrees to continue posing as Luis' fiancée since the patriarchal legitimacy the engagement lends her will strengthen her bid for a child. Not only does this force the mismatched couple into close proximity but the adoption catalyses a thaw in relations between them. While Emma is outwardly caustic, moments of reflective solitude, notably in scenes showing her lovingly restoring furniture, create an impression of hidden sensitivity and the unexplained desire for a child – which we learn was strong enough to break up her previous, otherwise happy relationship – completes her mystification and feminisation. Even more striking is Luis' transformation, from self-styled cynic to overgrown lovelorn adolescent. Although the narrative sets up his growing interest in Emma earlier, it is the accidental viewing of footage of her potential adoptee which turns Luis dewy-eyed and immediately precedes a montage showing him heart-sick in Emma's absence, using his skills as a perfume-maker to attempt to (re-)create her smell. The two plot lines of (adoptive) maternity and romance are collapsed together in an ending that joins the couple to succeed in adopting the boy. Interestingly, the scene in which the adoption agency approves their bid, as though to compensate for the displacement of physical maternity in its main plot, sees the pregnant agency employee go into labour herself. The retrograde momentum of an ending that has Emma 'snare' the once marriage-hating Luis is redoubled by the narrative's inscription of romance as integration into conventional social order, making Emma and Luis' deeply un-sexy union answer to desire on the part of his matriarchal family – in front of whom it is largely played out – to see him married.

A number of rom-com resolutions realign procreation more overtly with paternal desire. The endings of *Pédale douce* and *Mauvaise foi* heighten their construction of the male view of procreation as sacrosanct by exploiting the classic narrative device of the deadline structure, building their climaxes around a father's race against time to prevent his partner aborting.[10] The pattern of tension then release generated by the narratives in each case cues us to welcome the outcomes, which see the unborn children 'saved' and with them their parents' relationships. The fact that these stories show mothers poised to undergo the abortion procedure suggests the serious challenges posed by the circumstances of each birth. In *Pédale douce*, it is gay Adrien and not the baby's incorrigibly womanising biological father Alexandre, at this point absent, who persuades Eva not to abort the child, then assumes its paternity. In *Mauvaise foi*, following bitter feuding around cultural differences relating to their ethnicities as, respectively, Arab and Jew, Ismaël and Clara have also separated and are disputing, until he learns of her plans to abort and rushes to the hospital. As in *Pédale douce*, the narrative cuts directly to shots of the couple bonding over their baby, avoiding many of the difficult issues that have until now come between them.

If marriage is overall less significant in the contemporary French rom-com than the more provisional commitments associable with the discourse of intimacy, reproduction can also represent one narrative strategy to achieve such a state of affairs. The terms of the old-fashioned, clichéd resolution (borrowed for the title of Attal's film) '*ils se marièrent et eurent beaucoup d'enfants*', or 'they got married and had lots of children' – already interestingly different from the English equivalent 'and they lived happily ever after' – are reversed in many of the films discussed in this section, since parenthood precedes or precipitates long-term commitment. The fact that this arrangement can nonetheless preserve patriarchal order is underlined by patronymic themes in more than one film. One of the questions over which Clara and Ismaël of *Mauvaise foi* fall out concerns the baby's name, with Ismaël threatening to insist on Abdelkrim. This also occurs in a significant secondary plot in *Ma femme est une actrice*, where Yvan's Jewish sister finally imposes her own choice of Moïse (Moses) on her son, despite her gentile husband's reluctance. As such feminists as Eve Kosofsky Sedgwick (1985) have argued, the heterosexual marriage plot turns on a partnership between two sets of men.[11] Fiona Handyside (2007: 223–4) has more recently remarked on the French obsession with 'the name of the father', evidenced by the debate around legislation in 2002 overturning the automatic bestowing of the father's name on legitimate offspring.

Nor is it accidental that in both these cases the children in question are male. Even in the tradition of Judaism, where the woman's role in generational continuity is valued, it is as a progenitor for the male representatives of the group. Although it does not include a racial dimension, the same point is also implicit in the ending of *Mensonges et trahisons*, where Raphaël is overjoyed to be able to name the son Muriel has produced for him. In fact, with the exception of *Gazon maudit*, in every one of these films that end after the birth or adoption of a single child and where its sex is known, they are sons – in direct contrast with the 1980s celebration of girls (usually alongside feminine utopian space as a whole) in such films as *Le Jupon Rouge/Manuela's Loves* (Geneviève Lefebvre, 1987) and the Franco-Italian co-production *Speriamo che sia femmina/Let's Hope It's a Girl* (Mario Monicelli, 1986) (or much earlier *Club de femmes/Girls' Club* [Jacques Deval, 1936]).

It is relevant to consider the authorship of films with maternal resolutions. In pre-2000 rom-com production, along with gay director Gabriel Aghion's *Pédale douce*, the major female auteur hits *Romuald et Juliette* and *Gazon maudit* chose to leave tensions between their main characters neutralized alongside, if not thanks to, the arrival of a child. However, it is remarkable that those post-2000 rom-coms that effect a similar move are almost all directed by men. These include *Ma femme est une actrice* (Attal, 2001), *Mensonges et trahisons et plus si affinités...* (Tirard, 2004), *Mauvaise foi* (Zem, 2006), *Ce soir, je dors chez toi* (Baroux, 2007), and, just outside the decade, *Une folle envie* (Bernard Jeanjean, 2011). 'Feminine' candidates for such a simplistic resolution prove considerably less totalising: in Balasko's *L'Ex-femme de ma vie* the pregnancy is not cast as pivotal to Nina and Tom's reconciliation; in *Au suivant!* (Biras, 2005), a baby is one detail of the film's final flash-forward vision of the central couple's idyllic partnership; and in one of several storylines in both *Tout pour plaire* (Telerman, 2005) and *Toi et moi* (Lopes-Curval, 2006) a character has a baby at the end – although it is noteworthy that in the latter film it is explicit (and in the former assumed) that the mother has kept her job. This issue is either ignored in the male-authored films, or, in *Ma femme est une actrice*, actively thrown into doubt, as the female lead ignores news about a starring role in Hollywood in favour of posing with a cushion under her jumper. The fact that her husband at this moment catches sight of his own reflection multiplied in facing mirrors underscores male domination, at the levels of both narrative interest and power relations, at the end of the film. The contrasting perspective offered by *Toi et moi* tallies with the high numbers of working mothers in France. Although motherhood endures as a central concern in recent rom-coms, the fact that in this traditionally pro-family genre women should of late be more circumspect about simplistic maternal resolutions – and men's frantic promulgation of them – suggests the increasing reach of a feminist discourse based on equality. At the same time, motherhood, and procreation as a whole, remain almost without exception positively configured in this genre of reconciliation and renewal – indeed, not a single film in the corpus presents a couple who are childless by choice. This appears particularly important in view of a recent Australian study indicating the extent to which maternal discourses influence women (Maher and Saugères 2007), as substantiated by the high birth rate in France.[12]

Renegotiating Roles

Where the films discussed in the preceding section portray motherhood as all-consuming and, generally, all-important, at least the presence of the father in and around delivery rooms or asleep in the same bedroom as partner and baby attests to a degree of change in the level of fathers' involvement with their offspring in relation to former eras. A handful of rom-coms go further, assuming the presence of children as a given and addressing the possibility of a more substantially equal negotiation of child-raising between the two parents.

By their nature, the rom-coms about divorce *Une semaine* and *LOL* explore fathering to an extent; however, in both cases paternal care is presented as inferior to that offered by the mother. Specifically, both fathers prioritise amorous affairs over their children's wellbeing: the contrast between the reversed hierarchies of romance and parenting for mother and father in each film is stark. In contrast, several films portray more nurturing fathers, as in secondary storylines presenting positive (divorced/separated) father-child relationships in *Irène* (2002) and *Je vais te manquer* (2009). In *Irène*, it is made clear that this character trait informs the broody heroine's attraction towards decorator François. Although his baby son is mainly a background presence, François is portrayed as a devoted father and parental responsibility is shown on occasion to intrude directly on their courtship. Moreover, a rift in his relationship with Irène follows her realisation of his ongoing involvement with and feelings for his ex, which are presented as difficult to extricate from their joint parental status. In this case, an open ending in which the couple remains on good terms but not explicitly in a relationship refuses to ignore these complexities.

Nurturing qualities also form part of the appeal of the male leads in *Le Bison (et sa voisine Dorine)* (2002), *Au suivant!* (2005), *Essaye-moi* (Pierre-François Martin-Laval, 2006) and *Si c'était lui* (2007). Only *Au suivant!* presents an actual father-child relationship, between Bernard (Clovis Cornillac) and his daughter. The film accommodates Cornillac's penchant for extrovert physical comedy by making him an actor, in a story that pairs him with casting director Jo. It is his status as a widowed single father that lends his otherwise wacky character psychological depth and is crucial in prompting Jo to see him not as an oddball but a protective, domestic godlike 'new man' in the Hollywood rom-com mould (see Burns 2011: 17). Thus visiting him at home, she finds him sparing no effort in preparing a birthday party for his daughter and his sunny, life-filled suburban garden contrasts strongly with Jo's apartment, which she refers to as a luxury but which, in its minimalist design and muted decor, remains sterile. Both *Le Bison* and *Si c'était lui* meanwhile have their male lead assume a paternal role towards the offspring of the female protagonist, which is in both cases constructed as equally beneficial to the grown men in question: an irresponsible hedonist and a vagrant respectively. Once again a well-known comic, Baer, inhabits the paternal role in the first film, blending comedian and romantic comedy to make the link between a talent for parenting and the indefatigably enthusiastic and childish comic sensibility. This linkage is even more heavily underscored in *Essaye-moi*, whose style as a whole is governed by a cartoonish aesthetic reminiscent of early Warner Brothers. Thus the slapstick physical behaviour associated with Yves-Marie (Martin-Laval) is paired with visual imagery that defies the laws of physics, such as when the romantic (anti-)hero falls through a door and leaves a man-shaped hole behind him. Although neither of the main characters in this film has a child of their own, they 'adopt' one belonging to a neighbour for the day, and Martin-Laval exploits the close-up to emphasise the fact that it is when Yves-Marie bonds with the boy that the face of his love-object Jacqueline first begins to register approval.

In *Essaye-moi* the wondrous dimension of romance is inseparable from that of childhood, as underlined by a prologue set during the couple's tender years, and which establishes the narrative's improbable premise that Yves-Marie has spent 20 years becoming an astronaut in order to oblige Jacqueline to fulfil a promise to marry him on the condition that he go to the moon. There is in fact a remarkable absence of sexual tension in all three of the comedian rom-coms described above. In *Au suivant!*, the ending replaces the classic kiss with shots of the couple, with Bernard's daughter and their new baby in tow, joking around. In *Le Bison*, more extremely, the two leads' relationship is not predicated explicitly on romance at all. Dorine is the older concierge in the building inhabited by the wealthy Louis (Baer), whose antisocial hours and habit of playing loud music in the flat next door to Dorine's family have earned him the nickname 'the bison'. When Dorine's husband, a boorish trucker played by Martin-Laval, leaves her penniless, saddled with four children and eight months pregnant, to run off with his mistress, Louis is forced by circumstance to step into the breach and help her out with her children. Despite the lack of sexual chemistry here, the couple's relationship enacts familiar rom-com conventions, as they bicker but he also takes the role of knight in shining armour to 'save' her from destitution, including finding her a lawyer to pursue her ex. Their 'romance' also bridges class differences, erasing the proletarian status of the concierge (a recent trend, also in evidence in drama *Le Hérisson/ The Hedgehog* [Mona Achache, 2009]), who is played by the film's director, famous comedienne Isabelle Nanty. At the end of the film, Louis, transformed into a responsible caregiver, is clearly enchanted by Dorine's new son and the final scene sees the entire gang drive off together into the distance. As well as constructing nurturing father figures, these films go one step further than having parenthood catalyse romance: in them, the ideal of family life supplants any interest in attraction or passion almost altogether.

Issues around children are, though, obviously more likely to arise in rom-coms about couples who are already together. In one storyline in ensemble rom-com *Tout pour plaire*, Florence loses an important contract at her job in advertising when her son falls ill and her husband refuses to cancel his business trip. This is one of a series of events leading up to her decision to leave him. *Ils se marièrent* itself also touches on the role of childcare in provoking marital difficulties in an early scene. When wayward Yvan leaves his wife Charlotte – who also works as an estate agent – to go and play poker with his male coterie, she points out reasonably that she too would like to go out with her friends. However, not only does Yvan go out anyway, and is – in contrast to the female-authored *Tout pour plaire* – duly forgiven by his wife; after flirting with a concern for this broadly feminine problem, the film abandons the question in favour of a focus on the more frivolous issue of adultery, constructed from a male perspective.

The film that explores most fully the possibility of repositioning the genders with regard to childcare and family organisation, *De l'autre côté du lit* (2008), does so in an ostensibly light-hearted mode. This effect is achieved through a high concept plot, in which a husband and wife swap roles, and a style which, by contrast with ensemble films' typical preference for unobtrusive naturalism, embraces a more Hollywood approach to narrating rom-com. Salient formal features include rapid editing; frequent montages; music that relentlessly reinforces mood; self-conscious camerawork and staging, designed to focus readers' attention on particular details; a pastel colour scheme, including wife Ariane's pink car; and an expressive approach to mise-en-scène altogether. For example, despite the film's superficial distance from reality, the mise-en-scène of the couple's home – undergoing refurbishments – draws attention to their emblematic post-modernity. Unlike traditional French homes, the flat-fronted, flat-roofed new-build is constructed around an open-plan interior complete with shelves, breakfast bar and other fittings painted in various bright shades to look as artificial as possible. Its cacophony of unnatural colours and geometric designs, also reminiscent of a sitcom set (director Pouzadoux's background is as a television actress), pastiches a certain kind of twenty-first century

Figure 14. Domestic disharmony: contemporary life closes in for Hugo and Ariane of *De l'autre côte du lit*. © Warner Home Vidéo

décor [Figure 14]. Its layout, moreover, figures visually the narrative themes of a lack of clear delineation of territory.

The film immediately advertises a focus on femininity by aligning the narrative point of view with working mother Ariane (Sophie Marceau), as her opening voice-over describes a life plagued by guilt. Then a rapid montage mimicking the frenetic pace of this existence shows her attempting to juggle motherhood with her job in a jewellers' and running a house undergoing renovation. This reflects the findings of surveys carried out in France and elsewhere that show the majority of domestic work still falls to women (Shelton and John 1993; Régnier-Loilier 2009). To address this miserable situation, Ariane masterminds a life-swap between herself and husband Hugo (Dany Boon), the upshot of which is that both characters perform a parodic version of the other's gender role. Thus Ariane takes a colleague out for lunch and eats and drinks him under the table, before throwing up in private, and seduces a male colleague partly for physical amusement. Hugo, meanwhile, dons a pink shirt, sips tea delicately and feigns a love of romance novels to make his jewellery sales, with Boon's soft, high-pitched voice and sensitive star persona adding to the camp. On the other hand, each character's success in the other's role depends on elements of their original identity. Ariane's experience as a woman allows her to come up with the marketing coup of complementing Hugo's company's tool-production with a service offering muscular young men to help female customers use the products (another wry subversion of woman's classic position as fetishized feminine object), while business brain Hugo strategizes a reorganization of the workshop to maximize the jewellery enterprise's productivity. Despite its overt simplicity, the film recognises the external pressure to conform to familiar identities, as Ariane's mother tries to undermine the couple's arrangement and their son – who has said he would prefer them simply to divorce like other parents – vandalises his classroom. More crucially for the main plot, Ariane herself begins to question her newfound identity because of the distance it introduces between her and the children. A scene in which she leaves the office to join them on the beach and wades into the sea in her work clothes to scoop them up reduces her to a clichéd glorification of motherhood as elemental. The fact that it is concern for the children which puts paid to adult desire to chart new territories in family organisation indicates again the increased focus on children visible elsewhere in the rom-com and in French cinema in general of late. The film's ending overlooks the details of the couple's final compromise in its celebration of their love, but the fact that Hugo sweeps their daughter out of harm's away while Ariane puts out a fire with masterful ease – unlike in an early scene – implies that a more even distribution of the work of family life has been the route to saving their marriage. In this light the film can be seen as a call for both a better balance of work and family life and for a more equal distribution of labour between parents. In the latter respect, it suggests there is still much territory for women to gain.[13]

Case Study: *La Bûche/Season's Beatings* (Danièle Thompson, 1999)

Released in the lead up to the last Christmas of the twentieth century, *La Bûche* is the directorial debut of prolific screenwriter Danièle Thompson, daughter of well-known comic director, writer and actor Gérard Oury. It is the first of the films that, along with other (romantic) comedies *Décalage horaire* (2002), Oscar-entry *Fauteuils d'orchestre* (2009) and *Le Code a changé* (2009) have assured Thompson's status as a successful popular filmmaker. French-funded and peopled by a host of top and middle-level domestic and more international stars including Claude Rich, Françoise Fabian, Emmanuelle Béart, Charlotte Gainsbourg, Sabine Azéma and Jean-Pierre Darroussin, the film drew 1.6 million spectators in France – the majority outside Paris, as you might expect for a family film.[14] In addition to its saleable cast, it is typical of French family rom-coms in marrying comedy with melodrama, as the English title's punning focus on conflict (as opposed to a straight translation of the French word for the chocolate log traditionally eaten on Christmas Eve) reflects. Indeed, the film recommends itself for a detailed analysis because it distils several of the key tendencies identified in this chapter, as well as raising a number of far-reaching familial questions of its own.

Like the film Thompson co-wrote with director Élie Chouraqui six years earlier, *Les Marmottes*, *La Bûche* focuses on relationships within an extended family, in this case grown-up sisters Louba (Azéma), Sonia (Béart) and Milla (Gainsbourg), their divorced and initially estranged parents Yvette (Fabian) and Russian-Jewish immigrant Stanislas (Rich), and their secret illegitimate half-brother Joseph (Christopher Thompson). The opening narrative sequence unites mother and daughters for the funeral of her second husband. The sound of a mobile phone ringing from inside the coffin at once sets the darkly comic tone and introduces another important secondary character, Janine, the second husband's first wife and still close friend, whom Yvette identifies as the likely caller, stretching the bounds of the *famille recomposée*. This opening death resonates too with the symbolic death of the patriarch in post-classical French cinema, while a heart attack that later comes close to killing the 'real' family patriarch, Stanislas, uses the device of a medical theme, common in the late 1990s, to destabilise French filmic representations of the family (see Vincendeau 2008).

La Bûche also bears comparison with *Un air de famille*, in its depiction of families' predisposition towards rigid role-assignment. In the context of Thompson's statements about the universal aspect of family themes, Vincendeau has noted that these can offer filmmakers a means of blending myth with psychology (2008: 16, citing Thompson 2005; see also Pion-Dumas and Delmas 1999). In *La Bûche*, as in Klapisch's film, an ensemble structure here juxtaposes the two, allowing for an interplay between characters' self-images and external construction. Initially, the three sisters are caricatured: Milla is the selfish workaholic youngest sister with no time for others, acerbic, makeup-free and clad in biker leathers or shapeless khaki; Sonia is the perfect bourgeois housewife and mother, with no worries beyond the Christmas decor; and Louba is the kind but childless and penniless other woman to married Gilbert (Darroussin), living with her father at 42. However, immediately following the opening sequence, Sonia and Milla are shown criticising one another, each in exaggerated terms that belittle the other: Milla is accused of meanness for bringing Sonia's daughter a hand-painted Christmas present, while twisted logic sees Sonia's offer that Milla can bring whomever she likes for Christmas dinner interpreted as a pose of tolerance to make Milla herself look intolerant. In this way, the process by which family stereotypes are reinforced is itself revealed. Given that the use of stereotypes both to announce a comic tone and also to facilitate spectators' negotiation of the network depicted has been identified as a staple of at least some multi-protagonist films (Mar Azcona 2010: 10), this subversion of the convention is unsettling. Furthermore, the spectator's initial cues to make the same reductive judgements as indulged in by the sisters themselves – that is, their costume, performance style and other details of physical appearance – reinforce the multi-protagonist film's impulse to draw the spectator into its network, in this case calling us to question our readiness to judge on the basis of such surface details.

As the narrative progresses, the destabilisation of roles is compounded further, by their interchangeability in the *choral* constellation. When Sonia tells Louba the story of Joseph's illegitimate birth, instead of sympathising with their mother, the victim of adultery, Louba, herself pregnant, identifies with the plight of Joseph's poor single mother, left to raise a clandestine son. Louba's refusal to judge is only vindicated by an earlier revelation by Yvette that she too cheated prolifically on Stanislas – just as we later discover that the outwardly prim Sonia is also cheating on her husband, with a 'rough and ready' butcher whom she barely knows. Even more strikingly, Janine, set up as occupying the familiar and negatively constructed rom-com position of the other woman, when she is accorded narrative space, turns out to be not a hateful rival but a pleasant and lonely elderly woman, with whom Yvette ends up becoming friends: a rare moment of female solidarity superseding romantic rivalry. A scene in which she and Yvette stand at the dead man's grave and the second wife tells the first that there is only one remaining space finds comedy in the slowness of traditional rituals to adapt to new social configurations. In common with the weekly dinner in *Un air*, Christmas constitutes another of these rituals. The holiday reveals the contradictory nature of relations between family members, which are at once, by their nature, familiar – in other words foregoing niceties – yet at the same time, on formal occasions, demanding of politeness and respect, even more so as the mercurial family acquires more distant members. This tension is evident in the disputes over attendance at the Christmas Eve dinner, at which both Yvette and Stanislas would like to be present, but not together, while Milla also threatens to pull out on the pretext of disliking Sonia's husband and children. A scene in which Sonia gives the expensive gifts she has just purchased to passers-by (after running into her husband's lover) highlights and undercuts the absurdity of formalities divorced from human meaning.

The Christmas setting also provides a fulcrum for the film's different generic participations. As befits melodrama, the characters of *La Bûche* are uniformly suffering in the build-up to the holiday: Yvette is newly widowed, Stanislas possibly dying, Sonia on the brink of divorce and Milla lonely and tearful. Because of her unexplained pregnancy, Louba tells Joseph she has 'the blues', only to have him second her sentiments, presumably because he is missing the young daughter for whom he is making a model as a gift. Even his ex Annabelle (Isabelle Carré) turns up tearful and defensive, mid-separation from her second husband. Cliché is furthermore taken to comical extremes when Louba's lover Gilbert pours his heart out to a stranger whom he mistakes for Milla (because of a motorcycle helmet), only to have the latter affirm that he is 'down in the dumps' as well! However, if melodramatic themes – explored in dark night-time sequences set in such locations as Joseph's humble and poorly lit dwelling or in a hospital waiting room – appear far removed from the magical space of romantic comedy, the festive backdrop, whose lights are celebrated in an opening credit sequence accompanied by a maniacally cheery rendition of 'Jingle Bells', is in fact typical of the new romance's displacement of events to a space outside the everyday.

Moreover, romantic plot-lines run alongside those of familial drama. Notably, Louba's adulterous relationship with Gilbert at once exploits and acknowledges the power of romance to mystify. Played out for the most part in strangers' apartments, whose keys are temporarily in the possession of estate agent Gilbert, their liaison is based on a wilful pretence about the pair's relationship to the objective world. The exoticism already associated with Louba, as a Russian dancer, is complemented on their Christmas Eve together by Gilbert's staging of a romantic dinner in a baroque luxury apartment worthy of Versailles, complete with a tropical fruit platter. Despite her age, or rather to counterbalance it, Louba is not only an overgrown daughter still living at home, but her manner is childlike, as with her girlish delight

Figure 15. Sabine Azéma is the exotic face of romance in *La Bûche*. © Pathé

over Gilbert's efforts to please her, disavowing her status as a 'homewrecker' and further facilitating a romantic ambience of wide-eyed wonder. On the other hand, this is a long-term relationship, and Louba's explicit acknowledgement that Gilbert loves her because she's 'Bohemian', and that he will not want to know about her pregnancy, foregrounds the paradoxical distance implicit in romance's idealistic construction of the other [Figure 15]. This tension between the ideal and the real is ostensibly dissipated in a highly romantic scene, set to violins, where Gilbert unexpectedly declares his commitment to Louba and her unborn child. The triumph of emotion over reason is apparent in Gilbert's allusions to what he wants 'in [his] heart', while the major economic problems we have been told a sixth child will present are brushed aside by his repeated promise that 'we'll manage'. This relationship's conclusion appears somewhat conservative, with Louba capitulating to Gilbert's patriarchal promise to help set her up in an apartment. Nonetheless, the reference to pragmatic concerns in the scene tempers the storyline's adherence to a purely romantic model.

Nor should resolutions be taken out of context. Notably, an earlier scene that invited the viewer to engage with Gilbert's current wife by showing him cuddled up with her, hand on her pregnant belly, undermines this resolution by leaving us to wonder about the fate of Gilbert's other unborn child. Elsewhere, too, the narrative returns repeatedly to the theme of the damage that adultery and divorce cause for children. Joseph recounts a bitter childhood experience arising from hatred of his father, while his efforts to make a present for his daughter suggest his anxiety that his own child should avoid such traumatic experiences. They also suggest how the combination of men's greater involvement in child-rearing combined with high divorce rates and increased mobility (his wife and child live elsewhere in France) can leave fathers emotionally adrift, as reflected by the emergence of organisations such as Fathers for Justice or, in France, SOS Papa. Milla and Sonia, too, describe being variously traumatised by their parents' breakup and the relationship with their step-father. Elsewhere, in another role reversal, Sonia assumes the role of bad parent, as she and her husband argue viciously in front of their young son. A secondary plot in which a hysterical Annabelle temporarily abandons her new baby son with Joseph further extends the suggestion that romantic trials impact negatively on the children who are their product. As Powrie has noted, preoccupation with the fate of French children from a socio-demographic and political perspective follows logically on from the nation's combination of high birth and divorce rates, with numbers of single mothers on the rise. In this respect *La Bûche*, like *LOL*, *Une semaine sur deux* and *De l'autre côté du lit* with their volatile teens and pre-teens, can be seen as a moderate alternative to the interest in child abuse and disturbed childhoods described by Powrie in the 2000s (2010: 59–60).

In spite of all this, Louba's impregnation at 42 is constructed overwhelmingly positively, suggesting that the trend for older women taking on roles formerly reserved for younger ones bears, too, on the issue of motherhood. Indeed, *La Bûche* is one of the few films to show a significantly older than average mother (the mean being just under age 30 in France towards the end of the 2000s [Hampshire 2008: 398]), reflecting the fact that more and more mothers are having children later in Western countries – although here Louba is perhaps atypical in that it is not her career that has prevented her from mothering. The pregnancy's effect on Milla is especially striking, in accelerating her transformation from no-nonsense professional associated with the 'masculine' world of computers to broody, soft-hearted family girl. (This prefigures Gainsbourg's character's similar arc in *Prête-moi ta main*, where it is also linked to maternity.) Visiting Gilbert unbeknown to her sister, Milla states that to deny Louba motherhood would be 'disgusting'; she promises her sister that 'we'll do whatever it takes' and, coming close to the anti-abortion discourses of *Pédale douce* and *Mauvaise foi*, she admits to her that 'I was afraid you might do something stupid'. There is also an implicit deadline imposed on this narrative by virtue of Louba's age. Additionally, the importance of filiation and heritage are emphasised in this film, through a scene in which Stanislas asks Sonia to give her son a childhood toy of his from Russia and explain its significance as a survivor of the Holocaust. Overall, the ending appears to bear out Stanislas' pronouncement that 'there is nothing more beautiful than family'.

However, just as I have argued that temporal contextualisation, looking back, undermines the celebration of Louba and Gilbert's love, equally a comparative perspective across different storylines at the film's close further prevents the romantic model from proving totalising. For example, in a reversal of Louba's trajectory, Sonia – for whom children have not proven enough to make her happy in the absence of a loyal husband – is newly, and willingly, alone. This is typical of the ensemble film's refusal of univocal messages. It should also be noted that, characteristically for Thompson, a degree of narrative reflexivity further contributes to the film's interest in the construction of stories and problematises straightforward interpretations. Notable here is the interpolation of intertitles counting down the days until Christmas and, especially, several instances of to-camera addresses, where characters narrate seemingly significant memories. These addresses are at odds with the film's otherwise broadly classical style, dislocating individual characters from the group compositions typical of the *choral* to suspend linear narrative progression in favour of an ostensible focus on psychology. Characters' tales range from historicised nostalgia (Stanislas' story of escaping from Russia) to trauma relived (Joseph's childhood) or starry-eyed romance (Yvette's tale of running away with her second husband) – all of which are clichés of autobiography. Interestingly, Sonia's story – the only one told to another character, Louba, but still filmed head-on as an address, reinforcing the spectator's positioning within the film's network of characters – contains a further playful intertext. At the end of her tether and about to leave her husband, she begins by rhetorically challenging her interlocutor as to her identity in the very terms according to which we are likely to have judged her at the start of the film: 'What do you know about my life? I'm strong, rich, married with kids... The rock.' Her combative, sarcastic tone appears to herald a contrastingly illuminating insight into her true psychology at this moment of emotional vulnerability. However, her subsequent tale of her childhood self and a friend bumping into her father with his girlfriend and illegitimate son contains the detail that they had been seeing classic New Wave triangular romance *Jules et Jim/Jules and Jim* (François Truffaut, 1962). This highlights the story's points of contact with another New Wave ur-text, Truffaut's *Les Quatre cents coups*. That is, Sonia's account mirrors a pivotal moment from the earlier film, in which protagonist Antoine Doinel and his friend famously cross paths with Doinel's mother and her lover. This reference makes a mockery of the still dominant school of post-Freudian thought seeking to root human psychology in childhood experience – the very model the film has elsewhere invited us to invoke. Dabbling in the kind of cinephilic referential play often reserved for auteurs in French cinema, and appropriating one of the defining films of the New Wave canon to her popular ends, Thompson thus constructs a level on which all narratives' fictionalising tendency is stressed and the significance of the family itself wholly undercut.

Finally, a particularly interesting detail of *La Bûche* is that romantic and familial plots do not in fact simply run in parallel; in one case, the boundaries begin to blur. Unaware of his identity as her father's son, Milla is attracted to Joseph. This is first signalled by shots showing her gaze lingering on his torso in the hospital as the family awaits news about their father. To underline the point, Thompson uses a jump cut, moving in on Joseph's body from Milla's point of view; in any case, Milla later explicitly admits to Louba that she is 'like jelly' before him. In typically ludic fashion, the narrative later further complicates their relationship by introducing the possibility that Milla may not in fact be related to Joseph at all, as she may be the child of her step-father Jean-Pierre. However, the film refuses to allow the uneasy spectre of incest to be easily dismissed. On the two occasions on which Milla's attraction to Joseph is conveyed, camerawork and dialogue at the same time highlight similarities between the two characters that seem to support the suggestion that they are in fact related. Thus when Milla's eyes devour Joseph in the hospital, consecutive shots show the characters smoking a cigarette in the same way, holding it in their mouths without hands; and when she discusses her feelings for him with Louba, she states explicitly that it is unusual for her carry a torch for a man with the same problems ('introversion, neurosis...') as herself. References to literal incestuous desire are rare in rom-com. This contrasts with the topic's relative prominence in French culture, where it has not only featured as a staple of classic comic cinema and contemporary auteur drama but recurs, for example, in popular songs.[15] In any case, its appearance in *La Bûche* is intended not to shock but to place in parallel the Freudian family and heterosexual romance narratives. This move highlights the two configurations' commonality as self-other relations. As Evans and Deleyto have noted, romance is ultimately a question of identity, approached via a dialogical model through which characters learn about the other in the self (1998: 3–4). The lifting of the incest taboo, even by implication, in *La Bûche* thus confronts the question of to what extent romantic attraction seeks out the self in the other. Characteristically for this film, no answer is given. The final scene maintains the sexual tension between Joseph and Milla as the pair, now both aware of their possible blood tie, pull back from a tantalising near kiss at the last moment. Milla invokes a classic romantic text of thwarted love, *Romeo and Juliet*, as if to round off the film's generic credentials, while Joseph places the final accent on matriarchal power with his remark that: 'Mothers know everything. They should be made to talk.' Unlike in Shakespeare's tragic tale, this statement reserves the possibility of a future for even this couple, on the basis that they may yet discover they are not related. In this storyline, too, Thompson therefore preserves the openness which I have argued is typical of female-authored family rom-coms. The fact that the actor playing Joseph is her own son again brings extra-textual detail to inform her narrative in a playful way, underlining her status as a mother who, as metaphorical 'speaker' or filmmaker, does not in fact 'know everything'. It represents, in other words, a final warning to the viewer against drawing facile conclusions, about either familial or romantic roles.

La Bûche's blurring of the parameters between romantic and familial love in fact makes overt the work done by many family rom-coms. This is highly significant in a social and to some extent generic context characterised by marriage in crisis and with the bonds between individual partners rendered flimsy, such that parenthood can provide an alternative structure for longer-term interpersonal commitment. This suggests procreation's status as itself an expression of the hedonistic imperative for individual self-fulfilment associated with the contemporary era – a linkage supported by a recent French survey of one thousand citizens' reasons for having children, where 73 per cent of respondents cited motives of personal gratification (Anon 2009c). It also reverses the dynamic set up at the start of this chapter whereby the love story is the *raison d'être* of the family unit, casting the desire for family – at its most basic, the human reproductive urge – as pivotal in ensuring the survival of dyadic partnerships in France today, even if these are for the most part re-imagined along less conventional lines.

5
Genre, Style and Transnationalism

This chapter examines the explosion of French romantic comedies during the 1990s and 2000s specifically from the perspective of transnational genre filmmaking, as this practice is expressed through thematic preoccupations but also, particularly, style. It will be divided into two sections: firstly, after defining the terms for understanding transnationalism in relation to genre, I will focus on the influence of external cinemas on the national genre before, secondly, moving on to examine how the French rom-com in turn puts its own spin on a global genre and re-packages it for export. The first section of the discussion will include a reception study of critical reactions to the rom-com in the French press, as a focal point for attitudes towards global culture and notably US cultural hegemony – a question that has attracted great critical debate in France. Finally, in-depth analysis of the transnational aspects of global hit *L'Arnacœur* (2010) will draw together many of the ideas from the rest of the chapter through concrete examples.

Global Romantic Comedy, the Other Within

Despite cinema's ties to the nation state, in this millennium it is the concept of transnationalism that has increasingly gained ground as a salient perspective from which to apprehend the medium, as it traverses international distribution and other public and private exhibition circuits. Thus cultural and film theorists including Charles Acland (2005), Sean Cubitt (2004: 356) and Elizabeth Ezra and Terry Rowden (2006) agree that cinema's role in not only 'trans-local understandings' (Vertovec and Cohen 1999: xvii) but also 'felt internationalism' (Acland 2005: 239) has speeded up in recent years. Ezra and Rowden elaborate on these ideas:

> As a marker of cosmopolitanism, the transnational at once transcends the national and presupposes it. For transnationalism, its nationalist other is neither an armored enemy with whom it must engage in a grim battle to the death nor a verbose relic whose outdated postures can only be scorned. From a transnational perspective, nationalism is instead a canny dialogical partner whose voice often seems to be growing stronger at the very moment that its substance is fading away. Like post-modernism and poststructuralism, other discourses that have complicated the notion of unmediated representation, transnationalism factors heterogeneity into its basic semantic framework. (2006: 4)

Recognition of the close ties between nationalism and transnationalism as 'dialogical partner[s]' undergirds my suggestion in this section that for French romantic comedy, the global romantic comedy is best seen as 'the other within'. As for heterogeneity, this chapter will underline the diverse componential roots and makeup of the corpus, visible at every turn in a genre born out of the encounter between an indigenous film tradition and a transnational genre that is already hybrid in 'its basic semantic framework'. It is significant, too, that the scholars cited above go on shortly after the quoted passage to recognise the ongoing, 'emotionally charged' (ibid) force of nationalism, which will be to the fore in my discussion of the rom-com's reception. The subjectivity implied by reference to emotion further informs the notion of the external genre as other – but an other that offers symbiotic benefits.

Given the extensive explanations of the understanding of rom-com shaping this work, it only remains at this stage to clarify what is meant here by *global* romantic comedy. Evidently the genre in its widest sense, as a negotiator of changes in gender relations from the perspective of comedy, exists in most if not all national contexts. In some, it is particularly widespread – for example, it seems likely that a form of rom-com is the dominant second genre in which most Bollywood musicals participate. Like other genres, it is transnational most immediately in a physical sense of being widely exported by various nations. While Bollywood film is marketed to non-resident

Indians and others internationally, some of the most successful British exports of recent decades have been rom-coms, on which more shortly. However, as with most film genres, in rom-com it is the Hollywood version that represents the most globally visible variant of the genre. In general, Hollywood has in the past routinely been invoked as the other in relation to which less internationally dominant film industries and practices must define themselves, whether this is seen as a relationship primarily of contrast, as with more artistically positioned products (Elsaesser 2005) or of comparison (Moine 2002). In Chapter 1 I cited Moine's recognition of the important influence of 'globalised neo-Hollywood model[s]' on French cinema. This phrasing captures the extent to which the very idea of Hollywood is coming to represent the global in cinema and film culture: as Ezra and Rowden observe in their discussion of the personae of transnational stars, national identity becomes sidelined in such a way that '[t]he performance of Americanness is increasingly becoming a "universal" or "universalizing" characteristic in world cinema' (2006: 2).

I have argued in this book that what is widely understood as the global rom-com originated in the USA. While fully recognising the caveats which must apply to such a form of short-hand, in this chapter 'global' means, primarily, deriving from Hollywood. This is not to say that other traditions do not show their influence – both Almodóvar and the British rom-com tradition have been cited in this study. However, even these examples find themselves complicated by virtue of their very success, which has immediately seen them partially absorbed into the Hollywood machine, whether at the level of reception or production. Two of Almodóvar's so-called muses, Antonio Banderas and Penélope Cruz, in fact constitute examples of the performed 'Americanness' of transnational stars cited by Ezra and Rowden, while the international popularity of *Four Weddings and a Funeral* (Mike Newell, UK 1994) was a major factor in the buyout of production company Working Title Films' Anglo-Dutch corporate backer Polygram Filmed Entertainment by Universal Studios in 1999, prior to the release of several more hit rom-coms penned by screenwriter Richard Curtis. It is more than mere Gallic simplification to refer, as French rom-com reviewers sometimes do, to 'les comédies anglo-saxonnes' (see for example Anon 2007a).

In this first section I will, then, approach the French rom-com from the same perspective adopted by Baudrillard (2010: 82) in his pronouncement on the topic of modernity, where he borrows film vocabulary to endow the US with the position of original version and Europe that of the dubbed or subtitled copy. That is, the focus will limit itself for now broadly to the question of global influence on the French genre conceived for the purposes of analysis as one-way traffic, before reversing the paradigm later in the chapter. However, even such a deliberately reductive working model finds itself immediately complicated, bearing in mind earlier allusions to the heterogeneity of transnational culture and practice per se. To give just one example of the difficulties of pinpointing cultural origins, the widespread legacy of the films of Woody Allen – more popular in France than in the USA (Mazdon 2000: 95) – has been a feature of this research. This illustrates the complexity of the transnational palimpsest, given the director's own well-known emulation of French and other European art cinemas, and therefore the impossibility of discussing influence in a straightforward way. Nonetheless, I will now attempt to analyse global reference points visible in the French genre, paying attention to what they say about French attitudes towards globalised film and culture. In the first place, I will look at examples of how French rom-coms borrow from global predecessors in a relatively implicit way and in the second, contrastingly, through pastiche in the sense of 'an imitation you are meant to know is an imitation' (Dyer 2007: 1).

Stylistic and Other Borrowings

This section examining the global rom-com's more subtle and diffuse presence in the French genre will be divided into two subsections examining, in turn, various stylistic and other generically convention-alised echoes of the global rom-com, including around the deployment of stars, followed by particular uses of music and language redolent of transnational predecessors.

I. Style and Genre

Many aesthetic features and generic conventions within French rom-coms are linked to their Hollywood ancestry. Starting with the first of these, one detail skimmed by my earlier overview of global rom-com conventions in Chapter 2 was visual style. While any comments on the texture and appearance of a whole genre remain necessarily over-generalised, this is a particularly important point given the key role played by visual style in feminist critiques of the classical rom-com historically (see Durham 1998: 61). In short, the classical Hollywood rom-com has been seen as emulating other films produced in that context in creating an ideologically suspect, because powerful (Ellis 1989: 66), illusion of truth. This illusion is to a considerable extent reliant on the classical style: notably, high-key lighting designed to show maximum detail in an unobtrusive way; classical composition and framing, such as one- and two-shots; continuity editing (normally complementing plot linearity), including such conventions as shot-reverse shots, eyeline and other matches and cross-cutting between different locales; and the use of montage sequences.

While French cinema has perhaps never been as wedded as has Hollywood to the goal of linear plot advancement in a concentrated, transparent manner characterised by a high degree of narrative redundancy (see Moine 2007b: 141), popular cinema from the classical to the mainstream in France has followed a basically continuous editing style. However, many of the traits listed above are less immediately identifiable with Gallic style but are quite common in the rom-com. Beginning with mise-en-scène and composition, most French rom-coms are generally brightly and evenly lit, eschewing naturalism. That they rely heavily on one- and two-shots, too, is a by-product of their focus on two-person relationships first and foremost – with ensemble films providing a notable exception in both lighting and composition. However, a film that stands out for revelling in showing off its performers, and high production values in general, through lushly lit shots including many medium close-ups, is *Hors de prix*. Featuring top-level stars Audrey Tautou and Gad Elmaleh and an opulent Côte d'Azur setting, the film intersperses grandiose long and overhead shots of palaces at Biarritz and Cannes, and especially the Carlton Hotel's impressively kept grounds and the surrounding area, with loving close-ups of the luxury consumer goods that are the object of desire of Tautou's shamelessly avaricious character Irène.[1] Much is made, too, of both Tautou and Elmaleh's appealing appearances, the plot contriving to bedeck them with sumptuous costumes designed explicitly to show off the physical attributes they are 'selling', as they both play at being gold-diggers amid the hotel's moneyed clientele. It might be noted here that high-key lighting also facilitates absolute narrative clarity, which is relevant to a superficially fairly densely plotted farce involving multiple levels of duplicity and role-playing. Both the setting and the plot organisation contribute to the film's pastiche of the screwball comedy. In addition, one reviewer notes specific echoes of Lubitsch in its use of accumulated concrete objects to signal both ellipsis and excess. Exemplary here is a scene in which Irène, in flirtatious mode, sticks a cocktail umbrella into her hair; we then dissolve to the same head decorated with multiple umbrellas... and pull back to reveal a drunken Irène (Anon 2006b). *Hors de prix*'s evocation of Americanness is not, though, strictly limited to the classical period. Notably, a credit sequence in the 'stick figure' style associated with the American 1950s and 1960s, set to sprightly piano, percussion and saxophone jazz chords, extends its referential universe at least beyond Lubitsch's lifespan.

Within a broadly continuous style, the specific editing devices of cross-cutting and montages are also disproportionately common in French rom-coms, by comparison with national practice as a whole. Reviewer François Ramasse (1989), writing in *Positif*, highlights the cross-cuts in early rom-com *Romuald et Juliette* between the protagonists' children's very different bathrooms (Romuald is a rich businessman and Juliette a cleaning lady and mother of five) to illustrate his suggestion that what director Serreau's style lacks in originality it makes up for in efficiency, a word immediately associable with the Hollywood narrative-centric approach to cinema. Cross-cutting becomes, then, a signature of emulated Americanness, also commented on in a review of another early rom-com, Akerman's overtly transatlantic, bilingual *Un divan à New York*, where the editing in early sequences is seen as so vigorously parallel as to become 'systematic' (Frodon 1996). These examples highlight the fact that parallel editing is a particular convention at the beginning of romantic comedies focused on two characters, where each is being introduced – and usually, as with Romuald and Juliette, contrasted in such a way as to set up humorous conflict later. It persists in numerous films as the genre takes hold.

As for the montage sequence, 'a segment of a film that summarizes a topic or compresses a passage of time into brief symbolic or typical images' (Bordwell and Thompson 2008: 479), this has endured as a stock feature of the Hollywood repertoire from the classical to the contemporary period, thanks to its ability to pack a great deal of narrative detail into a short space of time – efficiency as *modus operandi* again. *Ma femme est une actrice*, for instance, uses a montage to plunge us into the late 1970s – and to re-envision the 'city of lovers', Paris, through the lens of cinema's 'romantic playground', New York (Jermyn 2009: 12) – via a homage to the opening sequence of Allen's *Manhattan* (USA 1979). After announcing its transatlantic leanings through a credit sequence showing famous photographs of classical Hollywood divas, overlaid with Ella Fitzgerald's indolent rendition of 'Lullaby of Birdland', a montage of stills of Parisians going about their daily business is accompanied by the protagonist-narrator's (Attal) commentary in voiceover that with 1.4 million women in the city, or two for every man, the Parisian bachelor faces favourable odds in the dating game. As if this precise echo of Allen's film were not obvious enough, Attal then rams the point home with the afterthought: '...but not compared with New York, where [the ratio] is 5.2 to 1!', as we cut to an image of the Statue of Liberty. This self-alignment with a recognised master of the genre is about more than just marketing. I have argued in Chapter 2 that the self-questioning mode epitomised by Allen's romantic comedies and dubbed by Shumway 'intimacy' is the dominant romantic discourse on display in the French rom-com, for aesthetic reasons bound up with the French allegiance to realism and openness, as well as ideological ones. These relate to a certain reluctance on the part of French society, still more heavily patriarchal than in the US or Britain, to adjust to women's increased freedom and equality. As Richard Dyer (2007: 59) has shown, 'pastiche facilitat[es] the experience of the imitated work'. Accordingly one feature of the 'intimate' character of many French rom-coms is an Allen-esque sensibility which I have described in Chapter 3 in terms of Rowe's concept of the melodramatised male. The Allen example in this way again crystallises one of the complexities of discussing influence. Shumway in fact suggests that the use of 'various devices to frame the material, often with the effect of making the story seem like autobiography or confession' (2003a: 158) typifies intimacy. Voiceover is the most obvious example of such devices. In France, there is a history of male voiceovers commenting on romance too, in (Hollywood-indebted) New Wave films by Godard and, especially, Truffaut (*Tirez sur le pianiste/Shoot the Piano Player!* [1960] is a famous example). Certainly, self-analysing voiceovers recur so frequently in the French romantic comedy now as to have been integrated into the genre in a way that no longer *necessarily* overtly invokes Hollywood. At some point, in other words, influence ceases to be distinguishable as such and gains its own identity in a new context.

A rom-com more identifiable with contemporary Hollywood that makes substantial use of montage is *Prête-moi ta main*. This is a useful text for studying global influence given producer-actor Chabat's status as a Frenchman with offices in Hollywood, as well as his unashamed remarks about wishing to emulate the success of global rom-coms like those written by Curtis (Loison 2006). To this end, for *Prête-moi* Chabat hired a team of writers to script his own idea *à l'américaine*, with immediately visible consequences. The montage here encapsulates the strategy adopted by the script as a whole: a highly streamlined approach to narrative designed to wring maximum laughs from densely packed information, thanks to careful attention to comic timing. An early sequence is exemplary. The film opens in a colourfully flamboyant anti-realist mode that almost caricatures Hollywood practice. As protagonist Luis (Chabat) narrates in voiceover his romantic history, in a heady combination of generic signalling and character exposition, flashbacks in muted tones show him badly disguised as a 1980s version of himself. This introduction recalls Grossvogel's (2005: 73) stress on Hollywood's romantic heroes and heroines as 'functional figures of comedy' and elicits 'fear' from one reviewer, who likens it to a puppet show (Anon 2006d). The colour seeps further from the image as Luis is left by a girlfriend, until only her purple scarf remains, a monochromatic detail on a black and white background, constituting an out-of-place convention from photography and auteur cinema. Further cinematic conventions are parodied as melancholy piano notes accompany slow-motion shots of our beleaguered hero, then the camera spins in an overhead shot above him lying on his bed, plagued by adolescent angst, before the mood is lightened by the revelation that Luis' obsession with his lost love led him to recreate her smell and become a much sought-after perfumer. This highly telescoped interlude has taken a mere four minutes, 26 seconds. Just over eight minutes later, after the film's initial 'problem' – that Luis' sisters are refusing to continue acting as housewives for him and demand he marries – has been established (and we have been briefly introduced to the female lead), we are presented with a second, even tighter montage, showing the different candidates with whom Luis is set up on blind dates. This time the device is further denaturalised by the use of split screens and moving panels. Mastery of comic rhythm – so associated with Anglo-American culture that *le timing* is untranslatable – is displayed by a final, punchline-like, yet deliberately understated because short, shot in which the blind date is a man.

Alongside its use of montages, associable with Hollywood for many decades, the densely referential nature of this opening, creating a strikingly non-naturalistic impression, is more redolent of postclassical Hollywood cinema (see Tasker 1993: 61) than French filmmaking. Of course, Lartigau's use of not only bright lighting but a strikingly bright colour palette adds to this effect and is equally more associable with US than French cinema (see Selfe 2010: 158). This raises the question of stylistic evolution in Hollywood. According to Bordwell (2006: 121–38), mainstream Hollywood is now dominated by an 'intensified' continuity style characterised by fast editing, wide-ranging camera movements and 'extreme' focal lengths, especially the extensive use of the close-up. With regard to this latter convention, Vincendeau (1993; 2000: 10) has specifically underlined the use of the close-up as even in the classical era much more common in US than French cinema. Close-ups also have an amplified role in a genre focused on emotion and where the pairing of different combinations of known stars acts as an important marketing hook.

Bearing this in mind, the film that on its release in 2002, in addition to explicitly referencing Hollywood, emulated the style (including narrative organisation) of a contemporary US rom-com more closely than any previous French film was *Décalage horaire*. This is achieved by the counterpointing of the two main characters in the opening and a preference for close-ups, one-shots and short takes throughout. Related to framing conventions, a comment by *Screen International*'s reviewer that 'never before has Binoche exuded such a mega-watt star persona' (Goodridge 2002), and likening her to Meg Ryan, illustrates how the privileging of close-ups is in turn linked to Hollywood's hard-selling of stars.

Although it would be neither possible nor particularly informative to list further rom-com conventions like 'meet cutes' or wrong partners ubiquitous in both Hollywood and France, one more does merit attention here for its prevalence and possible links to a post-modern sensibility: the deception scenario. As touched on in Chapter 2, Krutnik has emphasised the recurrence of scenes in which lovers are forced by circumstance to 'play' at being lovers – before assuming the role in earnest – as symptomatic of the overt artifice characterising the contemporary new romance. Whether or not such fabrications are more to the fore in the recent cycle is actually unclear – the conceptually adjacent *quiproquo*, or case of mistaken or falsified identity is central, too, to classical screwball and is routinely cited by French reviewers as a stock generic feature; in his later discussion even Krutnik himself does acknowledge the presence of deception scenarios in the Hollywood rom-com as a whole. Such plot contortions also occur in the *comédie boulevardière* or, going back to the nineteenth century, in romantic ür-text *Cyrano de Bergerac* (Rostand: 2002 [1897]) – on which one of Krutnik's (2002: 141–4) key examples, *The Truth About Cats and Dogs* (Michael Lehmann, USA 1996) is based. On the whole, then, the plot convention of feigned romance is familiar to French audiences, but is probably still most associated with a global tradition. French rom-coms in which it appears include, in addition to *Prête-moi*, both *Quatre étoiles* and *Hors de prix*, *Pédale douce*, *De vrais mensonges*, *Cliente*, *Essaye-moi*, *Il ne faut jurer . . . de rien!*, *Ma femme est une actrice*, *Je vous trouve très beau* and *Quand la mer monte*. The fact that most of these examples occur in post-millennial films is congruent with the global genre's general progress towards consolidation within the French film landscape. That these examples range from a film that has been seen as so crassly commercial as *Je vous trouve très beau* (see for example Morain 2006a) to the multi-prize-winning *Quand la mer monte* speaks to the widespread reverberations of such a shift – and to the eclectic applications of generic approaches to cinema.

II. Love Songs and Language

In this section I examine the use of the English language and, secondarily, Franglais in the French rom-com, both through songs and elsewhere in the narrative, as an example of self-proclaimed allusion to a global tradition. The use of love songs elaborated in an 'Anglo-Saxon' context, and so in English if there are lyrics, is in fact so widespread in the French rom-com as to preclude a list. American classics are common ('As Time Goes By' in *Les Marmottes* or 'Lullaby of Birdsong' in *Ma Femme est une actrice*) but British music is also popular, from Spandau Ballet's 'I Know This Much is True' in *Ce soir, je dors chez toi* to 'London Calling' by The Clash, again in *Ma femme*, and Britpop hit 'Alright' by Supergrass prominently (including over the DVD menu) in *LOL*. Even in a lower budget film like *Essaye-moi*, a hymn to cartoonish Hollywood slapstick, presumably to avoid copyright clearance costs, director Martin-Laval introduces brief snippets of original English-language songs including Diana Ross and the Supremes' 'Where Did Our Love Go?' into a soundtrack predominantly originally composed by Belgian Pierre Van Dormael and performed by the Brussels Jazz Orchestra, but also in English. The theme song 'From the Very Start I Knew It Was You' imitates the style of real classics so perfectly as to sound like a minor, forgotten one. The key point is that alignment with an English-language music tradition is often actively sought out.

Other rom-coms integrate English into their dialogue. These can be usefully split into the categories of those that display anxiety about the spread of English and those that welcome it. Notable in the first category are the pair of transatlantic romances, *Un divan à New York* (1996) and *Décalage horaire* (2002), which both star Binoche. In the bilingual earlier film, she is cast opposite American William Hurt as Henry, whose neurosis manifests itself through aphasia. Linguistic failure is therefore expressly connected with the English language. It is moreover contrasted with the greater linguistic and existential ease demonstrated by Binoche's French-speaking character, who in this film actually takes over Henry's psychoanalysis practice and becomes his patients' preferred consultant, despite her lack of training (although, in a joke about psychoanalysis, both analysts' speech is generally limited to 'hmm'-ing during sessions). In *Décalage horaire*, six years later, aphasia is swapped for logorrhea to the same end of associating English with dysfunction. As Rollet (2008: 100) notes, one feature of male protagonist Félix's cultural disorientation is his Franglais, as he readily imports almost entire phrases – and often those with a particular cultural significance as American ('*les happy ends c'est du bullshit*'/'happy endings are bullshit'). It is also interesting that virtual communication looms large in Rose's Gallic indictment of the world from which Félix has hailed, in her spectacularly conceptually conflated allusion to the triptych of 'the web, globalisation and terrorism', revealing the extent to which this film addresses, albeit playfully, contemporary anxiety around 'famous high-tech solitudes under the empire of the internet' (Vasse 2008: 77) – the notion that the more resources of communication are open to us in the post-technological world, the less real exchange takes place. Here this negative apprehension bypasses technology per se to become simply associated with America itself. There is no doubt concern about the decline of the French language behind such vigorous endorsements of it in these narratives.

In contrast, the more recent (2008) film *LOL* is characterised by an enthusiastic embrace of cultural and linguistic hybridity, including at the level of dialogue. This fits with the narrative's youth-orientation (relatively new in French cinema, where explicitly youth-oriented films have been more associated with television), which is most obvious in a soundtrack stuffed with – mostly English-language – pop songs, from Rolling Stones classics to contemporary hits by the likes of, as well as Supergrass, Alvin and the Chipmunks. Additionally, not only does the film's rapid editing style flirt with a music video aesthetic, but the fact that here not only significant elements of English but especially Franglais are incorporated into its spoken idiom speaks to the younger demographic's association with linguistic experimentation and change. Thus the *lycéens* on whom the film focuses – and especially those like Isabelle de Peyrefitte who are associated with a self-consciously cool pose – routinely insert single English words into their statements, usually where a French word would have done just as well (for example, '*Elle va passer la meilleure soirée de sa life* [not *vie*]'/'She'll have the night of her life'). Of course, the main area in which Franglais has flourished precisely because the French language will arguably *not* do as well is in the realm of the digital and technological revolution. Virtual communication – via text and online messaging – is also a major mode of communication here, as acknowledged by the title's quotation of an acronym that evolved in these arenas. Unlike in *Décalage horaire*, the ever-increasing reach of US-led global culture is celebrated by an exuberant portrayal of friendship and romance facilitated by communications technology, which is seen as inseparable from the penetration of English into the French language. Moreover, the film reflects the encroachment of the English language onto not only youth culture but especially feminine youth culture, as through women's fashion magazines or *la presse people*.[2]

The soundtrack of *LOL* also illustrates the ongoing relevance of a comment by Grossvogel (2005: 73–4): that romantic comedies often introduce incongruous elements into their love-songs. Grossvogel alludes specifically to new interpretations of old favourites, which for him allows them to preserve their nostalgic value with a pinch of humour. Incongruous versions further stress songs' status as quotation and incongruousness can come, too, from English itself. This occurs in *LOL* with Jean-Philippe Verdin's 'Little Sister'. This song is for the purposes of the narrative performed by the male lead Maël, teen heartthrob (since the film's success) Jérémy Kapone, during a central sequence providing a turning point in his relationship with the eponymous Lola, when they begin to admit their romantic leanings more openly. Thematically, it mythologises Lola and Maël's relationship, based on friendship ('We used to say that we were brother and sister'). What is unusual is that, unlike with the simulated Americanness of *Essaye-moi*'s English-language song, this piece is performed in a slightly accented French whose charm is magnified by the context and the performance's initial breathy hesitancy. In other words the sense of quotation is here cultural rather than specific: the number deliberately masquerades as not only a borrowing but an imperfect translation.

It is noteworthy that these films, as well as invoking the English language, tend too to pastiche global genres: primarily the teenpic in *LOL*, the most formulaic strain of rom-com itself in *Décalage* and musical romance in *Un divan*, which closes on a version of Cole Porter's 'Night and Day' and which one critic calls a 'postmusical', likening the dialogue to spoken songs and the background sounds during certain sequences to music (Martin 1997: 39). Similarly, sections of dialogue in *Mariages!* are in English thanks to a proportion of British guests at the titular wedding: upper-class bores exported straight out of *Four Weddings*. A rumour that Kenneth Branagh may be attending further cements the film's alignment to a tradition that is in this case more immediately recognisable as British than American.

There is a distinction to be made here, too, between the light in which British and American cultures are constructed, even through a common language. The mention of Branagh in *Mariages!* references British comedy as rooted in the venerated Shakespearean tradition. Another paradigmatic example is *Le Goût des autres*, in which protagonist Castella's exclusion from the intellectual clique whose membership he covets is demonstrated memorably by a cringe-making scene in which he declares his love to the English teacher Clara through a rudimentary love poem written in an English full of errors and misconceived metaphors, such as 'when I look at this woman my hearts gets a tan'.[3] This view of British culture as the preserve of an intellectual elite is a far cry from stereotypes of brash America. Yet, as we will see in reviewing reception later in the chapter, more often than not the two are in fact to greater or lesser extents lumped together in the French rom-com. These and other texts, then, locate the effects of globalisation, and their ambivalence about it, in the realm of language. In line with the variety of attitudes to globalisation tracked in this chapter, while some films betray a protectionist attitude paralleling the cultural bemoaning of Anglicisms' increasing purchase on French, others appear to welcome the phonic and semantic possibilities afforded by the English language's burgeoning status as a *lingua franca*. It is worth reminding ourselves, though, that such films nevertheless remain dominated by the French language with all its national and cultural associations. Nowhere is this paradigm of dabbling in the external within a recognisably French context better summed up than on a first viewing of the DVD version of *LOL*, as Supergrass' 'Alright' over the menu gives way to the French language – although transnationally produced – song '*Je ne veux pas travailler*' by Pink Martini during the opening credits.[4] As if this were not enough, as protagonist Lola's voiceover introduces shots of herself and her girlfriends, she explains that the film is played in slow-motion as 'that's what happens when you meet the best-looking girls in American TV series', adding, 'OK, we don't do that much in France, but it's stylish'. This comment resumes the film's attitude towards American narration (slow-motion entrances occur not only in American television but also numerous iconic Hollywood films of recent decades, from *Reservoir Dogs* [Quentin Tarantino, USA 1992] to the rom-com *Clueless* [Amy Heckerling, USA 1995]) and provides a convenient bridge to discussing overt transatlantic reflexivity in French rom-coms.

Reflexive Romance

As modes of communication, pastiche and cinephilia may enjoy more importance today than ever before in cinema (Hoesterey 2001: 46) and they are of paramount importance in contemporary French cinema specifically (Palmer 2011: 195–215). Romantic comedy is no exception. In this section I will briefly examine just two French films that exemplify the dominant new romantic trend for explicit citation of pre-existing romantic texts by referring insistently to hit Hollywood rom-coms. These are *Décalage horaire* and Marc Gibaja's less successful but no less generically interesting *Ma vie n'est pas une comédie romantique/It Had to be You* (2007). Finally, I will briefly show how a film from the end of the period, *Les Emotifs anonymes/Romantics Anonymous* (Jean-Pierre Améris, 2010), translates awareness of the rom-com's ongoing status as an immigrant even as it is increasingly integrated into French cinema.

Initially conceived for Hollywood production by a writer-director who has lived in the USA, *Décalage horaire* distinguishes itself in being the only French rom-com to date to have received a sustained critical commentary as such – also from the perspective of transnational exchange, explicitly contrasting the film with Hollywood predecessors (Rollet 2008). The key intertexts for this film are a screwball comedy, *It Happened One Night* (Frank Capra, USA 1934), and two more recent hits, *When Harry Met Sally* and paradigmatic new romance *Pretty Woman*. Resonance with Capra's film occurs through the couple's meeting in an airport, updating the classic film's bus station, and because a large chunk of the narrative takes place in the hotel bedroom which they are forced by circumstance to share, prompting gentle squabbling across the central axis.

Jumping forward half a century, *When Harry Met Sally*'s status as a reference point will already be obvious from the comparison cited earlier in this chapter, offered by one review, between Binoche and Meg Ryan. This is particularly manifest during a dinner scene in which Rose re-enacts Sally's iconic frankness about the female orgasm (Sally fakes one loudly in a restaurant), with a more sophisticated nuance. When Félix asks Rose how she could enjoy sex with a man she no longer loves (her ex), Rose unexpectedly replies that she has been 'faking it' for years with a man whom she still loves – although, we know, she has elected to leave him because he is abusive. Binoche's knowing, teasing smile as she delivers the line, the measured and deliberate manner in which she reveals a potentially shocking detail and, above all, a languorous, licking play of cutlery at her mouth all combine to put the knowing viewer immediately in mind of the moment that defined *When Harry*'s then audaciously modern sensibility.

As for the intertext with *Pretty Woman*, not only does Reno's neurotic businessman Félix recall Richard Gere's misunderstood Wall Street shark Edward (both also blighted by unresolved Oedipal complexes) and Binoche's emotional, initially heavily 'done-up' beautician Rose Julia Roberts' 'tart-with-a-heart' Vivian, but specific narrative moments echo those of the earlier film. One of these is the classic device of revealing the female character's true beauty, through the removal of a wig in *Pretty Woman* and the layer of clownish makeup in *Décalage*. The other concerns dialogue book-ending Thompson's film with a post-modern frame that invokes *Pretty Woman* and a certain simplistic conception of Hollywood entertainment as a whole: an opening voiceover in which Rose wishes life could be like films where 'whores marry millionaires' and a closing one where Félix reflects that 'Hollywood happy endings are bullshit'.

Multiplying the intertextual echoes reverberating through this film is one way in which my own analysis differs from Rollet's, since she only acknowledges the classical allusion – a more 'respectable' reference point for French cineastes than contemporary Hollywood, as I will argue in more detail in discussing this genre's reception later in this chapter. I also wish to add a transnational dimension to her feminist reading of the film. Specifically, in relation to the revelation of beauty scene in *Décalage*, for Rollet (2008: 103) Rose's shedding of her 'mask' of makeup represents liberation from society's rules regarding femininity. While this is true, it ignores the comically excessive character of the makeup. Its shedding represents a return to Binoche's naturalistic dramatic persona, which is iconically French *par excellence*. This visual intensification of Binoche's representation of Frenchness only parallels the recuperation of Hollywood star Reno by the French industry in the film, humorously acknowledged in the narrative by the fact that his character is a French chef who has 'defected' to the US only to find misery and divorce. His romance with Rose, who is so attached to French heritage she cries when the news shows footage of the Fourth Republic, represents the comforting return to the motherland – or perhaps the fatherland, given the unconventional ending uniting him not (physically) with his new love but with his estranged father, in rural Burgundy. Since the two – both chefs – fell out over Félix's unorthodox cooking ideas, there is also an implication of a return to traditional French methods in this arena. National values thus triumph at both textual and extra-textual levels and it is ultimately not just Rose and Félix who are brought together, but the Hollywood rom-com and the French film industry, on the latter's terms.

Rollet's interpretation of *Décalage*'s self-aware framing dialogue, meanwhile, reproduces an anti-Hollywood prejudice she identifies with French film studies as a whole. She claims that this example of reflexivity constitutes a specifically French touch of originality to 'elevate [...] the film to more than a genre film, or at least to superior genre fare' (2008: 99–100). This argument is untenable in view of the fact that self-referentiality is now a well-established, defining feature of contemporary Hollywood rom-coms. Not only that but in fact Félix's closing remarks pastiche the ending of *Pretty Woman*, where a street performer proclaims: 'This is Hollywood, land of dreams'. In other words, while Rollet makes convincing arguments about the adaptation of a US model for French audiences, such as through the use of local locations and stars, she somewhat overstates the radical originality of the French version against the Hollywood model.

The other French example of this highly self-reflexive transnational trend, *Ma vie n'est pas une comédie romantique*, also invokes more than one specific pre-existing rom-com. Here the key quotations are all more recent: *Sleepless in Seattle*, *When Harry Met Sally* and *Love Actually* (Richard Curtis, UK/USA 2003). The film opens with a black screen, while a male voiceover tells us that people who love rom-coms tend to be suspected of having failed in their own emotional life, then discusses such texts' power to manipulate the viewer's emotions: 'like a fool, you always feel a lump in your throat'. After the voice has confirmed that 'this rom-com fan' *is* a failure in love, we hear snippets of the narrative-defining radio broadcast dialogue from *Sleepless in Seattle*, then see images from the film, before a reverse shot shows its male viewer reclining on a sofa in front of the television on which it is playing. The apartment surrounding our 'speaker' is being emptied of furniture: it is the home (his voiceover tells us) he shared with the girlfriend with whom he has recently broken up. This melodramatic opening strongly recalls Ephron's tale of male bereavement and dysfunctional singlehood, an impression reinforced when we 'meet cute' our hero Thomas' (Gilles Lellouche) future love object, bubbly Ryan-esque blonde Florence (Marie Gillain).

At the same time, this initial meeting – which takes place in the wall-to-wall pink of a toilet roll aisle at a supermarket – marks a turning point towards Ryan's earlier hit rom-com, *When Harry Met Sally*, in that the protagonists are old schoolmates (and sweethearts). This intertext dominates the central body of the narrative. When Thomas inadvertently prompts Florence's split from her long-term partner (by listing the giveaway signs of adultery as he experienced them from his ex), the two become close friends who share their romantic and other fears, as in Reiner's film. Although this narrative is set over a shorter space of time than its predecessor (a few months rather than many years), the meandering pace of a narrative constructed around individual scenes and vignettes, with little effort made to connect them, recalls the earlier film. So does the couple's habit of calling each other by their full names and maintaining forced formality at times, such as by shaking hands with one another. The comparison is further underlined as the narrative progresses, both by the presence of a poster for Reiner's film visible in the background at a cinema's 'Romantic Comedy Week' and by a sequence at a New Year's Eve party (like the climax of *When Harry*) in which Florence's permed hair and 1980s bouffant-necked, off-the-shoulder dress make her Sally's double. Most recognisable of all is the pivotal scene in which the friends fall into bed together, in both cases following on immediately from the man's encounter with his significant ex and his resulting arrival at the woman's house late at night for support. Afterwards, too, there is a direct parallelism in the way we cut to each member of the couple discussing the event with a third party, as well as in their transparently insincere insistence that sexual relations should not continue lest they jeopardise the friendship.

Only in the final act does *Love Actually* make a – less explicit – appearance. Firstly, a scene in which Florence's ex conveys his ongoing love for her via written placards pastiches Mark's (Andrew Lincoln) declaration to Juliet (Keira Knightley) in Curtis' film. Shortly afterwards, a conversation between Thomas and Florence's son Lucas about the young boy's lovelife, played with deadly seriousness, imitates the relationship between *Love Actually*'s widow Daniel (Liam Neeson) and his romantically precocious stepson Sam. Finally, it is this plotline, too, that is echoed in the climactic sequence of *Ma vie n'est pas*, set in an airport, when – like Sam – Florence tries to force her way past an official in order to reach her love before they fly away to the USA.

The fact that, unlike Sam, Florence fails to get past the official in *Ma vie n'est pas* relates to the precise nature of this film's relationship to pre-existing rom-com models. Where *Décalage horaire* commented on Franco-US relations as a whole, this text is in dialogue with the generic tradition itself and, as its title promises, this is not limited to an unquestioning embrace. Precisely by invoking not just general but specific conventions and models, the text is consistently pointing up its own artifice – the same contrivance which its opening voiceover at once vaunts and deplores ('like an idiot, you feel a lump in your throat'). This extends to anti-realist aesthetics, intensifying the look and sound of the rom-coms mimicked at times to the point of caricature. One example is an acting style that veers between broad naturalism and performativity (Lellouche's histrionic 'crying' scenes). Occasional highly pictorial figure arrangement, as when Thomas and his colleague are momentarily shot from overhead lying on a black background with yellow polka-dots, reminiscent of a board game, with no narrative explanation, tends too to make of them stick figures. In general, the appearance of sets is even more jarring than the acting style. The pink toilet roll scene is representative of the film's use of bright colours and extreme contrasts, notably in Florence's new-build home (not unlike the backdrop to *De l'autre côté du lit*), where white walls are decorated with bright red stencilled flowers. This is matched at one point by deliberately fake-looking splodges of red on her face as she cleans, complete with tea-towel tied theatrically round her head. Another special effect so obvious as to appear intentionally foregrounded is the occasional use of flat, almost cartoonish rear projections, while a head-on shot of Thomas and a friend 'driving a car', with the surroundings shrouded in darkness, looks more static than equivalent efforts from the 1930s.

Such creakily ersatz visual illusionism, underlining the distance of this film from its apparent ancestors, is complemented by a heavy-handed score. This is so insistently composed of cheerily repetitive, plonking piano jazz as to completely cull any emotional impact from several key scenes. Not only that but more than one English-language classic is used but rerecorded in a strangely distorted version, as with a slowed down, croaky-voiced, oddly mournful rendition of 'Let's fall in love' during the first sex scene. This evokes the couple's own hesitant relationship with the romantic notion of *falling* in love; rather, they initially decide on a strictly rule-governed agreement to remain friends while sleeping together – which fails when their feelings conform to the romantic stereotype of overcoming them.

Despite a romantic thread coursing through the narrative, the happy ending is enacted in an even more heavily self-questioning mode than the rest of the film. The final act opens with the *Star Trek*-themed mock wedding of Florence's daughter Lisa to Thomas' colleague Bill. By forcing Florence and Thomas to see one another again, the wedding speaks to the true practical difficulties associated with the break-up of long-term relationships where families are concerned and actually casts the romantic marriage narrative, one version of life-long commitment, as science fiction. In this setting, Florence makes her final love declaration, only to have Thomas tell her she has left it too late and he is going to New York. She then chases him to the airport, in an archetypal Hollywood climax sequence around a deadline structure, only to have an official block her path to the plane. After 'miraculously' attracting Thomas' attention using sun reflected off her compact mirror, she meets him on the runway, the two running to each other in a joyous slow-motion that accentuates the moment's impact, only to have this 'impact' literalised as a bus runs Thomas down. This second *deus ex machina* plot event is so abrupt that it emphasises the contrivance of final sequences like this one. With the audience well and truly shaken up, Florence turns, for the first time, directly to the camera and gives a gentle shake of her head, before we dissolve to a present day shot of the pair filmed head-on. Now both the passage of time and the shaking off of the couple's earlier, generically stereotyped personae are signalled by the loss of Thomas' beard and Florence's newly dark hair, as they explain to the audience that this was not of course how it happened. Rather, more prosaically, Florence simply accompanied Thomas to New York, an admission that prompts banal remarks – and a bickering dynamic – around the sale of her house. Romance is replaced, in other words, by everyday practicalities: as Florence and Thomas put it, 'routine, basically'. In a final flourish, however, just when the film appears to have declared its hand, a reverse shot shows that the couple are seated before a view of Manhattan and the Brooklyn Bridge. As Deborah Jermyn (2009: 10–13) has noted, New York – and 'the island' especially, often seen over the Hudson river – 'has evolved as the preeminent and most memorable location adopted by the Hollywood rom-com', 'constitut[ing] the quintessence of faith in the possibility and attainability of romance'. Reinforcing this romantic overlay, Florence's muffled conversation with Thomas suggests that 'things have never been so perfect'.

The vacillating ending of *Ma vie n'est pas une comédie romantique*, torn between romantic idealism and clear-sighted realism, epitomises the film's overall stance of wishing both to 'have its cake and eat it', to enjoy romantic clichés while recognising them as such. Although this is typical of Hollywood new romance, it must be said that in including such a large volume of blatant allusions to its own status as a formulaic text, the film appears by and large to have failed to work as an involving narrative, given that it drew only 104,000 spectators in France, by comparison with the subtler (and more star-led) *Décalage horaire*'s over a million. Both films, though, demonstrate their filmmakers' felt need to acknowledge the influence of the Hollywood rom-com on the French genre as formative and inevitable, but as a source of creativity rather than constraint.

This influence is much more diluted yet still perceptible by 2010 in *Les Emotifs anonymes*. A high-concept rom-com following rigorously the arcs of two characters beset by pathological shyness, the film stars actors who are well-known in France but barely recognisable elsewhere, Isabelle Carré and comic A-lister Benoît Poelvoorde. It is set in a French provincial town against the backdrop of the hand-crafted chocolate industry. In addition to its extreme Frenchness, however, this setting lends a flavour of anachronism, which creates a converse effect of distance comparable to those achieved by the highly self-reflexive acknowledgements about texts' cultural provenance included in the previous examples. The genre appears in all cases deterritorialised.

This section has attempted to illustrate some of the ways in which the films of the corpus invoke a so-called Anglo-Saxon tradition through content, form, aesthetics and language, as well as, often, thematic allusions too numerous to enunciate. In so doing it has sketched an overview of the French rom-com's position as a genre in relation to which many of the concepts more typically associated with migrant cinemas, such as 'double occupancy' (Elsaesser 2005: 108) and 'accented cinema' (Naficy 2001), apply. While these labels have designated films associated with diasporic and hyphenated identities, whether in the context of cosmopolitan elites or economic migrants, it is no exaggeration to say that today European citizens – like others – occupy more than one identity and that our secondary, 'global' identity is determined principally by the influence, recognisability and cultural currency of US culture. The following discussion will focus on one particular recurrent theme of the French rom-com that is highly revealing about filmmakers' attitudes towards that culture.

The Anglo-Saxon Other... (Wo)Man

A particularity of some French rom-coms is to cast the conventional rom-com character of the 'other man' – or occasionally woman – as

American or, less often, British. This occurs often enough to be remarkable and to betray French filmmakers' complex attitude towards the (trans-)national otherness these characters represent. In short, the identity termed in France Anglo-Saxon is in this way made doubly other, by being allotted a negatively constructed generic position defined as lacking knowable subjectivity.

In the cases of American other men, the definitive status of this nationality as sufficient to stand in for more three-dimensional characterisation is apparent in a tendency for this to be almost these characters' *only* distinctive trait. So it appears in *Ce soir, je dors chez toi*, when hero Alex is confronted in a hotel room by a romantic rival who is bland in appearance and polite if distant in the momentary snatch we glimpse of him. Before setting upon him, Alex calls him simply a 'fucking American'. Similarly – but substituting British-ness – in *Je crois que je l'aime*, protagonist Lucas' unseen former girlfriend, who turned out to be a spy for a rival company, is known simply as '*l'Anglaise*' ('the Englishwoman'). A trusted chauffeur immediately tells Lucas how much he prefers the new lady on the scene, Elsa, played by respected star Sandrine Bonnaire.

Elsewhere, as if to heighten the implication of American 'greatness' in the sense of global visibility, the trait of this nationality is coupled with celebrity status, as in *Ma vie n'est pas une comédie romantique* and *Ils se marièrent et eurent beaucoup d'enfants*. In the first film, Thomas runs into his ex on the arm of a friendly black – and therefore also racially other – American, to whom Florence later refers as '*the* Dexter Coleman?'. Thomas' humiliation is heightened by the fact that he is in the middle of an acupuncture session and has needles hanging out of his face. His confusion and shock are betrayed by his mumbled and incoherent attempt to speak English, as he responds to the news that the couple met in New York with the dumb pronouncement 'New York, yes yes, zee buildings'. The fact that at the end of the film Thomas 'conquers' New York – and presumably the English language – by relocating there traces a narrative movement to neutralise fears of exclusion from the globalised world. In *Ils se marièrent*, the other man vying for Vincent's place in his wife Gabrielle's romantic universe is played by pin-up Johnny Depp (although British actor Keith Allen also makes a brief appearance before being gently rebuffed by Gabrielle).

Cultural and linguistic fear of the Anglo-Ameriocan other is even more clearly on display in Attal's earlier film *Ma femme est une actrice*.

Despite extensive references to American musical and film culture, conceived as explicit quotation or homage, in the film's opening, thematically the text conflates a portrayal of French masculinity in crisis with an exploration of French nationality in crisis, largely through the dialogical other of British culture.[5] The narrative follows Attal's character Yvan during his wife's sojourn in London on a shoot, as he becomes increasingly paranoid about her acting opposite an older but much lusted after British actor, John, played by 1960s icon Terence Stamp. The fact that Stamp has enjoyed a stellar film career including working with the canonical auteur Pier Paolo Pasolini, given Attal's would-be auteur status and this film's overt focus on the difficulties for an ordinary man of being married to a celebrity, constitutes a self-flagellating joke of its own. In terms of national belonging, Yvan's exclusion-anxiety – from his wife's friendship with John and generally from the anglophone culture to which Gainsbourg famously belongs on her mother's side – is played out through language, in one humorous scene in particular. Following Yvan's sudden arrival in London, prompted by paranoia about John's reputation, the trio converse awkwardly in the restaurant trailer on the shoot. Initially, Yvan is unfriendly, answering John's polite small-talk with monosyllables. Catching his wife's reproachful eye, though, he explains that the language barrier is stopping him from saying more (although not, he adds pointedly, from observing all proceedings with a careful eye). There follows a banal passage in which John compliments Yvan on his English but mispronounces his name as the woman's name *Yvonne*, prompting an immediate correction from Yvan. Shortly afterwards, as talk turns to matters Gallic, it is the Frenchman's turn to get his own back, looking blank when faced with John's mediocre but passable pronunciation of French proper names, including a place name and a type of cheese, before correcting them with gusto. What is interesting here is the way in which Frenchness is emasculated, through the feminised label *Yvonne*, prompting the petty display in which Yvan regains the linguistic high ground for a moment – although later scenes including a nationalistically-inflected fantasy of shoving a large cheese into John's face confirm that his paranoia is far from having been assuaged. In terms of spectator positioning, because Yvan is both the ultimate master of the discourse in this scene and the film's auteur and main protagonist, we are aligned with his perspective in mocking the Anglo-Saxon other. The phrase Anglo-Saxon (rather than simply British) is particularly apt considering

John's depiction as a star who, despite clipped speech and 'European' cultural pretension, also has something of California and the global Hollywood movie-star about him (cf. Smith 2011: 89), as through his penchant for Tai-Chi before breakfast.[6] It is not insignificant that, although Charlotte and John do not have an affair, several narrative details (John's solicitous friendliness towards her and pointed echoing of her own 'silly' love of the Eiffel Tower, his roué behaviour in flirting with a young crew member when Charlotte is unavailable) suggest Yvan was right to fear him as a rival. At the end of the film, threats to Yvan's marriage are swept aside by Charlotte's pregnancy, or the absorption of any residual foreignness into French futurity, rather than any kind of *détente* with the feared other.[7]

The other man is not the only position occupied by Britons and Americans in French romantic comedy. Elsewhere, depictions are sometimes even more insulting, as with an American film producer in *Au suivant!*, apparently inspired by Samuel Fuller, whose portrayal as a capricious and unreasonable bully prompts *Les Inrockuptibles*' reviewer to denounce the comparison as entirely unjustified (Anon 2005a). Sometimes, too, they are considerably more favourable. Although I have argued that *Décalage horaire* and *Un divan à New York* constitute reassuring appropriations of global models within French parameters, the fact that the American(/ised) characters in these films are the leading men and not the rival suggests a greater willingness to engage with otherness. This is also the case more recently in *Jusqu'à toi* (Jennifer Devolder, 2009). *Cliente* goes further, having director-actress Balasko's character Irène emigrate to a Wild West landscape with an American Indian, who is idealised as an 'exotic' romantic hero. These examples give a sense of the variety of reactions to the global, English-speaking other on show in the genre. I will now turn to its critical reception in order to trace a similarly broad and complex spread of attitudes.

Reception of the Rom-Com

While the anxieties aired by rom-com narratives around other men and outsiders can be seen to relate to globalisation in a generalised way, today it is primarily in the realm of culture – indeed, in the postwar years perhaps first and foremost film culture – that the threat of envelopment by US 'imperialism' has been most keenly debated (see Kuisel 1993: 230). This section will examine the way in which press reaction to the incorporation of the rom-com genre in France enters into this debate.

The first point to note is critics' increasing recognition of the genre in the French film landscape over the period, broadly in tandem with the shift by distributors and marketing agencies towards promoting films more overtly as romantic comedies. Before the mid-2000s, films are almost without exception simply not described as *comédies romantiques* by distributors or critics but rather by such adjacent titles as *comédies sentimentales* or *comédies de moeurs* (roughly, 'comedies of manners'), with telltale adjectives like 'light-hearted' or 'tender' in descriptions giving away their generic allegiance (and sometimes providing a compass for this research). One of the first direct allusions to the genre's explosion appears as late as February 2005, in weekly news magazine *Le Nouvel Observateur*'s review of Balasko's *L'Ex-femme de ma vie*, immediately casting the genre as exogenous with the remark that 'making a romantic comedy *à la française* is French cinema's current fad' (Anon 2005c). Nearly two years later, another weekly news magazine, *L'Express*, in response to the success of *Je vous trouve très beau* (2005), *Hors de prix* and *Prête-moi ta main* (both 2006), dedicates an article to the phenomenon (Carrière 2006). This article, revealingly, pinpoints reluctance on the part of French directors to embrace the term *comédie romantique*, quoting both *Hors de prix* director Salvadori and also the director of 2006 rom-com/drama *Quand j'étais chanteur/The Singer*, Xavier Giannolli. This bears out the suggestion that filmmakers themselves internalise anti-Hollywood prejudice (see Rollet 2008: 94). Giannolli also duplicates this same prejudice, by claiming (like Rollet) that French cinema subverts rather than reproduces generic codes (before contradicting himself by suggesting that romantic comedy is a French genre invented by Marivaux). This article appears to capture a watershed moment following which the press begins a rapid about turn towards acceptance of romantic comedy's existence as a French genre. Indeed, the same year, *Télérama* refers to *Toi et moi* as a '*comédie romantique labelisée*' (Guichard 2006), or 'formulaic rom-com'. This magazine appears a little ahead of the curve here: the following year, an article in weekly news magazine *Marianne* entitled 'The Boom in Sugar-Coated Films of the Heart' reviewing *Je crois que je l'aime* (2007) by Jolivet, a director associated with socially committed comedies (see O'Shaughnessy 1997: 57; 66), refers to this film as a *comédie romantique*, but in inverted commas (Anon 2007b). Subsequently, the distancing quotation marks disappear definitively from reviews of many comparable films and by the end of the decade the label is entirely standardised at all levels of the written press.

Beyond this picture of gradual acceptance, the ways in which articles in the mainstream and cinephilic press frame the French rom-com as a US import reveal several trends that are worth analysing in more detail. I will divide these into the following categories: articles denigrating the global genre, articles decrying the failings of the French genre in the light of its relationship to global models and, finally, straightforward celebrations of the global genre and its legacy for France. Within these groups, a double standard with respect to classical and contemporary Hollywood is discernible. So too is a certain correlation between the manifestation of some discourses and particular strands of the press.

I. 'Hollywood Soup-Merchants'

While romantic comedy is belittled in both a global and a French context, the French press' circumspection about the genre is very frequently tied to its perceived Americanness. Some journalists and also filmmakers are quite explicit. For example, the anonymous (2004b) review of *Clara et moi* in *Le Nouvel Observateur* comments that this rom-com/drama exploring the issue of HIV compares favourably with what he calls simply '*les comédies* made in Hollywood'. In this locution, the American industry itself stands for unspecified negative values and the use of English underlines the writer's distasteful distance from his 'bad object'. Similarly, revered auteur Alain Resnais, whose films *Smoking/No Smoking* (1993) and *On connaît la chanson* (1997) merit attention from the generic perspective of the rom-com, when quoted in a review of the latter film, seeks to strategically distance himself from those filmmakers he curtly dismisses as 'Hollywood soup-merchants' (see Frodon 1997). As one might expect from an auteur, it is the commercial conception and bland sameness he imputes to Hollywood that for him are intimately bound up with its industrial context.

The charge of lack of originality, often levelled against Hollywood in recent decades especially, with the rise of film franchises, also underlies many other critiques, which reference the genre with phrases like 'yet another...' (Anon 2006e) or 'an umpteenth...' (Anon 2007c; Carrière 2004). These disparaging remarks make no direct allusion to Hollywood, but, as we have seen, the genre was only fully embraced as a label within the French press around the mid-2000s, suggesting that these writers can only be referring to the large body of global antecedents. Sometimes, too, a French film is favourably contrasted with a Hollywood one, on the grounds of having managed to 'renew' the genre (Anon 2004b).

More interesting are those critiques that take exception to a particular aspect of Hollywood cinema, such as Frodon's (2006: 38) lukewarm review of *Prête-moi ta main* for *Cahiers du cinéma*, which displays characteristic hostility to the anti-auteurist US method by remarking that Lartigau might as well take his name off the credits, except 'it's the law, in France, that a film must have a director'. Occasionally, too, observations about cinema are situated in a much wider cultural field, as for example when popular director Aghion directly follows a pejorative assessment of what is often known in French discourse as 'American political correctness' with the rousing statement: 'If comedy is a way of reaching a broad public and raising audience figures for European films, then long live comedy!' (see Tinazzi 2003). In such cases, it is apparent to what extent a single film provides a fulcrum for the expression of a politico-cultural anti-Americanism.

II. Pale Imitations

In opposition to the tendency to write Hollywood off, there emerges a self-abasing strand in the French press that holds Hollywood up as the more expert 'other' to purportedly lacklustre domestic genre filmmaking. For instance, the Communist daily *L'Humanité*, reviewing *Filles perdues, cheveux gras/Hypnotized and Hysterical (Hairstylist Wanted)* (Claude Duty, 2002) – which contains a 'rip-off' of the iconic scene from gross-out rom-com classic *There's Something About Mary* (Bobby and Peter Farrelly, USA 1998) in which a beloved pet flies out of the window – elaborates on his summary assertion that the French are poor at making comedies by calling the film 'more anodyne than the Farrelly brothers' (Anon 2009b). More flatteringly to Hollywood, *L'Humanité* (again) argues that *Ma Vie n'est pas une comédie romantique* is much less moving than American versions (thereby arguably missing the point of its self-conscious genre spoofing) (Anon 2007d). Interestingly, too, such an attitude can even be found in publications cited earlier as equally guilty of belittling Hollywood fare, such as when finance-focused newspaper *Les Échos* states that French rom-coms do not usually attain the same level of quality as the model on which they are based (Anon 2003a). Even a publication that offers more fully elucidated comparisons of the two national cinematic traditions, *Les Inrockuptibles* – a self-consciously 'cool' weekly magazine dedicated to culture and that is famously pro-American/pro-global in its musical criticism – is guilty of a polarising slant. Thus Pierre-Marie Prugnard (1999) suggests in his review of *La Nouvelle Eve* that the influence of a US tradition 'in which love thrives on opposition' – the once again nameless rom-com tradition – makes the backdrop of Parisian intellectual cinema less lifeless, before lamenting the filmmaker's inability to avoid reproducing certain current French cinematic fads.[8]

When French reviews invoke concrete contrasts with Hollywood and cast the latter as superior to French practice, the contrasts are more often than not made against classical films, particularly in more intellectually constructed and cinephilic publications. If repetition with too little variation is the scourge of some French genre critics, it is in some ways logical that contemporary rom-coms should receive shorter shrift than classical ones, by virtue of their belatedness. However, a fondness for classical Hollywood is also one of the defining traits of the pro-auteurist New Wave critics and filmmakers, whose legacy endures. It is hardly surprising, then, that filmmakers aligned with the auteur tradition like Jolivet and Corsini should call upon such giants of the classical American rom-com as Howard Hawks and Blake Edwards for Corsini (Grasseri 1999) or Lubitsch for Jolivet (Lipinska 2007) to contextualise their work. At the journalistic level, meanwhile, to cite just a couple of examples, *Positif*'s allusions in their review of *Décalage horaire* to director Thompson's 'unbearable attempts to cast Binoche as a faux "funny face" breakfasting at Roissy' (Anon 2002a), or *L'Humanité*'s desultory assessment of *Modern Love* as 'a pathetic imitation of former Hollywood models' (Ostria 2008), are typical.

These apparent contradictions in French critical practice confirm my key argument that generic structures are compatible with and can foster creativity. That is, while the New Wave critics tended to locate the brilliance of auteurs in their transcendence of the genre, my own perspective resituates such success as a virtuoso mastering of the genre's conventions. Since self-reflexivity is constitutive of genre as a concept, this includes playing with those conventions in such a way that auteur 'masterpieces' are as available for reinvention as any other texts – the very issue on which the criticisms cited in this section appear to hinge. The double standard that results from this blind spot, like the two broader trends for either condemning or praising Hollywood, corroborates Jameson's observation of the way in which value itself 'fatally programs every binary opposition into its good and bad, positive and negative, essential and unessential terms' (1992: 16). It also supports a Foucauldian perspective on identities as based on (mis)recognition of close others, most obviously exemplified by patriarchy's polarisation of women into whore and virgin figures, with attendant repressed or desirable qualities attached to each respectively.

III. American Greats

However, there is some relief from this hitherto excessively single-minded picture. Some reviews at all ends of the journalistic spectrum praise Hollywood without offering France as a negative other. At the 'high' end especially, praise does tend to remain limited to classical Hollywood. Thus the generally complimentary review of *Romuald et Juliette* offered by *Positif* compares the film to *Sullivan's Travels* (Ramasse 1989) – not an obvious reference. Even the less specialised *L'Express* invokes Hollywood icons of old Buster Keaton and Cary Grant, rather than contemporary slapstick comedians such as the equally pertinent Jim Carrey or Steve Martin, in its generally positive review of *Essaye-moi* (Libiot 2006).

Elsewhere, the contemporary US mainstream also appears as a positive reference point for French rom-coms. Rather unexpectedly, financial daily newspaper *La Tribune Desfossés* shows some tolerance for this cultural referent in a review of *La Nouvelle Eve*, invoking US sitcoms like *Ally McBeal* as positive models for the film. However, this attitude is tempered by the fact that later in the same article US television is actually cast as a refuge for auteurs too 'seditious' for Hollywood to handle (Bonnard 1999). A similar trend for qualified celebration of things American is discernible in *Télérama*, a listings magazine descended originally from Catholic publication *Radio-Télévision-Cinéma*, which counted André Bazin as its most illustrious contributor. While more mainstream than *Cahiers* and *Positif*, *Télérama* remains at the auteurist end of the weekly magazine spectrum: it is known for its arts coverage and in its genre is the 'bible' *de rigueur* for the educated middle-classes. A hospitable attitude towards transnational influence emerges, for example, in the review of *Toi et moi* featured in this publication, which judges the film to have benefited from elements taken from *Sex and the City* (Guichard 2006). It should be noted that at the time of writing *Sex and the City* had not yet become a film and so was not strictly speaking a Hollywood product, suggesting the same further double standard as in *La Tribune*, where it is easier to relinquish cultural superiority in the uncontested realm of television than in nationally beloved film culture. All the same, it is important that some reviews identify the possibilities for enrichment of French film offered by global paradigms. The review of *Toi et moi* moreover goes further, isolating positive aspects of a US tradition recognisable as linked to Hollywood and not just television, namely efficiency and charm. It simultaneously, though, mentions a feature which I have argued is more characteristic of French comedy: melodrama, described here as 'the hidden face of all good comedy'. This suggests a celebration of transnational hybridity that is more sophisticated than the usual take on the question of influence offered by many cinephilic newspapers and journals. The same is also true of *Les Inrockuptibles*, which seeks not only to compare but also on occasion to effect a rapprochement of French and US practices. Its review of *2 Days in Paris* is one example that bucks the trend, by praising the film not only through comparison with Sturges but also by vaunting its accommodation of a smattering of 'French bad taste' within an overall frame seen as more immediately American (Kapriélian 2007). In this case, the eulogy is still, though, limited to the work of 'hip' auteur Delpy.

A clearer-cut distinction in attitudes towards North American models is visible in the reception of more mainstream films in the truly popular press, such as many daily newspapers or such publications as *Première*, *Studio* and *Cinélive* (or since 2009 the merged magazine *Studio-Cinélive*). A salient example is *Décalage horaire*. While I have already detailed some of the hostile reaction to Thompson's film in the cinephilic press, by contrast *Studio* dubs the film a 'magical' success (Fabre 2002) and *Première*'s Stéphanie Lamome (2002a) describes it in the following terms:

> Amid the deluge of French comedies coming out for the start of the school year, here is one that provides some light relief from the cynicism our filmmakers hold so dear. At last a director (a woman, no less) ventures into the genre of sentimental comedy '*à l'américaine*' and earns her fairy-tale stripes. What is more, Danièle Thompson takes the risk – this time

a very French one – of shooting in a single location by focusing on two characters, unlike with the gallery of scattered portraits gone over with a fine tooth comb in *La Bûche*, the first outing for this brilliant screenwriter as director.

These comments present a number of revealing points. First is the implication that 'cynicism', the antithesis of the rom-com ethos, is a highly regarded value in French filmmaking circles. Second is the way in which the powerful links between popular and feminine modes as culturally 'inferior' are highlighted by the parenthetical aside '(a woman, no less)'. The ironic resonance of this barb is a function, in turn, of author Lamome's own female gender, stamped in her name at the bottom of the page. Next, the contrast this critic draws with Thompson's first film, ensemble piece *La Bûche*, suggests that her identification of the specificity of what she calls 'a sentimental comedy "à l'américaine"' (since in 2002 relatively widespread ease with the term 'romantic comedy' was still another four or five years away) resides pre-eminently in a dyadic narrative structure. This supports the argument that this rom-com format bears the imprint of a North American culture that more openly prizes individualism than does France's. Lamome, however, does not make any such potentially censorious link between aesthetics and ideology. If anything, in fact, this particular contrast between American and French models is obscured, by the conflation of the dyadic focus with the apparently 'very French' (itself a dubious assertion) practice of shooting in one location. The vitality of a syncretic blend of Gallic and American traditions is in this way asserted. Going one step further, Lamome finally makes a virtue of another detail that might elsewhere have been construed as a negative aspect of Thompson's profile: her background as a successful screenwriter, including for television – the very history that assures her exclusion from the auteur category. In other words, Lamome goes out of her way to panegyrise Thompson. If she bends observable fact to this end, this can be attributed to the position of 'inferiority' from which Thompson – and to an extent she herself, as a female journalist working for a popular magazine – is operating. For Lamome's purposes, then, as with the many female filmmakers working in romantic comedy, Hollywood provides a reference point untainted by the insidious Gallic sexism circulating in national film discourse around popular entertainment as distinct from 'high art'.[9]

It is also crucial to consider secondary coverage of films in addition to reviews and thereby the overall picture of how – and how extensively – rom-coms are represented in the French press. Here films' positioning as auteur or mainstream fodder is if anything even more important. *Première*'s review of *Décalage*, for instance, is complemented by a glossily illustrated two-page spread constructed around an interview with Thompson but also exploiting Binoche's star status, through stills from the film and through its title 'Pretty Juliette' (Lamome 2002b) (also of course a reference to *Pretty Woman*, again championing cultural mixity). When we consider the question of space dedicated to films in this way, a particularly striking double standard applies to the more recent, unapologetically mainstream *De l'autre côté du lit*. Despite drawing 1.8 million spectators to the French box office, this broad comedy featuring domestic mega-stars Boon and Marceau as a husband and wife who swap lives, and set in a household that looks like the set of an American sitcom, within the collections held by Paris' *Bibliothèque du Film*, is only the subject of short, fairly neutral reviews by four French newspapers.[10] These are *France-soir*, the more middle-class *Le Figaro* and its sister publication *Le Figaroscope* and finally – proving itself open-minded about cinema again – *La Tribune Desfossés*. This parsimonious coverage contrasts extremely with the response to popular auteur Balasko's *Cliente*, released the same year. Despite attracting only slightly more than a third of the cinema spectators of Pouzadoux's film (just under 700,000 entries), *Cliente* features in 15 of the general interest (or listings) newspapers and magazines held by the library and is also reviewed within *Cahiers du cinéma*, among its specialist periodicals. It might be noted that this film was not universally admired by critics any more than audiences. However, details like its blend of tones, its multiple protagonists and a naturalistic aesthetic make it feel French. At the same time, Balasko's popular auteur/star identity guarantees that the film enjoys the status of a cultural event, an effect reinforced by her frequent appearance on television chat shows not only to promote her own work directly but as a commentator on cultural and other current affairs.

Rom-Com for Export

Despite the ongoing deprecation of popular and especially 'Americanised' fare in the cinephilic press, some reviews show that this rather self-negating and complex-ridden narrative is not the only one that can be and is beginning to be attached to the rise of the French rom-com *à la franco-américaine*. In this section I will argue that the French rom-com can be seen as transnational not only in the sense of having incorporated originally 'foreign' paradigms but also in feeding back into global film culture and so enhancing transnational cinema with particularities which are local in origin. With this aim, I will examine several cases whereby such transformed texts are positioned either in vain or successfully for export or remake abroad. It is important to note before proceeding that films less obviously produced with an eye on international markets may also find export opportunities, following domestic success – as for example with French mega-hit *Le Goût des autres*, which garnered over half a million dollars in the US as well as notching up profits in Europe, despite the lack of transnational reputation of its stars and its unspectacular Parisian milieu setting. However, my focus in this section is on those films that strike me as conceived intentionally for travel.

While scholarship in film studies often focuses on the dissemination of US culture, attention has also been given to the historical importance of on-screen 'Frenchness' as a reference point in global film culture, both in the post-war period (Schwartz 2007) and more recently, notably through stardom (see for example Vincendeau 2000b; Moine 2007b: 138–40). The French adoption of the rom-com can be seen in this light as a commercial strategy to extend the local industry's transnationally conceived market share. Of course, it is also the case that global culture is part of French culture – that is, the same recourses that might appear to align a film with transnational modes can merely be intended to lend it a cosmopolitan 'cool' at home. Beyond this strategy, though, many rom-coms *have* exported internationally and in several cases remake rights have also been sold to Hollywood.[11]

Thompson's films provide a notable example of the rom-com's export potential. First *La Bûche* did modest business (just under $150,000) in the USA. More significantly, *Décalage horaire*, originally conceived for Hollywood production by a director who lived in the US for many years, was distributed in 31 territories and took a respectable half a million dollars at the US box office. As for *Fauteuils d'orchestre*, benefiting from its choice as France's foreign-language Oscar entry, this film passed the $2 million mark in America, as well as being released in almost as many territories as *Décalage*. This relative global success is no doubt due in part to Thompson's choice of globally known actors, including Charlotte Gainsbourg, Emmanuelle Béart, Juliette Binoche, Jean Reno and Cécile de France. More recently, the export of films starring Audrey Tautou (*Dieu est grand, je suis toute petite*, *Hors de prix*, *De vrais mensonges*) confirms the key role played by transnational stars in selling films abroad. So does the substantial international success of Julie Delpy's *2 Days in Paris*, which received no French funding (Anon 2007a) and stars the transnational director-actress herself opposite known American actor Adam Goldberg in stereotypically French and American roles (she is promiscuous, he is uptight) and which, thanks above all to the additional coup of choosing to film in English, grossed over $4m. Furthermore, appearing in a rom-com that has exported can alter and broaden the international image of a French star. This is the case with Binoche, who since *Décalage* has appeared in the Hollywood rom-com *Dan in Real Life* (2007), where she plays an exotic, cosmopolitan eccentric (nationality unspecified) opposite Steve Carrell's all-American widower and father-of-three.

Prête-moi ta main – again perhaps thanks to Gainsbourg's presence – is a rom-com that enjoyed a UK release and has also sold its remake rights to Hollywood. Moreover, its producer and star Chabat has an office there dedicated to developing similar products, suggesting the possibility of further French-inflected Hollywood rom-coms. In the case of *LOL*, director Azuelos has already gone on to make a US version of the original, starring A-lister Demi Moore and child superstar Miley Cyrus. While the politics of remakes are enormously influenced by anti-American sentiment, and it is true that alternative versions tend to foreclose the possibility of the original film's release in a given territory, this example shows how the French rom-com enters into the transnationalisation of the film industry itself, through individual trajectories.[12] It also indicates a major potential amplification of the international exposure and success of filmmakers concerned. It is no accident that it should be a film such as *LOL*, that so knowingly emulates global models, which finds itself circulating back again into international film distribution channels. Relevant here is Giddens' description of the process of 'disembedding', which creates global culture and by which he means 'the "lifting out" of social relations from local contexts of interaction and their restructuring across indefinite spans of time-space' (1990: 21). The key term here is 'restructuring' with its implied result: a new hybrid identity in which

French and global elements are enmeshed, ultimately to the point of indistinction. It cannot be overemphasised to what extent even the most unashamedly 'Hollywood-style' French rom-coms remain markedly French. This is most apparent in their main language and stars, but many films examined in this chapter are also marked by other tendencies specifically identifiable with the French genre, as illustrated earlier in this study. For example, well over half of the films dicussed here treat in some form the issue of maternity discussed in Chapter 4, whether through the relationship between the female protagonist and her own mother or daughter or through the issues of pregnancy and childbirth. It is elements like these that bring us back to Ezra and Rowden's description of a transnational perspective as shot through with elements of a national identity that appears simultaneously to be growing stronger and fading away.

On the other hand, few of the films discussed in this chapter contain significantly 'dark' elements of the kind I have identified with French rom-coms, while none of those I have discussed at any length as ostentatiously globally-informed are based on ensemble structures. Perhaps it is in these features, then, of mixing tones and following multiple protagonists that rom-coms become most truly 'French'.[13] Certainly ensemble films are markedly less likely to be described as rom-coms in the French press – and among these, those which also contain typically French generic elements, such as rom-com/family film *Le Premier jour du reste de ta vie*, are more likely to be compared with Gallic forefathers (in this case Claude Sautet and Klapisch [Lacomme: 2007]). This is not to say such films do not participate in romantic comedy, as my analyses of them elsewhere in this book attest: rather, there is a sense of the genre's national consolidation over the period in question, and therefore an ease with mixing global and local features. Self-consciously syncretised films such *Les Emotifs anonymes* and *LOL* suggest that in 2010 the rom-com has by and large been integrated into French filmmaking practice rather than, as yet, entirely seamlessly assimilated.

As films such as *Décalage horaire* and *L'Arnacœur* – not to mention *Amélie* with its nostalgically re-imagined tourist-zone Montmartre, or the extreme national stereotypes on display in *2 Days in Paris* – show, this may include making cultural difference another sales tool by 'playing up' films' very Frenchness, a felicitous impulse in the context of a culture already widely associated with romance. Indeed, at the level of marketing, the strap-line to the US DVD cover of *Décalage horaire* contributes further to this strategy, fusing American screwball and French erotic cinematic traditions neatly in the phrase: 'The battle of the sexes just got sexier'. In the case of *L'Arnacœur*, one English-language poster was emblazoned with the statement from critic Leonard Maltin that '[i]t puts most of Hollywood's recent romantic comedies to shame and proves that there's still vibrant life in the genre'; another cited *Vogue*'s pronouncement of the film as 'utterly chic'. As Steve Fore has put it in a discussion of marketing 'peripheral' (primarily Hong Kong) cinemas globally, 'difference is not ignored but foregrounded, though typically only within carefully regulated parameters; these products usually provide only a superficial tourist's gaze at unfamiliar people, places and beliefs' (Fore 2001: 132–3).

In the contemporary cosmopolitan film marketplace, several French rom-coms represent another example of a situation described by Fore in terms of a reconfigured 'mediascape' flowing in a direction opposite of the norm. This is hardly without precedent in French cinema – from the New Wave and popular postwar cinemas to, more recently, the international success of Luc Besson and his production and distribution company Europacorp (as in, for instance, the *Transporter* franchise). All the same, at this point in its life the French rom-com's intervention in the usual flow of films and capital has already partially dislodged the boundaries of the global genre, reconfiguring the meaning of romantic comedy for global viewers, with implications for both the international fortunes and also the cultural prominence of French cinema.

In sum, although it is true that most French rom-coms have failed to tap into the large foreign markets to which most filmmakers would presumably welcome access, the second half of the 2000s has overseen a discernible shift, in the UK at any rate, with the rom-com for the first time becoming identifiable in the eyes of a broad public as a French genre. This notably thanks to the group of films starring Tautou and also to the success – in this case global – of *L'Arnacœur*, to whose analysis I shall now turn.

Case Study: *L'Arnacoeur/Heartbreaker* (Pascal Chaumeil, France/Monaco 2010)

Co-produced by Focus Features International alongside several French companies, distributed in multiple territories and achieving a worldwide box-office gross in excess of $44m, television director Pascal Chaumeil's debut feature – written by among others *Prête-moi* co-writer Laurent Zeitoun and American Jeremy Doner and filmed in Monaco and on the Côte d'Azur – also sold its remake rights to Universal Pictures in the USA.[14] Beyond this, its narrative displays a high degree of self-consciousness about its cross-breed status, constantly defining itself in relation to Hollywood and the global rom-com.

The film's pre-credit prologue sequence establishes the complex relation to acknowledged forefathers that will characterise the narrative. This twelve-minute interlude introduces us to the central protagonist Alex (Romain Duris) in an initially oblique (because we first meet inconsequential secondary characters) but ultimately one-dimensional fashion, as the 'con-artist of the heart' promised by the French title's play on words (*arnaqueur* is a confidence trickster and *coeur* the translation of heart): a gigolo who lures women away from their unsuitable partners. Its status as a comical prelude to the central action, which also telescopes instant character exposition, speaks to contemporary Hollywood comedy. Humour is signalled above all through the sequence's style. For example, at the moment when Alex is shown wooing the girl in question during a heart-warming (staged) humanitarian intervention in an Arabian desert, a cutaway reveals the contrastingly dull and frustrating experience of her boorish partner, who has opted to remain at the hotel in order to witness a wet T-shirt competition that does not materialise. The rapid editing and mobile camera, too, mirror the frenetic pace of intensified continuity, while the tenor of performances is histrionic. It is also performance that first definitively reveals the staged nature of the sequence as a whole, when we see Alex turn away from his female 'prey' and pull a grotesque face intended to make him well up into tears [Figure 16]. This act disrupts any suspension of disbelief on the part of the audience by pointing up the fakery of acting itself, especially in highly conventionalised mainstream genres. In this way it effects the same self-reflexive and distancing action as the whole sequence, whose subject matter is the ability of good looks and charm to seduce us into believing lies, at a speed so breathless no time is left for reflection. In other words, the high production values and advertising feel of the photography associated with the exotic setting are revealed as an alluring smokescreen for underlying banality, in this case that of paid work. This denaturalising drive is reinforced by excessive references to convention, as the prologue develops into a montage sequence

Figure 16. Foregrounding performance in *L'Arnacœur*. © Revolver Entertainment

coupled with a male voiceover giving *Manhattan*-esque statistics about women, set to US rap. This sequence's function is to introduce key secondary characters and to set up, partly through to-camera addresses, the 'rules' of Alex's company: a business run with his sister and brother-in-law that involves being paid to prevent women from settling down with partners deemed unsuitable by a close relative or friend. One shot from the images illustrating this *métier* recalls the iconic but itself humorous (because, as Etta James' 'I Just Want to make Love to You' underlines, daringly saucy) advertisement for Diet Coca Cola featuring a workman outside the window of an office full of women. Shortly after, snippets showing Alex speaking multiple languages including Japanese are designed to elicit a laugh, at such an audacious eschewal of verisimilitude in favour of flashy style. With this dense opening, by the time the intertitle reading '*L'Arnacœur*' announces the beginning of the main plot, Chaumeil has laid out a typically post-modern new romantic position that at once undercuts conventions and seeks to engage the viewer through their deployment.

If Hollywood in general (and secondarily advertising) is pastiched-cum-parodied in the prologue, as the narrative progresses generic references become more specific. When the central project, for Alex to come between heiress Juliette (Vanessa Paradis) and her fiancé Jonathan (Andrew Lincoln), is set up – in order to facilitate a conventional deception scenario via which the two protagonists can be brought together – Chaumeil draws on the resources of the spy film. These include point-of-view shots through a long range camera and a gently suspenseful percussion and strings score, to show Alex's team gathering data on Juliette. Here the parodic element comes from the fact that petite, manicured antiques expert Juliette is a poor stand-in for a dangerous spy. Later in the film, it is the spectacular and violent action sequence whose contrivance is brought to the fore, when Alex's sister Mélanie, threateningly disguised in a full-face helmet and black leathers on a motorbike, steals Juliette's handbag in an aggressive drive-by incident, in order that Alex – who is masquerading as her bodyguard – can stage the bag's rescue. When Mélanie is unmasked round the corner, all the edge-of-the-seat adrenaline evaporates as the 'mugger's strength and menace is revealed as pure illusion. Furthermore, the pain associated with real violence is graphically demonstrated by Alex's reluctant submission to being punched in the face, in order to provoke a nose-bleed and so lend his escapade authenticity.

However, the fact that this film does not simply scorn Hollywood conventions is apparent in a joke that gently mocks those who pretend to be above mainstream culture: a scene where sophisticated self-styled ice-queen Juliette hides her face because she is unable to resist mouthing the words to Wham!'s 'Wake Me Up Before You Go Go' on Alex's car radio. Later, too, when the couple discovers their mutual (though in Alex's case invented to match Juliette's) love of classic 1980s rom-com *Dirty Dancing* (Emile Ardolino, USA 1987), there is a hint of teasing in the disingenuous remark by fully debriefed Alex that he thought she would be more 'art-house' (*'films d'auteur'*) – not to mention her admission of her preconceived idea of him as more into action films. It is through the *Dirty Dancing* intertext and in its romantic trajectory in general that the film moves away from laughable parody and into affecting pastiche. For example, in a reversal of the explicit and sometimes distorted uses of known songs I have referred to often in this chapter, at one point here the strains of the signature tune from Ardolino's hit, 'Time of My Life', are discernible as background to a scene showing Alex and Juliette's blossoming relationship. However, the notes are so scattered that, overlaid too with an ambient, mainly string score, they are not intended so much to be recognisable as to lend a revitalised romantic impression. It is also particularly striking that the climactic romantic exchange between the couple expresses itself through their dance of the finale number from *Dirty Dancing*, which we have earlier witnessed Alex learning in order to seduce Juliette. To heighten the parallelism, the cotsumes and editing closely mirror those of the earlier film. This is a prime example of the way in which 'pastiche is compatible with the impression of feeling' (Dyer 2007: 168): we are supposed to be moved despite our knowledge that this is a set-up. This paradox applies to Alex's project and characterisation as a whole, which demand that we simultaneously admire or at least engage with his seduction and believe that he at some point starts falling for Juliette. This well-trodden rom-com narrative path, where a protagonist falls in love through feigned love, in this case invokes transnational models to make the point, not without profundity, that discourses produce realities. Equally determined to have it both ways in terms of romance and post-modern self-awareness, the ending is constructed around a series of flippant reversals, as Alex decides to return to Juliette rather than board a plane, but nonetheless offered up in earnest, setting up a romantic kiss whose intended iconicity is reinforced by its multiplication across several cuts and camera angles.

Beyond allusions to Hollywood, *L'Arnacœur* also draws on a host of national stereotypes in revealing ways, primarily through its two leads. The choice of Duris and Paradis is enormously significant in terms of its transnational positioning, particularly bearing in mind remarks by Adrien Thollon, from production company Médiamétrie, detailing how the difficulties which arose in seeking finance for the film centred around questions over Paradis' bankability (Lutaud 2010), alongside Zeitoun's wry reflection that the team could have raised the money in a flash with Mathilde Seigner (and French comic giant Kad Merad) (Libiot 2010a). Popular actress Seigner is well-known in France, where in 2010 Paradis had only patchy acting credentials. However, as the producers who stuck to their guns surely understood, Paradis is a global celebrity, both through her persona as a singer and model and above all thanks to her (now broken) relationship with Hollywood superstar Johnny Depp – which, moreover, aligns her with an anglophone tradition. Additionally, she was known for her rejection of celebrity and as something of an enigma, the couple being famously protective about their private life (see Catroux 2010). This perfectly complements the air of perceived Gallic sophistication that arises notably from her association with the Chanel brand. As for Duris, while he is also a successful actor at home, his lead roles in Klapisch's trans-European narratives *L'Auberge espagnole/Pot Luck* (2002) and *Les Poupées russes/Russian Dolls* (2005), and to a lesser extent in such exported auteur and mainstream films as *De battre mon cœur s'est arrêté/The Beat That My Heart Skipped* (Jacques Audiard, France 2005) and *Molière* (Tirard, 2007) have lent him some fame outside France. In the Klapisch films, his Frenchness is axiomatic, representing as he does the Gallic presence in an international mix, while his embodiment of French literary icon Molière extends this association to comprehend national heritage.

L'Arnacœur plays on both these images. Juliette is cast as unattainable and mysterious, as with unreadable views of her, often in profile, at key moments in Alex's bid to win her over. Her association with Anglophilia, meanwhile, is borne out by her engagement to Jonathan. On the other hand, her expertise in antiques and wine and her love of fine dining and Chopin feed into the image of elegant Frenchness that suffuses the text as a whole – and exploit the international marketability of French luxury goods and settings. However, this is not the only French stereotype constructed by the film: it also accommodates once more an earthier vision, primarily associated with Alex. This character's corporeality, manifested by the bloody nose, is in fact repeatedly palpable in the effort it costs him to achieve impressive and athletic feats, as he comically huffs and puffs, not always making it to the scene of the action in time. Meanwhile Juliette's inner French peasant comes to the fore with the revelation that she eats Roquefort for breakfast. Vincendeau (2010: 245–7) has shown the extent to which this coarse stereotype characterises external views of France propagated by British television and cinema, and ultimately *L'Arnacœur* brings together its central couple through a shared Frenchness that resides in their 'real' conversations about smelly breath and snoring.

The flipside of Paradis' recuperation away from her global, partially anglophone persona is disparagement of the latter culture, condensed in the character of Jonathan. Although the film is for the most part at pains to stress this wrong partner's niceness, alongside such other attributes as his success, wealth and philanthropy, like television actor Lincoln's symmetrical, blue-eyed but somewhat blandly pleasant appearance, his character is depicted as *too* pleasant to be interesting – as Juliette's father tells her near the close, 'he'll bore you to death'. His boy-scout piety is conveyed by the straightforward colour symbolism of his pale and often white attire and his impeccable manners. Among the few glimpses of Lincoln's character the film gives us, it is no accident that on one occasion we see him washing his face, recalling Rollet's (2008: 101) claim that in France the US (again, Britain here stands in) is associated with excessive cleanliness. And anglophone cleanliness extends to figurative purity, or what the French often refer to as 'Anglo-Saxon puritanism': a stereotype invoked by an unsubtle portrayal of Jonathan's parents as uptight prudes, who are dismayed at the sight of scantily clad women. The contrast with licentious Alex's five o'clock stubble, black suits and air of danger could not be greater. Additionally, Alex's tendency to pose (self-critically) before the mirror, Duris' slight physique and his character's love of and agility in dancing, suggest his feminisation. This further stereotype of French masculinity exists both outside (Vincendeau 2010: 245–50) and within (see Vincendeau 2000b: 223–30; Mazdon 2000: 59) the country, its most prominent cinematic embodiments including New Wave actors like Jean-Pierre Léaud, Jean-Claude Brialy and Sami Frey. Consequently, the stereotype plays to both audiences.

L'Arnacœur, second only to *Amélie* as a French rom-com to make its mark at the international box office, realises in this way the transnational genre's disparate but not necessary conflicting impetuses: to reinvent Frenchness in a global image and to reaffirm Frenchness on the world stage. Perhaps because of its smart textual self-consciousness it was on the whole praised at both the popular and the more cinephilic end of the spectrum. An article in *L'Express* comparing this film with the drama *Sturm/Storm* (Hans-Christian Schmid, Germany/Denmark/Netherlands/Sweden/Bosnia & Herzogovina, 2009) comments perceptively on the film's transnational generic status, so much so that I will close this analysis by quoting it:

> Do these films of American ancestry herald a sea-change here [in Europe]? Of course not. National cultural specificity remains – and so much the better for it. But I also applaud to see cinema, a land where imagination and reality exist in harmony, open itself up to diversity. *Which should not be confused with the unstoppable spread of globalisation.* (Libiot 2010b; my emphasis)

Concluding Remarks: Rom-Com into the 2010s

A number of striking features have emerged from this analysis of contemporary French romantic comedies, and these are developing in particular ways in the 2010s. Melodrama, realism and a fairly overt focus on contemporary social issues (urban fragmentation, ethnic diversity) appear particularly widespread in the French genre. These issues connect to broader trends in French cinema and society, notably France's status as epitomising an Old Europe that is resistant to the modernisation of, for example, working patterns (witness 2011's furious revolt over pension reforms); equally, the nation has a large immigrant population, helping to explain the slightly increased prominence of inter-ethnic romances in rom-coms there in comparison with Hollywood – a trend continued with the most successful rom-com of the last four years in the domestic market, *Un bonheur n'arrive jamais seul/Happiness Never Comes Alone* (James Huth, 2012) (box-office admissions 1.8 million), starring Sophie Marceau and Gad Elmaleh (although Elmaleh's difference is minimised as he plays Jewish, not North African).[1] A linked formal particularity to emerge in the French genre is the recurrence of multi-protagonist (*choral*) rom-coms, which are associable with the pragmatic sensibility of the discourse of intimacy, as opposed to romance. This is remarkable given the importance of seduction and (especially feminine) mystique in French culture, yet which in rom-coms now comprise central narrative elements only rarely and usually in a self-knowing way.

One of the most obvious sites in which 'legitimate' gender roles prove fundamental is the family unit, a structure that constitutes a lower-order but still striking preoccupation in France. It is also noteworthy that in a few films the impulse to be part of a family actually seems to vye with or even replace romantic desire as a driver for heterosexual coupling, once more the case too in *Un bonheur n'arrive jamais seul*, where 'happiness doesn't come alone' because it comes with three children, as well as *La Stratégie de la poussette/The Stroller Strategy* (Clément Michel, 2012). There is arguably a French character to such narratives' stress on the social function of the couple, as opposed to the elevation of the individual typical of global new romances. Indeed, the influence of the neo-traditional new romance in France is relatively limited, although recent deception scenario-based films, from festival circuit auteur piece *L'Art d'aimer/The Art of Love* (Emmanuel Mouret, 2011, clearly indebted to *The Truth About Cats and Dogs*) to popular hits *Un plan parfait/A Perfect Plan* (Pascal Chaumeil, 2012; 1.2 million admissions) and *20 ans d'écart/It Boy* (David Moreau, 2013; 1.4 million admissions), suggest the recent Hollywood fad for an ironically attenuated return to romantic values – including dyadic narrative structures – is catching on fast in France. The success of the (also internationally exported) film *Populaire* (Régis Roinsard, 2012; 1.2 million admissions), starring rom-com favourite Duris and Deborah François of Palme d'Or-winning *L'Enfant/The Child* (Jean-Pierre and Luc Dardenne, 2007) fame, further supports this statement.[2] Its 1950s and part US setting also attests to both the ongoing deterritorialisation of the rom-com in both time and space and – alongside the casting – the continued drive to sell the genre abroad. It is both highly apt and ironic that Duris' character proclaims towards the close of this film that if it is the French who do love best, it is the Americans they should look to for lessons in business!

While (typically negative) appraisals of 'ironic' post-feminist rom-coms made in a global context cannot apply as simply in France due to the different identities and periodisation of feminism there, homing in on particular issues throws up more concrete facts about the French rom-com's gender politics, some of which speak to notions of backlash. The rom-com's formal tendency to give ample space to female perspectives – both in terms of subject matter and point of view – already feeds into a movement towards legitimising narratives of female experience in France. It also affords lucrative and culturally significant new opportunities to female stars in national comedy, where their agency is more likely to be accentuated than is the case in most other genres. As regards *how* the genre depicts female trajectories, it is important that overall even this narrative form focused on coupling on the whole ratifies the normalcy of female professionalism. However, a number of films emulate one trend in 'post-feminist' global texts in stressing female dissatisfaction with work, alongside female loneliness connected to the demands of employment. Even if this is not explicit, women's jobs tend to be constructed as an incidental, non-defining aspect of their lives almost across the board, in films by both men and women. This trend appears to be solidifying: the two rom-coms showing on my most recent visit to Paris in January 2014, *Jamais le premier soir* (Melissa Drigeard) and *A coup sûr* (Delphine de Vigan) (like *Un bonheur n'arrive jamais seul* and *20 ans d'écart*) both portrayed women working in media organisations in whose offices the films were partly set. Although both films were directed by women, the first demonstrates work to be so unfulfilling that all three female protagonists are over-invested in highly flawed romantic relationships and one joins a cult (also picking up a trend for recognising spiritual emptiness as a feature of contemporary life), and in the second case the film's premise is the obstruction that the heroine's 'professional' attention to efficiency and quality outputs represents for her sexual and emotional life. Not only must she consult a prostitute for tips on seduction, but quitting her job is finally a prerequisite to finding love, albeit with an ex-colleague. Men's jobs, by contrast, even if they are not the rom-com's main focus, are not belittled – except temporarily in cases where love goes hand in hand with professional self-realisation (*Un bonheur*, in which Elmaleh's talented musician Sacha puts on a hit show before settling down, is once more exemplary), rather than obviating it, as is typical for female characters (a trend set up in *Décalage horaire* and still pervasive). It is also the case that the genre's middle-class aspect ignores the most troublesome ongoing inequalities of not only economy (and here the distance from texts associated more strictly with realism is apparent) but gender itself. As French sociologist François de Singly (2004: 221–2) has noted, while the sexual revolution has narrowed the professional gap between highly educated men and women, it has increased the gap between the latter and their less privileged sisters.

Equally problematic are the images of femininity, and by extension the nature of the female stardom, facilitated by the rom-com. While several 1990s films promoted female comics whose appeal lay in their performance skills first and foremost, later in the period beauty, and being set up as desirable or seductive – as opposed to *principally* charismatic – becomes more important. Although global rom-com stars like Meg Ryan, Julia Roberts, Jennifer Aniston or Katherine Heigl do not deviate substantially from ideals of female attractiveness or slimness, they have generally been seen as relatively attainable, even 'girl-next-door', archetypes. The couture models populating the most prominent examples of the French genre, including extreme waifs like Audrey Tautou, are further removed from everyday life – even if comic elements in their performances somewhat narrow the distance. A subtrend for unthreatening, childlike visions of femininity incarnated by such actresses as Tautou, Cécile de France and Julie Gayet (and many others, from Marion Cotillard to Mélanie Doutey) is also significant, although perhaps lessening in recent years as less ethereal, blonder and indeed often brassier actresses in the American mould – such as Diane Kruger (*Un plan parfait*) or Virginie Efira (*La Chance de ma vie*, Nicolas Cuche, 2011; *20 ans d'écart*) – multiply. With a gradually growing frequency these are older women, targeting France's mature audience; but the latter are still (presented as) disproportionately attractive, as for example with Fanny Ardant in Marion Varnoux's recent *Les Beaux jours/Bright Days Ahead* (2013), about a retired female dentist who falls in love with an IT lecturer – even if the longevity of figures like Ardant, Baye and Deneuve itself provides something of a counterpoint to the girlish waif trend. Older female characters are also often higher-status than their partners: *20 ans d'écart*, in which pretty Efira's magazine editor catapults *joli laide* Pierre Niney's student to the titular 'it boy' (in the English translation) status, is even more emblematic. The spectrum of attractiveness for Frenchmen in rom-com is much wider, including not only physically unremarkable or unconventional-looking figures like Edouard Baer, Romain Duris or Jean Reno but also 'plain' actors such as Alain Chabat and Michel Blanc. The norms of appearance promoted by this genre are particularly significant in that its central project is to construct its protagonists as attractive mating prospects.

There emerges from this picture a remarkable contrast between female rom-com heroines' presentation as professional women and the genre's ultimate reliance, in its working over of heterosexual desire, on 'the production of discrete and asymmetrical oppositions between "masculine" and "feminine"' (Butler 1990: 17). To the extent that such a division provides a barometer of the real state of affairs in contemporary France, this suggests a gulf separating public and private spheres in a country where numbers of working women are increasingly high across most professions (including filmmaking), yet looking good is still today a way of life for many women. As I have suggested, the French tendency to place in opposition rather than equate masculinity and femininity is also a key factor in the high birth rate in France, where other European nations' have declined of late: a further apparent contradiction given women's increasing penetration of professional walks of life. The difficulty of reconciling these gendered aspects of French social life reflects a cacophony of incompatible notions at play in national culture that has surely influenced the nation's exceptionally low marriage rate – a major change with respect to its long-term history. Certainly the current situation appears precarious. Notably, a slight decline in female-authored promotions of motherhood in recent rom-coms would appear to bear out the likely accuracy of Badinter's (2010) prediction that France's high birth rate will not endure the influence of external discourses.[3]

Finally, as regards the genre's filmic identity, popularity is the salient feature, with many rom-coms cited in this book featuring in the top ten (in fact almost always five) French films at the domestic box office every year since 2005. This growing popularity should be understood in the context of bumper years in terms of both cinema attendance and French film consumption specifically in France at the end of the 2000s. Nonetheless, since 2010 the rom-com's success has led to it becoming so common as to have gone from normalisation to total naturalisation. The global profile of a handful of French films means this is also the case from an external perspective. *Amour et turbulences/Love is in the Air* (Alexandre Castagnetti, 2013), released – albeit in a limited way – in 15 countries, is another recent example. It is also one that, by virtue of its transatlantic setting (it takes place mostly on a plane, continuing the trend for staging romantic encounters in places of transience, but also exploits both Parisian and New York locations) and the casting of internationally known actress Ludivine Sagnier, underscores a partial bifurcation of the genre in terms of those films primarily targeting domestic or else – increasingly of late – international markets. Delpy's English-language films *2 Days in Paris* (2007) and its sequel *2 Days in New York* (2012), both of which took a few million dollars internationally (but less at home) are the most obvious example of this development. The success of the French 2011 Oscar-winning film *The Artist*, a silent nostalgia piece mobilising several rom-com tropes, can also be seen to feed into such a move, that takes in at the same time that it exceeds rom-coms.

In view of Kuisel's argument that France has perceived threats to its national values almost exclusively in terms of US cultural imperialism since 1990 (the moment when the rom-com begins to flourish), the appropriation and repackaging of a notionally global/Hollywood genre gains political as well as economic significance. Above all, it should be recognised that adeptness on the part of professionals working in France at reading transnational demand for rom-coms is an important factor in the French film industry's status as the Western world's second-largest. This is one aspect of Gallic cultural life that looks set to remain intact for the foreseeable future.

Notes

Introduction

1. For France, Carrie Tarr with Rollet (2001:1) cite 14 per cent for the 1990s; Kate Ince (2008: 281) cites around 14.4 per cent for the years 2000–2007 and Ginette Vincendeau (2010) finds this to rise to 19.4 per cent in the year 2009, all basing data on CNC statistics; for Hollywood, see Silverstein (2014).
2. Figures sourced from Simsi (2000).
3. An updated version of this argument appears in English in Sellier (2008).
4. All translations from texts written or spoken in French are my own.

1 Romantic Comedy – and its Discontents

1. Auteur director Marion Vernoux has discussed the usefulness of romance as a trope for making sense of real experience (Dobson 2010).
2. http://www.urbandictionary.com/define.php?term=romantic%20comedy&defid=1995126. Accessed 20 July 2012.
3. Moine has noted that certain films of the late 1960s and early 1970s by Deville, de Broca, Rappeneau and others were known as *comédies à la française* to denote their similarity to American screwball films (2005: 218).
4. See for example Palmer (2011: 99–106) analysing the *Mesrine* franchise, while despite claims to the contrary his study as a whole avoids engaging with truly mainstream fare; regarding heritage films, Hayward (2005: 304) argues that even Phil Powrie (1999: 2), whose contribution to re-envisioning popular French cinema as a revealing socio-historical document is impressive, over-privileges the genre as the nation's 'hegemonic' cinema in the 1990s, to the detriment of comedy.

2 Romance Today

1. The title of this section is a quotation from George Orwell's satirical novel *Keep the Aspidistra Flying* (2000 [1936]) – later borrowed by Nancy Mitford – in recognition of capitalism's status in underpinning the changes discussed here (like the society critiqued by Orwell).
2. Same-sex marriage and adoption have also been made legal since the period of this research, in 2013.
3. The internet features prominently in a more positive way in adolescent social interaction within the school peer group in teenpic crossover rom-coms *LOL* and *Une semaine sur deux (et la moitié des vacances scolaires)* (Ivan Calbérac 2009).
4. This is also the case in *Je vous trouve très beau*, analysed in the next chapter.
5. Deleyto (2009b) has also suggested the possible beginnings of a trend for multi-protagonist organisation in US rom-coms very recently.
6. The early precursor to the current cycle *Romuald et Juliette* is here an exception.
7. See Stanley Cavell (1981: 20) argues the absence of adultery distinguishes screwball comedies focused on married couples from contemporaneous French farces.
8. Sellier discusses the legacy of the tradition of 'male libertinage' for New Wave cinema.
9. For a fuller discussion of the significance played by screwball behaviours in the contemporary French rom-com see Harrod (2013).
10. Examples given are *French Kiss* (Lawrence Kasdan, UK/USA 1995), *Kate and Leopold* (James Mangold, USA 2001) and *Someone Like You* (Tony Goldwyn, USA 2001); see also Negra 2008.
11. The same argument is rehearsed in Harrod (2012: 229–30).

3 Gendered Identities in Love

1. For a fuller summary of Méda's research on the incompatibility of contemporary female professionalism and other French cultural attitudes about gender and social organisation see eternautes.free.fr/decouv/02lect.doc. Accessed 5 November 2014.
2. A comparable move is effected by the resolutions of *Toutes les filles sont folles* and *Cliente*, with pairs of sisters, and in *LOL* and *Une semaine sur deux* with mother-daughter duos.
3. It is instructive to observe some of the self-confessed parallels between Juliette and Seigner herself. An article on the actress that appeared in *France-soir* following the release of *Tout pour plaire* focuses on her search to find a man. In an interview, Seigner pronounces herself too frank and

suggests that she has as yet failed to find a partner with whom she can really laugh (Gianorio 2003).
4. See also Radner (1993) on *Pretty Woman*'s staging of the contradictions of post-feminism.
5. As for Dujardin's Oscar-winning turn in *The Artist* (Hazanavicius, 2011), this film undercuts the good looks of a matinée idol as inert and empty.
6. For further analysis of the depiction of older heroines in recent Hollywood rom-coms see Jermyn (2011) and, in both global culture and specifically *Something's Gotta Give* (Meyers, USA 2003), Wearing (2007).
7. For further discussion of this film's treatment of the theme of female ageing see Harrod (2012: 232–3).
8. Figures sourced from INSEE France http://www.insee.fr/fr/themes/document.asp?ref_id=EEC05. Accessed 8 January 2013.
9. http://www.eternautes.free.fr/decouv/02lect.doc. Accessed 7 November 2014.
10. Figures sourced from INSEE France http://www.insee.fr/fr/publications-et-services/default.asp?page=dossiers_web/dev_durable/ecart_revenu_salaire_hommes_femmes.htm. Accessed 8 January 2013.
11. For international statistics on female doctors see http://www.nationmaster.com/graph/lab_fem_doc-labor-female-doctors. Accessed 22 June 2012.
12. Royal has since been somewhat recuperated as the 'woman behind the great man', i.e. in her 'proper place', following her former partner François Hollande's election as president in 2012.
13. The French buddy rom-com does not, however, share the same identification with youth culture seen in some US films. This may be linked to the older average age of the French cinemagoing public as a whole.
14. Delanoë's time in office appears from today's perspective to have paved the way for the arguably more radical election in April 2014 of Paris's first female mayor, Anne Hidalgo.
15. This double standard is reproduced in Alain Brassart's *L'Homosexualité dans le cinéma français* (2007), in which he omits to discuss even lesbian-themed mega-hit *Gazon maudit*.
16. This is a pan-European distinction splitting Mediterranean countries, broadly, from Protestant Northern European ones. According to Maks Banens (2011), all countries in the first group, which decriminalised homosexuality early (1791 in France), today pursue universalist policies for gay rights, while those in the second group, which decriminalised it much later (1967 in the UK), pursue differentialist ones, forging stronger gay community identities.
17. For a fuller discussion of Chouchou's contradictions, also from a postcolonial analytical standpoint, see Rosello (2011).

4 Family Affairs

1. France's birth rate is topped only by the Republic of Ireland, where abortion is still illegal.
2. Interestingly, Emma Wilson (2005: 221) has also proposed a familial angle for women's mode of production, because certain actresses have gone on to direct and because the same actresses often feature recurrently in female-authored work. Both tendencies can be traced across rom-com production and especially in the ensembles.
3. For example Kristeva (1993).
4. It is nonetheless as well to recall here that the variety of female profiles accommodated by the French rom-com is interpretable in more than one way. The instability and multiplicity of feminine identities has been cited as a source of woe for feminists wishing to present a united front against men, whose life goals appear, contrastingly, characterised by striking singularity of purpose (see for example Hakim 2000: 37–9). Indeed, the concept of choice as a whole has become a byword for a host of arguably regressive post-feminist discourses.
5. For recent examples of absent or deficient patriarchs in French cinema see also Powrie (2007: 296–9).
6. In addition to *Le Premier jour*, further examples from the rom-com include *La Bûche* (see case study) and, more recently, *Je vais te manquer* (2009).
7. The others are adultery, up until the early 1990s, then medical issues.
8. Palmer (2011) has recently observed that French cinema of the 2000s in general explores parenting more often than its American equivalent.
9. See for example Kristeva (1986: 298).
10. *Tout pour plaire* also includes a missed abortion appointment but without a deadline structure.
11. Shumway (2003: 12) observes that New Comedy, based on the exchange of women, is probably the ur-story of romantic discourse.
12. All 100 subjects interviewed, whether or not they had children, revealed themselves to be affected in some way by these discourses.
13. A condensed version of the preceding two subsections appears in Harrod (2012).
14. The exact figures are: 1,615,815 (France), 270,718 (Paris). Figures sourced from Simsi (2000).
15. For example 'Scandale dans la famille', sung by Sacha Distel and others, or compositions by Serge Gainsbourg, both sung (his notorious hit 'Lemon Incest') and filmed.

5 Genre, Style and Transnationalism

1. Needless to say, many of the luxury goods featured – from settings to fashion, gourmet food and fine wine – are at the same time French-accented international exports, contributing to this film's saleability in multiple territories including the UK and USA.
2. For a further discussion of the use of English and Franglais in these and other recent French comedies see Harrod (2015).
3. For a fuller analysis of this scene from the point of view of expressing love see Harrod (2013).
4. Later, *LOL's* soundtrack alludes to a truly French cinematic past, borrowing a refrain from *La Boum*, the breakthrough film for Marceau and another story about a teenaged girl which provides a constant reference point for reviewers.
5. These two crises are also spliced together elsewhere in French cinema, often made a source of nervous humour, as for example in auteur and comic hits respectively *La Haine* (Mathieu Kassovitz, 1995) and *Brice de Nice* (see also Chion 2008: 138–44; 168–73).
6. Indeed, Smith (2011: 187) reproduces statements made by Attal in an interview about choosing to set the film partly in London as a means to pay homage to the glamour of certain Hollywood comedies.
7. A similar version of the preceding paragraph appears in Harrod (2015: 151–2).
8. French reviews of Salvadori's Lubitschean *Hors de prix* are interesting, repeatedly picking out its debt to classical Hollywood – and once again *Les Inrockuptibles* finds the French film lacking by comparison (Kaganski 2007); yet US reviews, which were more positive overall, stressed the film's Europeanness.
9. A relatively high number of rom-coms reviews across the board are the subject of reviews by female critics, attesting to the genre's continued association with femininity, even as it becomes associated with both male performers and directors. However, women are not of course alone in championing mainstream genre films. For instance, Christophe Narbonne's (2003) review of *Laisse tes mains sur me hanches* in *Première*, while mixed, is more positive than most on its popular status, such as the deployment of director-actress Lauby's persona, known from television especially (she is part of the comic troupe *Les Nuls*) and the 'effectiveness' of its comedy.
10. While the BiFi collection is itself incomplete, its selection of reviews of *De l'autre côté* is indicative of the film's critical marginalisation.
11. It should be noted, though, that it is common practice for remake rights to be bought out by Hollywood in a fairly blanket fashion with higher

concept and/or more successful foreign films and in many cases does not lead to a remake.
12. For a fuller discussion of the history of perceived economic relations between French films and their remakes see Mazdon (2000: 4–5).
13. Graphic sex scenes are also absent from the more obviously Hollywood-inflected narratives, whereas somewhat more explicit sexual material sometimes features elsewhere in the French genre, as per my discussion of *L'Art (délicat) de la séduction*, or in films like *Embrassez qui vous voudrez* that seek to shock; however this is still not particularly common.
14. While this is not unusual, the film is being considered for remake by other production companies should the option become available again. For instance, Isabel Freer, executive at UK-based FilmWave, has told me of the company's interest in the film.

Concluding Remarks: Rom-Com into the 2010s

1. http://www.allocine.fr/film/fichefilm_gen_cfilm=191481.html. Accessed 22 July 2014.
2. http://www.allocine.fr/film/fichefilm_gen_cfilm=193877.html, http://www.allocine.fr/film/fichefilm_gen_cfilm=209732.html and http://www.allocine.fr/film/fichefilm_gen_cfilm=197289.html. Accessed 22 July 2014.
3. Badinter's principal focus in her study is in fact on how 'ecological' discourses promoting 'earth mothering' are set to erode French women's willingness to have children while desiring to keep working.

Bibliography

Abel, R. 1984. *French Cinema: The First Wave 1915–1929*. Princeton: Princeton University Press.
Acland, C. 2005. *Screen Traffic: Movies, Multiplexes, and Global Culture*. Durham: Duke University Press.
Akass, K. and J. McCabe (eds). 2004. *Reading Sex and the City*. London and New York: I.B.Tauris.
_____ 2004. 'Ms. Parker and the Vicious Circle: Female Narrative and Humour in *Sex and the City*.' In K. Akass and J. McCabe (eds), *Reading Sex and the City*. London: I.B.Tauris, pp.177–201.
Ali, S. 2012. 'Visual Analysis.' In C. Seale (ed.), *Researching Society and Culture*. London: Sage, pp.283–302.
Allen, R.C. 1999. 'Home Alone Together: Hollywood and the "Family Film".' In M. Stokes and R. Maltby (eds), *Identifying Hollywood's Audiences: Cultural Identity and the Movies*. London: BFI.
Ang. I. 1985. *Watching Dallas: Soap Opera and the Melodramatic Imagination*. London: Methuen.
Anon. 1994. 'La Beauté selon Deneuve.' *Elle*, 26 October.
_____ 1999. '*La Nouvelle Eve*,' *Positif* no. 456 (1 February): 45.
_____ 2000. 'Tous les garçons et les filles.' *Les Inrockuptibles* no. 247 (13–19 June): 25.
_____ 2002a. '*Décalage horaire*.' *Positif* no. 501 (1 November): 45.
_____ 2002b. '*Irène*.' *La Croix*, 26 June.
_____ 2003a. 'French comédie.' *Les Echos*, 17 March.
_____ 2004a. '*Ils se marièrent et eurent beaucoup d'enfants*.' *L'Humanité*, 25 August.

―――― 2004b. '*Clara et moi.*' *Le Nouvel Observateur*, 1 July.

―――― 2005a. '*Au-suivant!*' *Les Inrockuptibles*, 6 June.

―――― 2005b. 'En France, le concept de film gay n'est pas clair.' *Le Monde*, 30 February.

―――― 2005c. '*L'Ex-femme de ma vie.*' *Le Nouvel Observateur*, 3 February.

―――― 2006a. 'L'Amour à trente ans.' *Les Echos*, 27 June.

―――― 2006b. '*Hors de prix.*' *L'Humanité*, 13 December.

―――― 2006c. '*Mauvaise foi.*' *Le Canard enchaîné*, 6 December.

―――― 2006d. '*Prête-moi ta main.*' *Les Echos*, 31 October.

―――― 2006e. 'Un vrai roman-photo.' *Les Echos*, 8 March.

―――― 2007a. '*2 Days in Paris.*' *Le Canard enchaîné*, 11 July.

―――― 2007b. 'Le boom du cinéma rose tendre.' *Marianne*, 17 February.

―――― 2007c. '*Si c'était lui.*' *La Tribune Desfossés*, 12 December.

―――― 2007d. '*Ma vie n'est pas une comédie romantique.*' *L'Humanité*, 19 February.

―――― 2009a. '*Dieu est grand, je suis toute petite.*' *Le Monde*, 26 September.

―――― 2009b. '*Filles perdues, cheveux gras.*' *L'Humanité*, 11 September.

―――― 2009c. TNS-Sofres Survey 2–5 January. *Philosophie magazine* no. 27 (March).

―――― 2010c. 'Sophie Marceau: "Etre une femme, c'est génial et difficile."' *Elle*, 7 May, pp.134–137.

Attali, D. 2006. 'Une *mauvaise foi* enthousiasmante.' *Le Journal du dimanche*, 3 December.

Audé, F. 'La place du rieur: gentillesse et complaisance dans les comédies françaises.' Unpublished paper delivered at the Popular European Cinema conference, University of Warwick, September 1989.

Augé, M. 1995. *Non-places: Introduction to an Anthology of Supermodernity*, trans. John Howe. London: Verso.

Austin, G. 2003. *Stars in Modern French Film*. London: Hodder and Arnold.

―――― 2008. *Contemporary French Cinema*. Manchester: Manchester University Press.

Babington, B. and P.W. Evans. 1989. *Affairs to Remember: The Hollywood Comedy of the Sexes*. Manchester: Manchester University Press.

Badinter, E. 1980. *L'Amour en plus: histoire de l'amour maternel, XVIIe – XXe siècles*. Paris: Livre de Poche.

―――― 2003. *Fausse route*. Paris: Odile Jacob.

―――― 2010. *Le Conflit: la femme et la mère*. Paris: Flammarion.

Bakhtin, M. 1981. *The Dialogic Imagination: Four Essays*, trans. C. Emerson and M. Holquist, ed. M. Holquist. Austin: University of Texas Press.

―― 1984 [1941]. *Rabelais and His World*, trans. H. Iswolsky. Bloomington: Indiana University Press.

Balides, C. 2004. 'Immersion in the Virtual Ornament: Contemporary "Movie Ride" Films.' In D. Thorburn and H. Jenkins (eds), *Rethinking Media Change*. Cambridge, Mass.: MIT Press.

Banens, M. 2011. 'PaCS and Civil Partnerships: Similarities and Discrepancies.' Paper delivered at The Association for the Study of Modern and Contemporary France annual conference, 'Continuities and Discontinuities?: France Across the Generations.' University of Stirling, 1–3 September.

Bard, C. 1999a. 'Les antiféministes de la deuxième vague.' In C. Bard (ed.), *Un siècle d'antiféminisme*. Paris: Fayard, pp.301–328.

―― 1999b. 'Pour une histoire des anti-féminismes.' In C. Bard (ed.), *Un siècle d'antiféminisme*. Paris: Fayard, pp.21–38.

Barnett, E. 2003. '*Essaye-moi*.' *Les Inrockuptibles*, 15 March.

Barrette, P.B. 2002. '*Ma femme est une actrice*.' *24 Images* no. 114 (1 December), p.58.

Barthes, R. 1977. 'Introduction to the Structural Analysis of Narratives.' In *Image/Music/Text*, trans. S. Heath. London: Fontana Press, pp.79–124.

Bartky, S.L. 1982. 'Narcissism, Femininity and Alienation.' *Social Theory and Practice* 8, no. 2: 127–143.

Baudin, B. 2002. 'Danièle Thompson, vies en transit.' *Le Figaro*, 30 October.

―― 2006. 'Roschdy Zem, un acte de tolérance.' *Le Figaro*, 6 December.

Baudrillard, J. 2010. *America*, trans. Chris Turner. London and New York: Verso.

Bauman, Z. 2003. *Liquid Love: On the Frailty of Human Bonds*. Cambridge: Polity Press.

Bazgan, N. 2010. 'Female Bodies in Paris: iconic urban femininity and Parisian Journeys.' *Studies in French Cinema* 10, no. 2: 95–109.

Beauvoir, S. de. 2004. *Le Deuxième sexe*, ed. Ingrid Galster. Paris: Presse de l'Université Paris-Sorbonne.

Bergson, H. 1911. *Laughter: An Essay on the Meaning of the Comic*, trans. C. Brereton and F. Rothwell. New York: Macmillan. First published in 1900.

Bernard, L. 1998. 'Gay et juif à la fois.' *L'Evènement du jeudi*, 12 March.

―― 1999. 'Eve, une invitation à croquer la pomme.' *La Tribune Desfossés*, 27 January.

Bordwell, D. 2006. *The Way Hollywood Tells It: Story and Style in Modern Movies*. Berkeley and Los Angeles: University of California Press.

―――― 2008. *Poetics of Cinema*. New York and London: Routledge.

Bordwell, D. and K. Thompson. 2008. *Film Art: an Introduction*. New York: McGraw Hill.

Brassart, A. 2007. *L'Homosexualité dans le cinéma français*. Paris: Nouveau monde.

Brey, I. 2014. 'Paris in Christophe Honoré's *Love Songs*: The Capital, Elaborating Families.' Paper delivered at the *Studies in French Cinema* Annual Conference, 4 April.

Brunsdon, C. 2000. 'Post-feminism and shopping films.' In J. Hollows, P. Hutchings and M. Jancovich (eds), *The Film Studies Reader*. New York and London: Oxford University Press.

Bruyn, O. de. 2006. 'De A à Z: notes sur les films: *Fauteuils d'orchestre*.' *Positif* no. 541 (1 March): 47.

Brysk, A. 2004. 'Children Across Borders: Patrimony, Property or Persons.' In A. Brysk and G. Shaffir (eds), *People Out of Place: Globalization, Human Rights and the Citizenship Gap*. London: Routledge.

Bukatman, S. 1998. 'Zooming Out: The End of Offscreen Space.' In J. Lewis (ed.), *The New American Cinema*. Durham, NC: Duke.

Burch, N. and G. Sellier. 1996. *La Drôle de guerre des sexes du cinéma français*. Paris: Editions Nathan.

Burns, A. 2011. '"Tell me all about your new man": (Re)Constructing Masculinity in Contemporary Chick Texts.' *Networking Knowledge: Journal of theMeCCSA Postgraduate Network* 4, no. 1. Online. Accessed 11 August 2012.

Butler, J. 1990. *Gender Trouble: Feminism and the Subversion of Identity*. New York and London: Routledge.

Cairns, L. 2006. *Sapphism on Screen: Lesbian Desire in French and Francophone Cinema*. Edinburgh: Edinburgh University Press.

Carrière, C. 2003. 'Qui joue quoi?' *L'Express*, 14 March.

―――― 2006. 'Il l'aime, elle non plus.' *L'Express*, 2 November.

Carroll, R. 1988. *Cultural Misunderstandings: the Franco-American Experience*, trans. Carol Volk. Chicago: University of Chicago Press.

Catroux, S. 2010. 'Vanessa Paradis l'intouchable.' *France-soir*, 17 March.

Cavell, S. 1981. *Pursuits of Happiness: the Hollywood Comedy of Remarriage*. Cambridge, Mass. and London: Harvard University Press.

Chapman, R. 1988. 'The Great Pretender: Variations on the New Man Theme.' In R. Chapman and J. Rutherford (eds), *Male Order: Unwrapping Masculinity*. London: Lawrence and Wishart, pp.225–248.

Cixous, H. 1980 [1975]. 'The Laugh of the Medusa,' trans. K. Cohen and P. Cohen. In E. Marks and I. de Courtivron (eds), *New French Feminisms*. Brighton: Harvester, pp.245–264.

Clark, K. and M. Holquist. 1984. *Mikhail Bakhtin*. Cambridge, Mass.: Harvard University Press.

Coste, B. '*Crustacés et coquillages*: logique et esthétique de l'identité post-gaie.' In F. Grandena and C. Johnston (eds), *Cinematic Queerness: Gay and Lesbian Hypervisibility in Contemporary Francophone Feature Films*. Oxford and New York: Peter Lang, 2011.

Cubitt, S. 2004. *The Cinema Effect*. Cambridge: MIT Press.

Davies, K. 1941. 'Intermarriage in Caste Societies.' *American Anthropologist* 43, no. 3: 376–395.

Deleyto, C. 1998. 'Love and Other Triangles: *Alice*.' In P.W. Evans and C. Deleyto (eds), *Terms of Endearment: Hollywood Romantic Comedies of the 1980s and 1990s*. Edinburgh: Edinburgh University Press, pp.129–147.

―――― 2003. 'Between Friends: Love and Friendship in Contemporary Hollywood Romantic Comedy.' *Screen* 44, no. 2: 167–182.

―――― 2009a. *The Secret Life of Romantic Comedy*. Manchester and New York: Manchester University Press.

―――― 2009b. *Woody Allen y el espacio de la comedia romántica*. Valencia: Ediciones de la Filmoteca.

―――― 2011. 'The Comic, the Serious and the Middle: Desire and Space in Contemporary Film Comedy.' *Journal of Popular Romance Studies* 2, no. 1 (October). http://jprstudies.org/2011/10/the-comic-the-serious-and-the-middle-desire-and-space-in-contemporary-film-romantic-comedy-by-celestino-deleyto/. Accessed 14 February 2012.

Desnos, R. 1966. *Cinéma*. Paris: Gallimard.

Doane, M.-A. 1987. *The Desire to Desire: Women's Film of the 1940s*. Indianapolis University Press: Bloomington.

Dobson, J. 2010. Round Table with Kate Ince and Carrie Tarr at 'Women's Filmmaking in France 2000–2010' conference, Institut Français and Institute of Germanic and Romance Studies, 2–4 December.

Douin, J.-L. 1974. 'La Dictature de la rigolade.' *Revue de Cinéma* (May).

Duchen, C. 1986. *Feminism in France: From May '68 to Mitterrand*. London and New York: Routledge and Kegan Paul.

―――― 1994. *Women's Right and Women's Lives in France 1944–1968*. London and New York: Routledge.

Durham, C.A. 1998. *Double Takes: Culture and Gender in French Films and Their American Remakes.* Hanover: University of New England Press.

Dyer, R. 1992. *Only Entertainment.* London: Routledge.

―――― 2007. *Pastiche.* London: Routledge.

Edelman, L. 2004. *No Future: Queer Theory and the Death Drive.* Durham, North Carolina: Duke University Press.

Ellis, J. 1981. *Visible Fictions: Cinema, Television, Video.* London: Routledge.

Elsaesser, T. 2005. *European Cinema Face to Face with Hollywood.* Amsterdam: Amsterdam University Press.

Eng, I. 1985. *Watching Dallas: Soap Opera and the Melodramatic Imagination.* London and New York: Routledge.

Evans, P.W. and C. Deleyto. 1998. 'Introduction: Surviving Love.' In P.W. Evans and C. Deleyto (eds), *Terms of Endearment: Hollywood Romantic Comedies of the 1980s and 1990s.* Edinburgh: Edinburgh University Press, pp.1–14.

Everett, W. 2005. 'Fractal Films and the Architecture of Complexity.' *Studies in European Cinema* 2, no. 3: 159–171.

Ezra, E, 2004. 'The Death of an Icon: *Le Fabuleux destin d'Amelie Poulain.*' *French Cultural Studies* 15, no. 3: 301–310.

―――― and T. Rowden. 2006. *Transnational Cinema, the Film Reader.* New York: Routledge.

Fabre, P. 2002. '*Décalage horaire.*' *Studio* no. 183 (November).

Ferriss, S. and M. Young. 2006. 'Introduction.' In S. Ferris and M. Young (eds), *Chick Lit: the New Women's Fiction.* NewYork and London: Routledge, pp.1–13.

―――― 2008a. 'Introduction.' In S. Ferriss and M. Young (eds), *Chick Flicks: Contemporary Women at the Movies.* New York and London: Routledge, pp.1–25.

―――― 2008b. 'Chic flicks: the new European romance'.' In S. Ferriss and M. Young (eds), *Chick Flicks: Contemporary Women at the Movies.* New York and London: Routledge, pp.175–190.

Fielding. H. 1996. *Bridget Jones' Diary.* London: Picador.

Firestone, S. 1979. *The Dialectic of Sex: The Case for Feminist Revolution.* London: Women's Press.

Fischer, L. 1989. *Shot/Countershot: Film Tradition and Women's Cinema.* Princeton: Princeton University Press.

Flahault, E. 1999. 'La Triste image de la femme seule.' In Christine Bard (ed.), *Un siècle d'antiféminisme*, pp.391–400. Paris: Fayard.

Flaubert, G. 2002. *Madame Bovary*, ed. and trans. Geoffrey Wall. London: Penguin.
Forbes, J. 1992a. *The Cinema in France: After the New Wave.* London: BFI.
—— 1992b. 'Design for Living: The Family in Recent French Cinema.' In R. Chapman and N. Hewitt (eds), *Popular Culture and Mass Communication in Twentieth Century France.* Lampeter: Edwin Mellen, pp.114–125.
Fore, S. 2001. 'Life Imitates Entertainment: Home and Dislocation in the Films of Jackie Chan.' In E.C.M. Lau (ed.), *At Full Speed: Hong Kong Cinema in a Borderless World.* Minneapolis and London: University of Minnesota Press: pp.115–142.
Foucault, M. 1981. *Histoire de la sexualité. Volume 1: an Introduction*, trans. R. Hurley. Harmondsworth: Penguin. First published 1976.
—— 1984. *Histoire de la sexualité*, vols. 2 and 3, *L'Usage des plaisirs* and *Le Souci de soi*. Paris: Gallimard.
Frederick, E.C. 1973. *The Plot and Its Construction in Eighteenth Century Criticism of French Comedy.* New York: Burt Franklin.
Freud, S. 1958. 'On the Universal Tendency to Debasement in the Sphere of Love.' In Freud, *The Standard Edition of the Complete Psychological Works of Sigmund Freud: Vols. I–XXIV*, trans. James Strachey, vol. 11. London: Hogarth Press.
—— 2002. *Wit and its Relation to the Unconscious*, trans. J. Crick. London: Penguin.
Frodon, J.-M. 1995. *L'Age moderne du cinéma français.* Paris: Flammarion.
—— 1996. 'Les quiproquos transatlantiques de Chantal Akerman.' *Le Monde*, 11 April.
—— 1997. 'La Question de vérité en chantant de bon coeur.' *Le Monde*, 13 November.
—— 2006. '*Prête-moi ta main*' *Cahiers du cinéma* no. 618 (December): 38.
Garrett, R. 2007. *Postmodern Chick Flicks: The Return of the Woman's Film.* New York and Basingstoke: Palgrave Macmillan.
Gavalda, A. 2004. *Ensemble, c'est tout.* Paris: Le Dilletante.
Gehring, W.D. 1986. *Screwball Comedy: A Genre of Madcap Romance.* New York, Westport and London: Greenwood.
Germain, D. 2010. 'Love story amnésique.' *VSD*, 23 September.
Gianorio, R. 2003. 'Seigner à tomber.' *France-soir*, 16 March.
—— 2005. 'Melki, l'ambition tranquille.' *France-soir*, 30 March.
Giddens, A. 1990. *The Consequences of Modernity.* Stanford: Stanford University Press.

_____ 1992. *The Transformation of Intimacy: Sexuality, Love and Eroticism in Modern Societies*. Cambridge: Polity Press.

Gilbert, N. 2008. *A Mother's Work. How Feminism, the Market and Policy Shape Family Life*. New Haven, CT: Yale University Press.

Gili, J. A. 2007. '*Ensemble c'est tout*: le goût de vivre.' *Positif* no. 553 (March): 26–8.

Glitre, K. 2001. 'The Same, but Different: The Awful Truth about Marriage, Remarriage and Screwball Comedy'. *CineAction* no. 54: 2–11.

Goodridge, M. 2002. 'Slick Star Vehicle Shows No Weariness.' *Screen International* no. 1374 (27 September), p.23.

Gordon, R.B. 2001. *Why the French Love Jerry Lewis: From Cabaret to Early Cinema*. Stanford: Stanford University Press.

Grasseri, S. 1999. 'Divine Karin.' *L'Express*, 28 January.

Greene, E.J.H. 1977. *Meander to Marivaux: The History of a Comic Structure*. Edmonton: University of Alberta Press.

Greenfield, L. 1992. *Nationalism: Five Roads to Modernity*. Cambridge: Harvard University Press.

Greer, G. 1971. *The Female Eunuch*. New York: McGraw-Hill.

Gross, M. 2001. 'Les nouvelles parentés.' In G. Ignasse (ed.), *Le Pacs, hier, aujourd'hui et demain, Actes du colloque de Reims des 13 et 14 novembre 2000*. Paris: L'Harmattan.

Grossvogel, D.I. 2005. *Marianne and the Puritan: Transformations of the Couple in French and American Cinema*. Oxford and Lanham, MD: Lexington.

Guichard, L. 2006. '*Toi et Moi*.' *Télérama*, 8 March.

Hakim, C. 2000. *Work-Lifestyle Choices in the 21st Century*. Oxford: Oxford University Press.

Hall, S. 1980. 'Cultural Studies: two paradigms'. *Media, Culture and Society* 2: 57–72.

Hallam, J. and M. Marshment. 2000. *Realism and Popular Cinema*. Manchester: Manchester University Press.

Hampshire, D. 2008. *Living and Working in France*. London: Survival Books.

Handyside, F. 2007. 'Girls on Film: Mothers, Sisters and Daughters in Contemporary French Cinema.' In M.-C. Barnet and E. Welch (eds), *Affaires de Famille: The Family in Contemporary French Culture and Theory*. Amsterdam and New York: Rodopi, pp.221–237.

Harris, S. 1997. 'The people's filmmaker? *Théâtre populaire* and the films of Bertrand Blier.' In S. Perry and M. Cross (eds), *Voices of France: Social, Political and Cultural Identity*. London: Pinter, pp.14–26.

―――― 2002. '*Ma femme est une actrice.*' *Sight and Sound* 12, no. 10 (1 October): 42.

Harrod, M. 2012. 'The *réalisatrice* and the rom-com in the 2000s.' *Studies in French Cinema* 12, no. 3: 227–240.

―――― 2013. 'Sweet nothings: imagining the inexpressible in contemporary French romantic comedy.' *Studies in French Cinema* 13, no. 2, pp.171–187.

―――― 2014. 'Auteur Meets Genre: Rohmer and the Rom-Com.' In L. Anderst (ed.), *The Films of Eric Rohmer: French New Wave to Old Master*. London: Palgrave Macmillan, pp.101–117.

―――― 2015. 'Franglais, Anglais and Contemporary French Comedy.' In M. Harrod, M. Liz and A. Timoshkina (eds), *The Europeanness of European Cinema: Identity, Meaning, Globalization* (London: I.B.Tauris, pp.145–159.

Hayward, S. 2005. *French National Cinema*. London and New York: Routledge.

―――― 2010. *French Costume Drama of the 1950s: Fashioning Politics in Film*. Bristol: Intellect.

Heathcote, O., Hughes, A. and J. S. Williams. 1998. 'Introduction: Reading Gay Signatures.' In O. Heathcote, A. Hughes and J. S. Williams (eds), *Gay Signatures: Gay and Lesbian Theory, Fiction and Film in France*. Oxford and New York: Berg, pp.1–25.

Henderson, B. 1978. 'Romantic Comedy Today: Semi-Tough or Impossible?' *Film Quarterly* 31, no. 4 (Summer): 11–23.

Hennessy, R. and C. Ingraham (eds). 1997. *Materialist Feminism: A Reader in Class, Difference, and Women's Lives*. New York: Routledge.

Henry, A. 2004. 'Orgasms and Empowerment: *Sex and the City* and Third Wave Feminism.' In K. Akass and J. McCabe (eds), *Reading Sex and the City*. London: I.B.Tauris, pp.65–83.

Hoesterey, I. 2001. *Pastiche: Cultural Memory in Art, Film, Literature*. Bloomington and Indianapolis: Indiana University Press.

Hollinger, K. 1998. *In the Company of Women: Contemporary Female Friendship Films*. Minneapolis and London: University of Minnesota Press.

Holmes, D. 2006. *Romance and Readership in Twentieth-Century France: Love Stories*. Oxford: Oxford University Press.

Ince, K. 2002. 'Queering the family: fantasy and the performance of sexuality and gay relations in French cinema 1995–2000.' *Studies in French Cinema* 2, no. 2: 90–7.

———— 2008. 'From Minor to "Major" Cinema? Women's and Feminist Cinema in France in the 2000s.' In '(Retro)projections: French Cinema in the Twenty-First Century', special issue of *Australian Journal of French Studies* 45, no. 3: 277–88.

Jackson, S. 1995. 'Women and Heterosexual Love: Complicity, Resistance and Change.' In L. Pearce and J. Stacey (eds), *Romance Revisited*. London: Lawrence and Wishart, pp.49–63.

Jameson, F. 1992. 'Reification and Utopia in Mass Culture.' In *Signatures of the Visible*. London: Routledge.

Jarvie, I.C. 1970. *Towards a Sociology of the Cinema*. London: Routledge and Kegan Paul.

———— 1978. *Movies as Social Criticism: Aspects of Their Social Psychology*. Metuchen, New Jersey: Scarecrow Press.

Jeancolas, J.-P. 1979. *Le Cinéma des français 1958–1978, La Cinquième République*. Paris: Stock.

———— 2009. 'Homme-com: Engendering Change in Contemporary Romantic Comedy.' In S. Abbott and D. Jermyn (eds), *Falling in Love Again: Romantic Comedy in Contemporary Cinema*. London: I.B.Tauris.

Johnston, C. 2002. 'Representations of homosexuality in 1990s mainstream French cinema.' *Studies in French Cinema* 2, no. 1: 23–31.

Jones, A.R. 1986. 'Mills and Boon Meets Feminism.' In J. Radford (ed.) *The Progress of Romance: The Politics of Popular Fiction*. London: Routledge and Kegan Paul, pp.194–218.

Jermyn, D. 2009. *Sex and the City*. Detroit: Wayne State University Press.

———— 2011. 'Unlikely Heroines? "Women of a Certain Age" and Romantic Comedy.' *CineAction* no. 85: 26–33.

Kaganski, S. 2001. 'Amélie pas jolie.' *Libération*, 31 May.

———— 2007. '*Hors de prix*.' *Les Inrockuptibles*, July 6.

Kaplan, E.A. 1992. *Motherhood and Representation*. London, USA and Canada: Routledge.

———— 1996. *Women and Film: Both Sides of the Camera*. London and New York: Routledge.

Kaprièlian, N. 2007. '*2 Days in Paris*.' *Les Inrockuptibles*, 10 July.

Karnick, K.B. and H. Jenkins. 1995. 'Introduction: Golden Eras and Blind Spots – Genre, History and Comedy.' In K.B. Karnick and H. Jenkins (eds), *Classical Hollywood Comedy*. London and New York: Routledge.

King, G. 2002. *Film Comedy*. London and New York: Wallflower Press.

Kosofsky Sedgwick, E. 1985. *Between Men: English Literature and Male Homosocial Desire*. New York: Columbia University Press.

Kristeva, J. 1986. 'A New Type of Intellectual: the Dissident.' In T. Moi (ed.), *The Kristeva Reader*, New York: Columbia University Press, pp.292–300.

―――― 1993. 'Le Temps des femmes.' In Kristeva, *Les Nouvelles maladies de l'âme*. Paris: Fayard, pp.297–332.

Krutnik, F. 1990. 'The Faint Aroma of Performing Seals: the "Nervous" Romance and the Comedy of the Sexes.' *The Velvet Light Trap* no. 26 (Autumn): 57–72.

―――― 1998. 'Love Lies: Romantic Fabrication in Contemporary Romantic Comedy.' In P.W. Evans and C. Deleyto (eds), *Terms of Endearment: Hollywood Romantic Comedies of the 1980s and 1990s*. Edinburgh: Edinburgh University Press, pp.15–36.

―――― 2002. 'Conforming Passions?: Contemporary Romantic Comedy.' In S. Neale (ed.), *Contemporary Hollywood*. London: BFI, pp.130–148.

Kuisel, R.F. 1993. *Seducing the French: The Dilemma of Americanization*. Berkeley: University of California Press.

―――― 2000. 'The Fernandel Factor: The Rivalry between the French and American Cinema in the 1950s.' *Yale French Studies* 98: 119–134.

Lacomme, J.-P. '*Le Premier jour du reste de ta vie*.' *Le Journal du Dimanche*, 20 July.

Lamome, S. 2002a. '*Décalage horaire*.' *Première*, no. 308 (October), p.54.

―――― 2002b. 'Pretty Juliette.' *Première*, no. 308 (October), pp.72–3.

Landrot, M. and L. Guichard. 1999. 'Les Fonceuses.' *Télérama* no. 2559 (27 January).

Lent, T.O. 1995. 'Romantic Love and Friendship: the Redefinition of Gender Relations in Screwball Comedy.' In K. Brunovska Karnick and H. Jenkins (eds), *Classical Hollywood Comedy*. London and New York: Routledge.

Leonard, S. 2001. '"I Hate My Job, I Hate Everybody Here": Adultery, Boredom, and the "Working Girl" in Twenty-First Century American Cinema.' In Y. Tasker and D. Negra (eds), *Interrogating Postfeminism: Gender and the Politics of Popular Culture*. Duke and London: Duke University Press, pp.100–131.

Levin, C. 1981. 'Introduction.' In J. Baudrillard, *Towards a Critique of the Political Economy of the Sign*, trans. Charles Levin. New York: Telos Press, pp.5–29.

Libiot, E. 2006. '*Essaye-moi*.' *L'Express*, 16 March.

―――― 2010a. 'Prestige de l'amour.' *L'Express*, 11 March.

―――― 2010b. 'Chronique: le cinéma d'Eric Libiot: l'union fait la force.' *L'Express*, 11 March.

Light, A. 1984. 'Returning to Manderley: Romance Fiction, Female Sexuality and Class.' *Feminist Review* no. 16 (Summer): 7–25.

Lipinska, C. 2007. 'Le Temps de l'amour.' *Le Nouvel Observateur*, 22 February.

Lipovetsky, G. 1993. *L'Ere du vide: essais sur l'individualisme contemporain.* Paris: Gallimard. 1st published 1983.

Loison, G. 2006. '*Prête-moi ta main.*' *France-soir*, 1 November.

Louis, M.-V. 1999. "Harcèlement sexuel et domination masculin.' In C. Bard (ed.), *Un siècle d'antiféminisme*. Paris: Fayard, pp.401–416.

Luhmann, N. 1986. *Love as Passion: The Codification of Intimacy*, trans. J. Gaines and D. L. Jones. Cambridge, Mass.: Harvard University Press.

Lutaud, L. 2010. '*L'Arnacoeur*: personne n'y croyait...' *Le Figaro*, 7 March.

Maher, J. M. and L. Saugères. 2007. 'To Be or Not to be a Mother?' *Journal of Sociology – The Australian Sociological Association* 3, no. 1: 5–21.

del Mar Azcona, M. 2010. *The Multi-Protagonist Film*. Chichester: Wiley Blackwell.

Marshall, B. 1998. 'Gay cinema.' In A. Hughes and K. Reader (eds), *Encyclopaedia of Contemporary French Culture*. London and New York: Routledge, pp.262–263.

Martin, A. 1997. '*Un divan à New York*.' *Cinema Papers* no. 120 (1 October): 39–40.

May, E.T. 1980. *Great Expectations: Marriage and Divorce in Post-Victorian America*. Chicago: University of Chicago Press.

Mazdon, L. 2000. *Encore Hollywood: Remaking French Cinema*. London: BFI.

McDonald, T.J. 2007. *Romantic Comedy: Boy Meets Girl Meets Genre*. London and New York: Wallflower.

Millet, K. 1969. *Sexual Politics*. New York: Ballantine Books.

Mitchell, J. 1966. 'Women: The Longest Revolution.' *New Left Review* no. 40.

Modleski, T. 1990. *Loving With a Vengeance: Mass Produced Fantasies for Women*. London and New York: Routledge. First published 1982.

——— 1991. *Feminism Without Women. Culture and Criticism in a 'Postfeminist' Age*. New York: Routledge.

Moine, R. 2002. *Les Genres du cinéma*. Paris: Nathan.

——— (ed.) 2005a. *Le Cinéma français face aux genres*. Paris: Association française de recherche sur le cinéma.

——— 2005b. 'Reconfigurations génériques de la comédie dans le cinéma français contemporain.' In R. Moine (ed.), *Le Cinéma français face aux genres*. Paris: Association française de recherche sur le cinéma, pp.214–223.

—— 2007a. 'Generic Hybridity, National Culture, and Globalised Cinema.' In I. Vanderschelden and D. Waldron (eds), *France at the Flicks: Trends in Contemporary French Popular Cinema*. Cambridge: Cambridge Scholars Publishing, pp.36–50.

—— 2007b. *Remakes: les films français à Hollywood*. Paris: CNRS Editions.

—— 2008. 'Remaking Romance: French-Style Love Story into US Romcom.' Graduate Seminar, King's College, London, 6 January.

—— 2010. '*Bienvenue chez les Cht'is*: la région ou la classe?' *Poli-Politique de l'image*, no. 2 (March): 37–49.

Moore, R.C. 2006. 'Ambivalence to Technology in Jeunet's *Le Fabuleux destin d'Amélie Poulain*.' *Bulletin of Science, Technology and Society* 26, no. 1 (February): 9–19.

Morain, J.-B. 2006a. '*Je vous trouve très beau*.' *Les Inrockuptibles*, 1 February.

—— 2006b. '*Fauteuils d'orchestre*.' *Les Inrockuptibles*, 15 February.

Morrissey, J. 2008. 'Paris and voyages of self-discovery in *Cléo de 5 à 7* and *Le Fabuleux destin d'Amélie Poulain*. *Studies in French Cinema* 8, no. 2: 99–110.

Mortimer, C. 2010. 'Romantic Comedy.' London and New York: Routledge.

Mulvey, L. 1985. 'Changes: Thoughts on Myth, Narrative and Historical Experience.' *Discourse* 7 (Autumn): 6–18.

Naficy, H. 2001. *An Accented Cinema: Exilic and Diasporic Filmmaking*. Princeton and Oxford: Princeton University Press.

Narbonne, C. 2003. '*Laisse tes mains sur mes hanches*.' *Première* no. 314 (April), p.40.

Neale, S. 1992. 'The Big Romance or Something Wild?: Romantic Comedy Today.' *Screen* 33, no. 3 (Autumn): 284–299.

—— 1999. 'Teenpics.' In P. Cook and M. Bernink (eds), *The Cinema Book*, 2nd Edition. London: BFI.

—— 2000. *Genre and Hollywood*. London: Routledge.

—— and F. Krutnik. 1990. *Popular Film and Television Comedy*. London: Routledge.

Negra, D. 2004. '"Quality Postfeminism?": Sex and the Single Girl on HBO.' *Genders Online* no. 39. http://www.genders.org/g39/g39_negra.html. Accessed 13 February 2012.

—— 2008. 'Structural Integrity, Historical Reversion, and the Post 9/11 Chick Flick.' *Feminist Media Studies* 8, no. 1 (March).

Orwell, G. 2000. *Keep the Aspidistra Flying*. London: Penguin. First published in 1936.

Ory, P. 1989. *L'Aventure culturelle française*. Paris: Flammarion.

O'Shaughnessy, M. 2007. *The New Face of Political Cinema: Commitment in French Film since 1995*. New York and Oxford: Berghahn Books.

Ostria, V. *'Modern Love.' L'Humanité*, 12 March.

Palmer, J. 1987. *The Logic of the Absurd: On Film and Television Comedy*. London: BFI.

Palmer, T. 2007. 'Threading the Eye of the Needle: Contemporary French Pop-Art Cinema and Valeria Bruni-Tedeschi's *Il est plus facile pour un chameau...*' In D. Waldron and I. Vanderschelden (eds), *France at the Flicks: Trends in Contemporary French Popular Cinema*. Cambridge: Cambridge Scholars Publishing, pp.89–103.

_____ 2011. *Brutal Intimacy: Analyzing Contemporary French Cinema*. Middletown, Connecticut: Wesleyan University Press.

Patterson, J. 2009. 'True Bromance,' *Guardian*, 11 April. http://www.guardian.co.uk/film/2009/apr/11/bromantic-comedy-love-you-man. Accessed 19 September 2011.

Pearce, L. and J. Stacey. 1995. 'The Heart of the Matter: Feminists Revisit Romance.' In L. Pearce and J. Stacey (eds), *Romance Revisited*. London: Lawrence and Wishart, pp.11–49.

Péron, D. 2006. '*Mauvaise foi*: alliance ethnique.' *Libération*, 6 December.

Perry, K. 1995. 'The Heart of Whiteness: White Subjectivity and Interracial Relationships.' In L. Pearce and J. Stacey (eds), *Romance Revisited*. London: Lawrence and Wishart, pp.171–185.

Pion-Dumas, L. and L. Delmas. 1999. 'Danièle Thompson, les secrets de famille.' *Synopsis* no. 5 (Winter).

Powrie, P. 1999. 'Heritage, History and the New Realism.' In P. Powrie (ed.), *French Cinema in the 1990s: Continuity and Difference*. Oxford, Oxford University Press, pp.1–21.

Powrie, P., A. Davies and B. Babington. 2004. 'Introduction Turning the Male Inside Out.' In P. Powrie, A. Davies and B. Babington (eds), *The Trouble with Men: Masculinities in European and Hollywood Cinema*. London: Wallflower Press, pp.1–15.

_____ 2007. 'La Famille (du cinéma) en désordre: Roudinesco and Contemporary French Cinema.' In M.-C. Barnet and E. Welch (eds), *Affaires de Famille: The Family in Contemporary French Culture and Theory*. Amsterdam and New York: Rodopi, pp.283–304.

_____ 2010. 'Unfamiliar Places: "Heterospection" and Recent French Films on Children.' In W. Higbee and S. Leahy (eds), *Studies in French Cinema: UK Perspectives 1985–2010*. Bristol: Intellect, pp.59–68.

Prédal, R. 1984. *Le cinéma français contemporain*. Paris: Editions du Cerf.
———. 1991. *Le Cinéma français depuis 1945*. Paris: Editions Nathan.
———. 1993. 'Le Cinéma français et les genres.' *Cinémaction* 68: 48–56.
———. 1998. 'La Déferlante.' In M. Marie (ed.), *Le Jeune cinéma français*. Paris: Nathan, pp.8–21.
———. 2008a. *Le Cinéma français depuis 2000: un renouvellement incessant*. Paris: Armand Colin.
———. 2008b. *Le Cinéma français des années 1990*. Paris: Armand Colin.
Prugnard, P.-M. 1999. *Les Inrockuptibles*, 27 January.
Radner, H. 1993. 'Pretty is as Pretty Does: Free Enterprise and the Marriage Plot.' In J. Collins, H. Radner and A. Preacher (eds), *Film Theory Goes to the Movies*. New York and London: Routledge, pp.56–76.
Radway, J.A. 1991. *Reading the Romance: Women, Patriarchy and Popular Literature*. Chapel Hill and London: University of North Carolina Press.
Ramasse, F. 1989. 'Les Films.' *Positif* 339 (May): 64.
Régnier-Loilier, A. 2009. 'L'arrivée d'un enfant modifie-t-elle la répartition des tâches domestiques au sein du couple?' *Population et Sociétés*, no. 461 (November).
Rollet, B. 2008. 'Transatlantic Exchanges and Influences: *Décalage horaire (Jet Lag)*, Gender and the Romantic Comedy *à la française*.' In S. Abbott and D. Jermyn (eds), *Falling in Love Again: Romantic Comedy in Contemporary Cinema*. London: I.B.Tauris, pp.92–104.
———. 2010. *Masculin/Féminin: La Rom-Com à la française*. Seminar paper delivered at L'Institut National d'Histoire de l'Art, January 15, as part of the series *Genre et Gender*, sponsored by l'IRCAV (Université Paris 3 Sorbonne Nouvelle).
———. 2011. 'Queer or Not Queer Others: Gender Trouble and Postcolonial French Cinema.' In F. Grandena and C. Johnston (eds), *Cinematic Queerness: Gay and Lesbian Hypervisibility in Contemporary Francophone Feature Films*. Oxford, Bern, Berlin, Brussels, Frankfurt, New York and Vienna: Peter Lang.
Rolot, C. and F. Ramirez (eds). 1997. *Cinéma: le genre comique*. Montpellier: Centre d'Etude du Vingtième Siècle, Montpellier 3.
Rosello, M. 2002. 'Auto-portraits glanés et plaisirs partagés: *Les Glaneurs et la glaneuse* and *Le Fabuleux destin d'Amélie Poulain*.' *L'Esprit Créateur* 42, no. 3 (Autumn): 3–16.
———. 2011. 'Dissident or Conformist Passing: Merzak Allouache's *Chouchou*.' *South Central Review* 28, no. 1 (Spring): 2–17.

Rostand, E. 2002. *Cyrano de Bergerac*, trans. A. Burgess. London: Nick Hern Books.

Roudinesco, E. 2002. *La Famille en désordre*. Paris: Fayard.

Roux, B. 2001. 'Les Vertiges de l'Intimité: *Amélie Poulain* et *Loft Story*.' *Positif* no. 487 (1 September): 64–65.

Rowe, K. 1995. *The Unruly Woman: Gender and the Genres of Laughter*. Austin: University of Texas Press.

Ruiz Pardos, M. 2000. 'Addicted to Fun: Courtship, Play and Romance in the Screwball Comedy.' *Revista Alicantina de Estudios Ingleses*, 13: 153–160.

Sarde, M. 1983. *Regard sur les françaises*. Paris: Stock.

Sarris, A. 1998. '*You Ain't Heard Nothin' Yet*': *The American Talking Film, History and Memory, 1927–1949*. Oxford and New York: Oxford University Press.

Scatton-Tessier, M. 2004. '*Le Petisme*, Flirting with the Sordid in *Le Fabuleux destin d'Amélie Poulain*.' *Studies in French Cinema* 4, no. 3: 197–207.

Schatz, T. 1981. *Hollywood Genres: Formulas, Filmmaking and the Studio System*. Austin: McGraw Hill.

Schwartz, Vanessa R. 2007. *It's so French: Hollywood, Paris and the Making of Cosmopolitan Film Culture*. Chicago: University of Chicago Press.

Selfe, M. 2010. '"Incredibly French?" Nation as an interpretative context for Extreme Cinema.' In L. Mazdon and C. Wheatley (eds), *Je t'aime . . . moi non plus: Franco-British Cinematic Relations*. New York and Oxford: Berghahn Books, pp.153–168.

Sellier, G. 1997. 'La Nouvelle vague, un cinéma à la première personne du masculin singulier.' *Iris* no. 24 (Autumn).

_____ 1998. '*Un air de famille* de Cédric Klapisch: un film d'auteur populaire.' In M. Marie (ed.), *Le Jeune cinéma français*. Paris: Nathan, pp.121–123.

_____ 1999a. 'Le Cinéma des années 1930.' In C. Bard (ed.), *Un siècle d'antiféminisme*. Paris: Fayard, pp.205–215.

_____ 1999b. 'Les Contradictions du cinéma des années 1950.' In C. Bard (ed.), *Un siècle d'antiféminisme*. Paris: Fayard, pp.285–298.

_____ 2005. 'Les films "Belle Epoque" dans le cinéma d'après-guerre. Invisibilité d'un genre féminin.' In R. Moine (ed.), *Le Cinéma français face aux genres*. Paris: Association française de recherche sur le cinéma, pp.151–162.

_____ 2008. *Masculine Singular: French New Wave Cinema*, trans. Kristin Ross. Durham and London: Duke University Press, pp.149–150.

_____ 2010. 'French New Wave Cinema and the Legacy of Male Libertinage.' *Cinema Journal* 49, no. 4 (Summer). Special Issue 'In Focus: The French New Wave at Fifty: Pushing the Boundaries': 152–158.

Shelton, B.A. and D. John. 1993. 'Does marital status make a difference? Housework among married and cohabiting men and women.' *Journal of Family Issues* 14, no. 3 (September): 401–420.

Shumway, D.R. 2003a. *Modern Love: Romance, Intimacy and the Marriage Crisis*. New York and London: New York University Press.

―――― 2003b. 'Screwball Comedies: Constructing Romance, Mystifying Marriage.' In B.K. Grant (ed.), *Film Genre Reader III*. Austin: University of Texas Press, pp.396–416.

Silverstein, M. 2014. 'The Celluloid Ceiling: Behind-the-Scenes Employment of Women on the Top 250 Films of 2011. http://blogs.indiewire.com/womenandhollywood/what-bigelow-effect-number-of-women-directors-in-hollywood-falls-to-5-percent#.T_r9RpH_yVo. (Accessed 9 July 2014.)

Simsi, S. 2000. *Ciné-Passions, 7e art et industrie de 1945 à 2000*. Paris: Dixit.

Singly, F. de. 2004. *Fortune et infortune de la femme mariée*. Paris: PUF. First published in 1987.

Slater, L. 2012. 'Don't change your face, you can still get sexy parts.' *The Times*, 10 March, Weekend supplement, pp.2–3.

Smith, A. 2011. 'Men in Unfamiliar Places: A Response to Phil Powrie.' In W. Higby and S. Leahy (eds), *Studies in French Cinema: UK Perspectives, 1985–2010*. Bristol and Chicago: Intellect, pp.177–191.

Sontag, S. 1997. 'The Double Standard of Aging.' In M. Pearsall (ed.), *The Other Within Us: Feminist Explorations of Women and Aging*. Boulder: Westview.

Sorlin, P. 1977. *Sociologie du cinéma*. Paris: Aubier Montaigne.

Stacey, J. 1990. 'Romance.' In S. Radstone and A Kuhn (eds), *The Women's Companion to International Film*. London: Virago, pp.345–346.

―――― 1994. *Star Gazing: Hollywood Cinema and Female Spectatorship*. London and New York: Routledge.

Stigsdotter, I. 2010. 'British Audiences and 1990s French Realism: *La Vie rêvée des anges* as Cinematic Slum Tourism.' In L. Mazdon and C. Wheatley (eds), *Je t'aime... moi non plus*. London: Berghahn Books, pp.169–181.

Swamy, V. 2006. 'Gallic dreams? The family, PaCS and kinship relations in millennial France.' *Studies in French Cinema* 6, no. 1: 53–65.

Tally, M. 2008. 'Something's gotta give: Hollywood, female sexuality and the "older bird" chick flick.' In S. Ferriss and M. Young (eds), *Chick Flicks: Contemporary Women at the Movies*. London and New York: Routledge, pp.119–131.

Tarr, C. with B. Rollet. 2001. *Cinema and the Second Sex: Women's Filmmaking in France in the1980s and 1990s.* London and New York: Continuum.

Tasker, Y. 1993. *Spectacular Bodies: Gender, Genre and the Action Cinema.* London: Routledge.

———— 1998. *Working Girls: Gender and Sexuality in Popular Cinema.* London and New York: Routledge.

———— and D. Negra. 2007. 'Introduction.' In Y. Tasker and D. Negra (eds), *Interrogating Postfeminism: Gender and the Politics of Popular Culture.* Duke and London: Duke University Press, pp.1–25.

Taylor, N. 2011. 'A Forensic Look at Infidelity.' BBC Radio 4, 11am 17 June.

Thiesse, A.-M. 1984. *Le Roman du quotidien: lecteurs et lectures à la belle époque.* Paris: Le Chemin Vert.

Thomas, D. 2000. *Beyond Genre: Melodrama, Comedy and Romance in Hollywood Films.* Moffatt: Cameron and Hollis.

Thompson, D. 2005. 'Interview de la réalisatrice et du co-scénariste.' Studio-Canal DVD edition of *La Bûche*.

Thompson, K. 1999. 'Introduction.' In *Storytelling in the New Hollywood.* Cambridge, MA and London: Harvard University Press.

Tinazzi, N. 2003. 'Gabriel Aghion exorcise *Belle Maman*.' *La Tribune Desfossés*, 10 March.

Tröhler, M. 2000. 'Les films à protagonistes multiples et la logique des possibles.' *Iris*, no. 29: 85–102.

———— 2007. *Offene Welten ohne Helden. Plurale Figuren-Konstellationem im Film.* Marburg: Schüren Presseverlag.

———— 2010. 'Multiple Protagonist Films: a Transcultural Everyday Practice.' In J. Eder, F. Jannidis and R. Schneider (eds), *Characters in Fictional Worlds: Understanding Imaginary Beings in Literature, Film, and Other Media.* Berlin/New York: De Gruyter, pp.459–477.

Truffaut, F. 1976. 'A Certain Tendency of the French Cinema.' In B. Nichols (ed.), *Movies and Methods: An Anthology*, vol. 1. Berkeley and Los Angeles: University of California Press, pp.224–36. Originally published in *Cahiers du cinéma*, 31.

Tudor, A. 1974. *Image and Influence: Studies in the Sociology of Film.* London: Allen & Unwin.

Valens, G. 2002. '*Embrassez qui vous voudrez*. Leçon de cinéma: le casting.' *Positif* no. 501 (1 November): 40–1.

Vanderschelden, I. 2005. 'Jamel Debbouze: a New Popular French Star?' *Studies in French Cinema* 5, no. 1: 61–72.

———— 2007. *Amélie.* London and New York: I.B.Tauris.

Vasse, D. 2008. *Le Nouvel âge du cinéma d'auteur français.* Paris: Klincksieck.

Vertovec, S. and R. Cohen. 1999. *Migration, Diasporas, and Transnationalism.* Cheltenham: Edward Elgar.

Vincendeau, G. 1987. 'Women's Cinema, Film Theory, and Feminism in France.' *Screen* 28, no. 4: 4–18.

―――― 1988. 'Daddy's Girls (Oedipal Narratives in 1930s French Films).' *Iris* no. 8: 70–81.

―――― 1992. 'Family Plots: the Fathers and Daughters of French Cinema.' *Sight and Sound* 1, no. 11 (March): 14–17.

―――― 1993. 'Hijacked." *Sight and Sound* 3, no. 7 (July): 22.

―――― 1996. 'Twist and farce.' *Sight and Sound* 6, no. 4 (1 April): 24–6.

―――― 2000a. '*La Nouvelle Eve.*' *Sight and Sound* 10, no. 5 (1 May): 56–7.

―――― 2000b. *Stars and Stardom in French Cinema.* London and New York: Continuum.

―――― 2001. 'Café Society.' *Sight and Sound* 11, no. 8 (1 August): 22–5.

―――― 2004. 'The Art of Spectacle: The Aesthetics of Classical French Cinema.' In M. Temple and M. Witt (eds), *The French Cinema Book.* London: BFI, pp.137–152.

―――― 2005. 'Miss France,' *Sight and Sound* 15, no. 2 (1 February): 12–15.

―――― 2008. 'Family Tales.' *Sight and Sound* no. 18 (8 August): 16–17.

―――― 2010a. 'The French Resistance through British Eyes: From '*Allo 'Allo!* to *Charlotte Gray.*' In L. Mazdon and C. Wheatley (eds), *Je t'aime . . . moi non plus.* London: Berghahn Books, pp.237–254.

―――― 2010b. 'The Rise and Rise of French Women Filmmakers: Victory for Feminism or French Exception?' Paper delivered at 'Women's Filmmaking in France 2000–201' conference, Institute of Germanic and Romance Studies, London, 4 December.

Waldron, D. 2001. 'Fluidity of Gender and Sexuality in *Gazon maudit.*' In L. Mazdon (ed.), *France on Film: Reflections on Popular French Cinema.* London: Wallflower Press, 2001.

―――― and I. Vanderschelden. 2007. 'Introduction.' In D. Waldron and I. Vanderschelden (eds), *France at the Flicks: Trends in Contemporary French Popular Cinema.* Cambridge: Cambridge Scholars Publishing, pp.1–15.

Welcomme, G. 2004. 'Yolande Moreau filme sur ses terres flamandes.' *La Croix,* 27 October.

Wearing, S. 2007. 'Subjects of Rejuvenation.' In Y. Tasker and D. Negra (eds), *Interrogating Postfeminism.* Durham and London: Duke University Press, pp.277–310.

Werner, D. 1996. 'Génération Kleenex.' *Elle,* 16 September.

West, J. M. 2001. '*Vénus Beauté (Institut)*.' *Cinéaste* 26, no. 2 (1 March): 46.
Weston, K. 1991. *Families We Choose: Lesbians, Gays, Kinship*. New York: Columbia University Press.
Wheatley, C. 2015. 'Christianity and European Film.' In M. Harrod, M. Liz and A. Timoshkina (eds), *The Europeanness of European Cinema*. London and New York: I.B.Tauris.
Wilson, E. 2005. 'Et à Présent: Contemporary French Women Filmmakers.' *French Studies* 59, no. 2: 217–223.
Wolf, N. 1991. *The Beauty Myth: How Images of Beauty Are Used Against Women*. London: Vintage.
Wright-Wexman, V. 1993. *Creating the Couple: Love, Marriage, and Hollywood Performance*. Princeton: Princeton University Press.
Žižek, S. 2000. 'No Sex, Please! We're Post-Human.' http://www.lacan.com/nosex.htm. Accessed 1 April 2011.

Websites

http://www.urbandictionary.com/define.php?term=romantic%20comedy&defid=1995126. (Accessed 20 July 2012.)

http://www.etymonline.com/index.php?search=ranch. (Accessed 12 March 2012.)

http://www.eternautes.free.fr/decouv/02lect.doc. (Accessed 7 November 2014.)

http://www.insee.fr/fr/themes/document.asp?ref_id=EEC05. (Accessed 8 January 2013.)

http://www.insee.fr/fr/publications-et-services/default.asp?page=dossiers_web/dev_durable/ecart_revenu_salaire_hommes_femmes.htm. (Accessed 8 January 2013.)

http://www.nationmaster.com/graph/lab_fem_doc-labor-female-doctors. (Accessed 22 June 2012.)

www.allocine.com. (Accessed 22 July 2014.)

www.imdb.com. (Accessed 4 August 2014.)

French rom-coms 1990–2010 with Box-Office Admissions[1]

Films with a *choral* or ensemble structure are marked '**C**'.

Age d'homme... maintenant ou jamais!, L' (Raphaël Fejtö, 2007)	198,344
Amour, c'est mieux à deux, L'/The Perfect Date (Dominique Farrugia and Arnaud Lemort, 2010)	1,115,726
Apprentis, Les (Pierre Salavadori, 1995) **C**	586,675
Arnacoeur, L'/Heartbreaker (Pascal Chaumeil, 2010)	3,770,345
Art (délicat) de la séduction, L' (Richard Berry, 2001)	296,658
Au secours, j'ai trente ans/Last Chance Saloon (Marie-Anne Chazel, 2004) **C**	223,159
Au suivant! (Jeanne Biras, 2005)	174,700
Battement d'ailes du papillon, Le/Happenstance (Laurent Firode, 2000)	62,087
Belle Maman/Beautiful Mother (Gabriel Aghion, 1998) Co-written with Danièle Thompson[2]	1,257,895
Bison (et sa voisine Dorine), Le (Isabelle Nanty, 2002)	559,792
Bûche, La/Season's Beatings (Danièle Thompson, 1999) **C**	1,623,563
Ce soir, je dors chez toi/Tonight I'll Sleep at Yours (Olivier Baroux, 2007)	516,669
Célibataires (Jean-Michel Verner, 2006) **C**	64,624
Celle que j'aime/The One I Love (Elie Chouraqui, 2008)	148,578

---

[1] Figures are sourced from www.allocine.com. Accessed 22 July 2014.
[2] I have noted cases where films include a female writer in their credits.

Changement d'adresse/Change of Address (Emmanuel Mouret, 2006)	210,056
Chansons d'amour, Les/Love Songs (Christophe Honoré, 2007)	321,068
Chouchou (Merzak Allouache, 2003)	3,824,376
Clara et moi/Clara and Me (Arnaud Viard, 2004)	145,655
Cliente/A French Gigolo (Josiane Balasko, 2008) **C**	703,272
Code a changé, Le/Change of Plans (Danièle Thompson, 2009) **C**	1,629,590
Coeur des hommes, Le /Frenchmen 1 (Marc Esposito, 2003) **C**	1,534,704
Coeur des hommes 2, Le /Frenchmen 2 (Marc Esposito, 2007) **C**	1,820,320
Comme les autres/Baby Love (Vincent Garenq, 2008)	524,774
Crustacés et coquillages/Cockles and Muscles (Olivier Ducastel and Jacques Martineau, 2005) **C**	197,462
Dans Paris/In Paris (Christophe Honoré, 2006)	216,888
De l'autre côté du lit/Changing Sides (Pascale Pouzadoux, 2009) **C**	1,807,470
De vrais mensonges/Beautiful Lies (Pierre Salvadori, 2010)	463,473
Décalage horaire/Jet Lag (Danièle Thompson, 2002)	1,058,339
Détrompez-vous (Bruno Dega and Jeanne Le Guillou, 2007) **C**	310,772
Dieu est grand, je suis toute petite/God is Great and I'm Not (Pascale Bailly, 2001)	351,979
Dieu, que les femmes sont amoureuses... (Magali Clément, 1994)	unrecorded
Dis-moi oui (Alexandre Arcady, 1995)	481,832
Divorces! (Valérie Guignabodet, 2009)	154,808
Embrassez qui vous voudrez/Summer Things (Michel Blanc, 2002) **C**	1,473,200
Emotifs anonymes, Les (Jean-Pierre Améris, 2010)	477,166
Ensemble, c'est tout/Hunting and Gathering (Claude Berri, 2007) Based on the novel by Anna Gavalda **C**	2,312,325
Enfin veuve/A Widow at Last (Isabelle Mergault, 2007)	2,247,376
Essaye-moi (Pierre-François Martin-Laval, 2006)	504,782
Ex-femme de ma vie, L'/Ex-Wife of my Life, The (Josiane Balasko, 2005)	907,021
Fabuleux destin d'Amélie Poulain, Le/Amélie (Jean-Pierre Jeunet, 2001)	8,516,999
Fauteuils d'orchestre/Orchestra Seats (Danièle Thompson, 2006) **C**	1,936,811

Filles perdues, cheveux gras/Hypnotized and Hysterical (Hairstylist Wanted) (Claude Duty, 2002) Co-written with Pascale Faure **C**	260,966
Gazon maudit/French Twist (Josiane Balasko, 1995)	3,990,094
Goût des autres, Le/Taste of Others, The (Agnès Jaoui, 2000) **C**	3,779,215
Homme de chevet, L' (Alain Monne, 2009)	245,241
Homme est une femme comme les autres, L'/Man is a Woman (Jean-Jacques Zilbermann, 1998)	504,730
Hors de prix/Priceless (Pierre Salvadori, 2006)	2,163,864
Il ne faut jurer de rien! (Eric Civanyan, 2005)	887,688
Ils se marièrent et eurent beaucoup d'enfants/...And They Lived Happily Ever After (Yvan Attal, 2004) **C**	924,053
Irène (Ivan Calbérac, 2002)	244,903
Je crois que je l'aime/Could This Be Love? (Pierre Jolivet, 2007)	848,539
Je ne suis pas là pour être aimé/Not Here To Be Loved (Stéphane Brizé, 2005) Co-written with Juliette Salles	283,949
Je préfère qu'on reste amis (Olivier Nakache and Eric Toledano, 2005) **C**	321,832
Je reste!/I'm Staying! (Diane Kurys, 2003)	826,617
Je vais te manquer/You'll Miss Me (Amanda Sthers, 2009) **C**	164,493
Je vous trouve très beau/You are so Beautiful (Isabelle Mergault, 2006)	3,514,923
J'me sens pas belle/Tell Me I'm Pretty (Bernard Jeanjean, 2004)	339,583
Jusqu'à toi (Jennifer Devoldère, 2009)	79,438
J'veux pas que tu t'en ailles/Please don't go (Bernard Jeanjean, 2007)	422,848
Laisse tes mains sur mes hanches/Leave Your Hands on My Hips (Chantal Lauby, 2003)	
LoL (Laughing Out Loud) (Lisa Azuelos, 2008) **C**	267,808
Love, Etc. (Marion Vernoux, 1996)	unrecorded
Ma femme est une actrice/My Wife is an Actress (Yvan Attal, 2001)	708,858
Ma vie en l'air (Rémi Bezançon, 2005)	396,861
Ma vie est un enfer/My Life is Hell (Josiane Balasko, 1991)	1,170,523
Ma vie n'est pas une comédie romantique/It Had to Be You (Marc Gibaja, 2007)	125,078
Mademoiselle Chambon (Stéphane Brizé, 2009) Co-written with Florence Vignon	527,005
Mariage Mixte (Alexandre Arcady, 2004)	211,030
Mariages! (Valérie Guignabodet, 2004) **C**	1,960,719

Marmottes, Les/Groundhogs, The (Elie Chouraqui, 1993) Co-written with Danièle Thompson **C**	820,239
Mauvaise foi/Bad Faith (Roschdy Zem, 2006)	771,072
Mensonges et trahisons et plus si affinités/The Story of My Life (Laurent Tirard, 2002)	743,217
Mes amis, mes amours/London mon amour (Lorraine Levy, 2008) **C**	676,017
Modern Love (Stéphane Kazandjian, 2008) **C**	236,574
Nouvelle Eve, La/New Eve, The (Catherine Corsini, 1999)	unrecorded
Odette Toulemonde (Eric-Emmanuel Schmitt, 2006)	882,209
On connaît la chanson/Same Old Song (Alain Resnais, 1997) Co-written with Agnès Jaoui **C**	2,670,877
On va s'aimer (Ivan Calbérac, 2006) **C**	263,131
Osmose (Raphael Fejtö, 2003) **C**	unrecorded
Où avais-je la tête? (Nathalie Donnini, 2007)	unrecorded
Palais Royal! (Valérie Lemercier, 2005)	2,679,789
Parlez-moi de la pluie/Let's Talk About the Rain (Agnès Jaoui, 2008) **C**	979,515
Passe-passe/Off and Running (Tonie Marshall, 2008)	279,594
Pédale douce (Gabriel Aghion, 1996) **C**	4,158,212
Pièce Montée/Wedding Cake, The (Denys Granier-Deferre, 2010) Based on a novel by Blandine Le Callet **C**	443,693
Plus beau métier du monde, Le/The Best Job in the World (Gérard Lauzier, 1996)	2,269,925
Pourquoi pas moi?/Why Not Me? (Stéphane Giusti, 1999) **C**	unrecorded
Premier jour du reste de ta vie, Le (Rémi Bezançon, 2008) **C**	1,211,670
Prête-moi ta main/I Do (Eric Lartigau, 2006)	3,628,669
Quand j'étais chanteur/The Singer (Xavier Giannoli, 2006)	960,753
Quand la mer monte/When the Sea Rises (Yolande Moreau, Gilles Porte, 2004)	412,505
Quatre étoiles (Christian Vincent, 2006)	747,935
Regrets, Les/Regrets (Cédric Kahn, 2009)	222,820
Reines d'un jour/Hell of a Day (Marion Vernoux, 2001) **C**	287,840
Roman de Lulu, Le (Pierre-Olivier Scotto, 2001)	106,547
Se souvenir des belles choses/Beautiful Memories (Zabou Breitman, 2001)	593,057
Si c'était lui/Perfect Match (Anne-Marie Etienne, 2007)	389,336

Smoking/No Smoking (Alain Resnais 1993) Co-written with Agnès Jaoui **C**	411,499[3]
Tellement proches (Olivier Nakache and Eric Toledano, 2009) **C**	781,052
Toi et moi (Julie Lopes-Curval, 2006) **C**	113,802
Tôt ou tard/Sooner or Later (Anne-Marie Etienne, 1999)	46,633
Tout ce qui brille/All That Glitters (Hervé Mimram and Géraldine Nakache, 2010) **C**	1,415,609
Tout pour plaire (Cécile Telerman, 2005) **C**	1,443,202
Toutes les filles sont folles/All Girls are Crazy (Pascale Pouzadoux, 2003) **C**	261,127
Tu vas rire mais je te quitte (Philippe Harel, 2005)	176,918
Tricheuse/So Woman! (Jean-François Davy, 2009)	25,665
Un air de famille/Family Resemblances (Cédric Klapisch, 1996) Co-written with Agnès Jaoui **C**	2,415,739
Un baiser s'il vous plaît/Shall We Kiss? (Emmanuel Mouret, France 2007)	210,056
Un divan à New York/A Couch in New York (Chantal Akerman, 1996)	unrecorded
Un grand cri d'amour (Josiane Balasko, 1998)	unrecorded
Une semaine sur deux (et la moitié des vacances scolaires) (Ivan Calbérac, 2009) **C**	509,443
Une vie à t'attendre (Thierry Klifa, 2004)	858,229
Vénus Beauté (Institut)/Venus Beauty Salon (Tonie Marshall, 1999) **C**	1,315,974
Vérité ou presque, La/True Enough (Sam Karmann, 2007) **C**	306,512
Virilité et autres sentiments modernes/Manhood and Other Modern Dilemmas (Ronan Girre, 2000)	unrecorded
Zèbre, Le/The Oddball (Jean Poiret, 1992)	1,866,623
2 Days in Paris (Julie Delpy, 2007)	287,605

---

[3] This figure was sourced from http://www.imdb.com/title/tt0108167/?ref_=fn_al_tt_1 as it was unavailable at allocine.com. Accessed 4 August 2014.

Index

2 Days in New York (Julie Delpy, Germany/France/Belgium 2012), 213
2 Days in Paris (Julie Delpy, France/Germany 2007), 37, 88, 195, 199, 200, 213
8 Femmes/8 Women (François Ozon, France/Italy 2002), 118
9/11, 29, 50, 55
20 ans d'écart/It Boy (David Moreau, France 2013), 209, 210, 211
40 Year-Old-Virgin, The (Judd Apatow, USA 1996), 113
71 Fragments of a Chronology of Chance/71 Fragmente einer Chronologie des Zufalls (Michael Haneke, Austria/Germany 1994), 47
500 Days of Summer (Marc Webb, USA 2009), 8

A coup sûr (Delphine de Vigan, France 2014), 210
À la vie, à la mort/'Til Death Do Us Part (Robert Guédiguian, France 1995), 46
Abel, Richard, 1
abortion, 51, 149, 161
Adam's Rib (George Cukor, USA 1949), 18
Adoption, 120, 127–128, 148–149
Adultery, negative portrayal of, 139, 152, 158, 160, 182
 romance and, 58–66, 67
 sanctioning of, 57, 58, 60, 112, 154
 theme, 58–66, 87, 108, 122, 126, 133, 136
Affaire du voile, l', 50
Agathe Cléry (Étienne Chatiliez, France 2008), 96
Âge d'homme... maintenant ou jamais!, L' (Raphaël Fejtö, France 2007), 55
Age, childlike adults, 35–39, 46, 77, 84, 114, 134, 159, 211
 the cult of youth, 60, 93, 106, 108, 143, 159

Age, childlike adults (*cont.*)
older women, 88, 97, 98, 100–102, 153, 161, 211
youth culture, 118, 138, 177
Aghion, Gabriel, 46, 55, 77, 127, 150, 192
Akerman, Chantal, 2, 70, 92, 171
Allen, Woody, 67, 95, 107, 113, 169
Allusionism (*see* Referentiality)
Ally McBeal (20th Century Fox Television/David E. Kelley Productions, 1997–2002), 193
Almodóvar, Pedro, 89, 110, 118, 123, 168
Altman, Rick, 20
American-ness 168, 171, 178, 191
Amores Perros (Alejandro González Iñárritu, Mexico 1999), 47
Amour et turbulences/Love is in the Air (Alexandre Castagnetti, 2013), 212
Amour passion, 58–59
Analysis, discourse, 10
Ang, Ien, 16
Anglo-Saxons, les, 168, 175, 186–189, 207
Anonymity, 29, 36, 40–44, 60
Anti-Americanism, 23, 26–27, 176, 181, 186–194, 199
Apatow, Judd, 113
Apprentis, Les (Pierre Salavadori, France 1995), 114–116
Ardant, Fanny, 46, 94, 118, 211
Aristotle, 18
Arnacoeur, L'/Heartbreaker (Pascal Chaumeil, France/Monaco 2010), 201–207

Art (délicat) de la séduction, L' (Richard Berry, France 2001), 96–99, 147
Art d'aimer, L'/The Art of Love (Emmanuel Mouret, 2011), 209
Artist, The (Michael Hazanavicius, France/Belgium/USA 2011), 213
Atomisation, social (*see* Living, urban)
Attal, Yvan, actor, 61, 95, 104, 112, 120, 126, 172, 188
director, 54, 61, 95, 104, 111, 120, 126, 149, 150, 187–188
Au secours, j'ai trente ans/Last Chance Saloon (Marie-Anne Chazel, France 2004), 103, 119
Au suivant! (Jeanne Biras, France 2005), 77, 103–105, 118, 147, 151–153, 189
Auberge espagnole, L'/Pot Luck (Cédric Klapisch, France/Spain 2002), 205
Audiences, 19, 37, 39, 80, 83, 100, 131–134, 211
Audry, Jacqueline, 21
Auteuil, Daniel, 83, 98, 108
Auteur(/ism) (*see* Authorship, and Comedy, auteur)
Authorship, female, 9, 62, 99–100, 131, 147, 150–151, 212
male, 41, 87, 144, 147, 150–151
Autonomy, female, (*see* Independence, female)
Awards, film, 22
Azéma, Sabine, 62, 156, 157, 160
Azuelos, Lisa, 24, 140, 199

INDEX

Babel (Alejandro González Iñárritu, France/USA/Mexico, 2006), 47
Bacri, Jean-Pierre, 62, 135
Badinter, Élisabeth, 1, 123, 129, 130, 138, 145, 212
Baer, Edouard, 26, 40, 51, 55, 111, 152, 153, 211
Bakhtin, Mikhail, 62, 83
Balasko, Josiane, auteur, 190, 197
 director, 2, 42–43, 63, 71, 87–88, 92, 99, 108, 148, 151, 189, 197
 performer, 63, 88, 95, 96, 189
Bard, Christine, 7, 107
Bardot, Brigitte, 39, 92, 102, 125
Barr, Roseanne, 63, 83
Baudrillard, Jean, 33, 168
Bauman, Zygmunt, 74
Baye, Nathalie, 42, 88, 100–102, 211
Bazgan, Nicoleta, 31, 34
Béart, Emmanuelle, 94, 156, 199
Beauty (*see* Myth, beauty)
Beauvoir, Simone de, 16, 24, 144, 145
Beaux jours, Les/Bright Days Ahead (Marion Varnoux, France 2013), 223
Beijing Bastards/Beijing Zadhong (Zhang Yuan, China 1993), 47
Belle Maman/Beautiful Mother (Gabriel Aghion, France 1999), 58, 78, 100, 126–127
Bergson, Henri, 110
Berry, Richard, 96, 99
Besson, Luc, 201
Beurs, 26, 54–57

Beuze, La/Dope, The (François Desagnat and Thomas Sorriaux, France 2003), 6
Bhaji on the Beach (Gurinder Chada, UK 1993), 46
Bibliothèque du film, la, 12, 197
Bienvenue chez les Ch'tis/Welcome to the Sticks (Dany Boon, France 2008), 6, 22
Binoche, Juliette, 83, 85, 94, 174, 176, 180–181, 193, 197, 199
Birth rates, 129, 145, 151, 212
Bison (et sa voisine Dorine), Le (Isabelle Nanty, France 2003), 103, 152–153
Bisset, Jacqueline, 62
Blanc, Michel, 65, 94–95, 99, 101, 109–110, 211
Bondage, 65, 95
Bonnaire, Sandrine, 105, 187
Boon, Dany, 6, 26, 155, 197
Border Line (Danièle Dubroux, France/Switzerland 1992), 146
Bordwell, David, 48, 132, 171, 174
Boum, La/Ready for Love (Claude Pinoteau, France 1980), 142
Bouquet, Carole, 65, 94, 95, 100, 101, 109, 118
Bourvil, 107
Brice de Nice/Brice Man, The (James Huth, France 2005), 6, 98
Bridget Jones syndrome, 38, 87
Broca, Philippe de, 21
Bromance (*see* Buddies, male)
Bronzés, Les/French Fried Vacation (Patrice Chéreau, France 1978), 109
Bruni Tedeschi, Valeria, 63, 94, 124
Brunsdon, Charlotte, 94

249

Bûche, La/Season's Beatings (Danièle Thompson, France 1999), 103, 156–165, 196, 198
Buddies, male, 113–117
Butler, Judith, 81, 212

Café théâtre, 88, 109
Canet, Guillaume, 45
Career (*see* Work)
Caricature, 53, 111–112, 121, 123, 184
Carné, Marcel, 33
Casablanca (Michael Curtiz, USA 1942), 75–76
Cassel, Jean-Pierre, 55
Cassel, Vincent, 55
Casting, 55, 89, 142
Cavell, Stanley, 18, 78
Ce soir, je dors chez toi/Tonight I'll Sleep at Yours (Olivier Baroux, France 2007), 68
Ce soir ou jamais/Tonight or Never (Michel Deville, France 1961), 21
Cécile Telerman, 90, 151
Celebration, The/Festen (Thomas Vinterberg, Denmark 1998), 46
Célibataires (Jean-Michel Verner, France 2006), 43, 49, 147
Celle que j'aime/The One I Love (Élie Chouraqui, France 2009), 147
Certeau, Michel de, 35
Cet obscur objet du désir/That Obscure Object of Desire (Luis Buñuel, France/Spain, 1977), 101
Chabat, Alain, actor, 26, 63, 79, 94–95, 108, 112, 121, 211
actor-producer, 173, 199

Chance de ma vie, La (Nicolas Cuche, France 2011), 211
Chansons d'amour, Les/Love Songs (Christophe Honoré, France 2007), 12, 125
Chaos theory, 19
Chaumeil, Pascal, 2, 201–207
Chick-flicks, 17
Children, 54, 93, 123, 130, 138–139, 140 (*see also* Fatherhood, Motherhood)
Chouchou (Merzak Allouache, France 2003), 98, 121, 123
Cinema, auteur, 9, 22–25, 85, 163, 173, 193, 197
digital, 35
European, 27, 169, 192
extreme, 85
popular, 1, 11, 20–25, 49, 72, 170, 197, 201
Cinephilia, 179–186
Cixous, Hélène, 24, 145
Clara et moi/Clara and Me (Arnaud Viard, France 2004), 36–41, 70–71, 77, 87, 191
Class, social, 15, 18, 36, 93, 106, 118, 133, 210
Cliente/A French Gigolo (Josiane Balasko, France 2008), 42, 88, 100–103, 175, 189, 197
Club de femmes/Girls' Club (Jacques Deval, France 1936), 150
Clueless (Amy Heckerling, USA 1995), 179
Cluzet, François, 114, 120
Coco avant Chanel/Coco Before Chanel (Anne Fontaine, France/Belgium 2009), 3

Code a changé, Le/Change of Plans (Danièle Thompson, France 2009), 41, 65, 156
Code inconnu/Code Unknown (Michael Haneke, France 2000), 47
Coeur des hommes, Le/Frenchmen 1 (Marc Esposito, France 2003), 100, 113
Coeur des hommes 2, Le/Frenchmen 2 (Marc Esposito, France 2007), 100, 113
Comedy, auteur, 2, 9, 12, 25
  boulevard, 5, 58, 59, 175
  classical, 5, 59, 170, 175, 181, 193
  comedian, 26, 111, 113, 152, 153, 194
  remarriage, 14
  screwball, 5, 18, 68–71, 171, 175, 180, 201
  sex, 68
  Shakespearian, 58, 59, 178
  theatrical, 5, 59, 77
  vaudeveille (*see* boulevard)
Comme les autres/Baby Love (Vincent Garenq, France 2008), 126, 127
Commitment, 79–80, 86, 150, 164, 185
Community, the, 28–29, 31–32, 44–48
Corsini, Catherine, 2, 86, 193
Cotillard, Marion, 113, 201
Couple, the, 7, 42, 72–73, 85, 125, 209
Crise, La/The Crisis (Coline Serreau, France/Italy 1992), 8
crisis of masculinity (*see* Masculinity, melodramatised)

criticism, film, 8, 16, 21–23, 189–197
Crustacés et coquillages/Cockles and Muscles (Olivier Ducastel and Jacques Martineau, 2005), 63, 64, 67, 78, 122–124
Cukor, George, 18, 38, 110
cultural studies, 10, 14–17, 19, 25, 56, 144
Curtis, Richard, 168, 173, 182, 183
Cycles, generic, 14, 74
Cyrano de Bergerac, 175

Dallas (Lorimar Productions/Lorimar Television, 1978–1991), 16
Dan in Real Life (Peter Hedges, USA 2007), 43, 199
Darrousin, Jean-Pierre, 136
De battre mon coeur s'est arrêté/The Beat That My Heart Skipped (Jacques Audiard, France 2005), 205
De France, Cécile, 39, 46, 55, 77, 84, 94, 96, 199, 211
De l'autre côté du lit/Changing Sides (Pascale Pouzadoux, France 2008), 143
De vrais mensonges/Beautiful Lies (Pierre Salvadori, France 2010), 148, 150, 175, 199
Death, 137, 146, 157
Décalage horaire/Jet Lag (Danièle Thompson, France/UK 2002), 36–37, 40, 70, 76, 175–180
  characters, 37, 83, 94, 103, 106, 189, 209
  reception, 2, 156, 174, 186, 189, 193, 195, 198, 200–201

Delanoë, Bertrand, 117
Deleuze, Gilles, 49
Deleyto, Celestino, 5, 15, 19–21, 59, 72, 84–85, 91, 108, 113–116, 164
Delpy, Julie, 37, 88, 195, 199, 213
Demy, Jacques, 21, 22
Deneuve, Catherine, 92, 100, 101, 118, 127, 211
Depardieu, Gérard, 60, 107, 109, 115, 121
Depp, Johnny, 61, 116, 187, 205
Deprecation of the rom-com, 16–27, 189–194
Derrida, Jacques, 19
Desire, 15, 17, 29, 35, 65–67, 73, 78, 116
  female, 17, 63, 64, 79, 80, 85, 87, 88, 89, 138
  gay, 120–122
Desperate Housewives (Cherry Alley Productions/Cherry Productions/Touchstone Television/ABC Studios, 2004–2012), 90
Détrompez-vous (Bruno Dega, France 2007), 65
Deville, Michel, 21
Dieu est grand, je suis toute petite/God is Great and I'm Not (Pascale Bailly, France 2001), 51–54, 55, 103, 199
Dirty Dancing (Emile Ardolino, USA 1987), 203
Dis-moi oui (Alexandre Arcady, France 1995), 100
Distribution, 2, 22, 27, 166, 199, 201

Divorce, 65–66, 130, 138–144, 152, 156, 160–161
Doisneau, Robert, 33
Doublure, La/Valet, The (Francis Veber, France/Italy/Belgium 2006), 6
Doutey, Mélanie, 113, 211
Drag, 77, 98, 109, 121, 123
Drôle de Félix/Adventures of Felix (Olivier Ducastel and Jacques Martineau, France 2000), 122
Duchen, Claire, 93, 103, 129
Dujardin, Jean, 98
Dumont, Bruno, 29
Duris, Romain, 202, 205, 207, 209, 211
DVD, 12, 131
Dyer, Richard, 11, 16, 92, 169, 172, 205

Efira, Virginie, 211
Elbaz, Vincent, 112, 137
Elmeleh, Gad, 26, 98, 121, 170, 208, 210
Elsaesser, Thomas, 168, 186
Embrassez qui vous voudrez/Summer Things (Michel Blanc, France/UK/Italy 2002), 132, 135
Emotifs anonymes, Les/Romantics Anonymous (Jean-Pierre Améris, France 2010), 180, 185, 200
Empowerment, female, (see Independence, female)
Endings, happy, 27, 59, 80, 125, 176
Ensemble, c'est tout/Hunting and Gathering (Claude Berri, France 2007), 39

Equality, 6–7, 18, 81, 91, 100, 151, 172
Essaye-moi (Pierre-François Martin-Laval, France 2006), 152–153, 175–177, 193
Ethnography, 10, 35
Evans, Peter William, 15, 18, 59, 108, 164
Ex-femme de ma vie, L'/Ex-Wife of my Life, The (Josiane Balasko, France 2004), 148, 151, 190
Exoticism, 123, 159, 189, 199, 202
Export, 9, 11, 25, 37, 166–169, 197–201
Ezra, Elizabeth, 31, 166–168, 200

Fabuleux destin d'Amélie Poulain, Le/Amelie (Jean-Pierre Jeunet, France/Germany 2001), 1, 29–39, 47, 53, 103, 135, 199, 207
Fairy-tales (*see also* Fantasy), 31, 75, 77
Family, the, 3, 9, 11, 15, 129–134, 209
   decline of traditional, 28, 35, 44–46, 122–128
Fantasy, 36, 75–76, 116, 122, 125, 132
Farce, 59, 108, 153, 176, 194
Fatherhood, 123, 127, 130, 137–138, 149–156, 161
Fauteuils d'orchestre/Orchestra Seats (Danièle Thompson, France 2006), 45, 46, 77, 103–106, 156, 198
Feminism, Anglo-American, 19, 94, 132
   first-wave, 110

French, 7, 38, 85, 93, 133, 145
   second-wave, 7, 16, 130, 145
   third-wave (*see* post-feminism)
Fernandel, 107
Ferriss, Suzanne, 3, 17, 26, 27
Filles perdues, cheveux gras/Hypnotized and Hysterical (Hairstylist Wanted) (Claude Duty, France 2002), 191
Film *choral*, the (*see* Structures, ensemble)
Film, the multi-protagonist (*see* Structures, ensemble)
Filmmakers, female, 6, 41, 98, 131, 138, 196
Fischer, Lucy, 19, 103
Flowers of Shanghai/Hai shang hua (Hou Hsiao-hsien, Taiwan 1998), 46
Forbes, Jill, 25, 126
Foucault, Michel, 15, 131, 144, 194
Four Weddings and a Funeral (Mike Newell, UK 1994), 167, 178
fragmentation, social (*see* Living, urban)
Franglais, 37, 175–177
Frenchness, 181, 186, 188, 198, 200, 206, 207
Friendship (*see also* Buddies, male), 120, 122, 140–142, 147, 154, 158, 183–184
Frodon, Jean-Michel, 23, 171, 191, 192
Funès, Louis de 107

Gainsbourg, Charlotte, 61, 79, 94–96, 104, 112, 126, 156–161, 188, 199
Garrett, Roberta, 3, 14

INDEX

253

Gayet, Julie, 37–39, 84, 211
Gazon maudit/French Twist (Josiane Balasko, France 1995), 63, 71, 88, 94, 108, 121–125, 148, 150
Gender studies, 24
Genre, 21, 24
Giddens, Anthony, 15, 67, 199
Globalisation, 50, 89, 148, 176, 179, 189, 207
Godard, Jean-Luc, 21, 172
Golden Girls, The (Touchstone Television/Witt/Thomas/Harris Productions, 1985–1992), 90
Goût des autres, Le/Taste of Others, The (Agnès Jaoui, France 2001), 73, 77, 83, 85, 103, 134, 178, 198
Grossvogel, David, 62, 132, 173, 177
Grotesque, the, 25, 83–85, 89, 94
Guattari, Félix, 49
Guédiguian, Robert, 29, 46, 211
Guignabodet, Valérie, 24, 73
Guitry, Sacha, 5

Haine, La (Mathieu Kassovitz, France 1995), 55
Hakim, Catherine, 130
Hall, Stuart, 10
Hansen-Løve, Mia, 16
Hawks, Howard, 23, 193
Hayward, Susan, 1, 2, 21, 22
He's Just Not That Into You (Ken Kwapis, USA/Germany/Netherlands 2009), 43
Hepburn, Katharine, 83, 86
Hérisson, Le/Hedgehog, The (Mona Achache, France/Italy 2009), 153
heritage film, the, 3, 25

Hitchcock, Alfred, 22
Hollinger, Karen, 89, 90
Hollywood, actresses, 174, 180, 182, 211
  classical, 23, 132, 170, 172
  contemporary, 3–8, 75, 84, 100, 104, 166–175, 179, 181–197
Holmes, Diana, 15, 29, 79, 80, 129, 131
Homme de chevet, L' (Alain Monne, France 2009), 143
Homme est une femme comme les autres, L'/Man is a Woman (Jean-Jacques Zilbermann, France 1998), 126
Homosexuality, 46, 62, 63, 65, 108, 117–128
Honoré, Christophe, 12, 125
Hors de prix/Priceless (Pierre Salvadori, France 2006), 78, 93, 97, 121, 175, 190
  performers, 68, 73, 78, 97, 121, 170, 171
  reception, 2, 189, 199
Houellebecq, Michel, 42, 44
Humour, 26, 83, 114, 123
Hurt, William, 98, 176
Hybridity, 20, 113, 131, 167, 195, 200

I Love You, Man (John Hamburg, USA 2009), 116
Ice Storm, The (Ang Lee, USA 1996), 45
identities, alternative gender
  (*see* homosexuality)
  French (*see* Frenchness)
  gay (*see* homosexuality)
  gender (*see* roles, gender)

Il ne faut jurer de rien! (Eric Civanyan, France 2005), 77
Illness/medical theme, 45, 119, 137, 163
Ils se marièrent et eurent beaucoup d'enfants/And They Lived Happily Ever After (Yvan Attal, France 2004), 111, 113, 120, 149, 154, 187
Immaturity (*see* Age, childlike adults)
Ince, Kate, 117, 118, 122–123, 125
Incest, 5, 6, 100, 163–164
Independence, female, 9, 82–84, 136, 172
Individualism, 29, 41, 66, 72, 92, 131, 196
Industry, French film, 1–4, 6, 12, 21–25, 181, 192, 213
Innuendo, 15
Internet, the, 20, 42–43, 90, 102, 139, 176
Intertextuality (*see* Referentiality)
Intimacy, homosocial, 114
    post-romantic, 57, 66–75, 79, 80, 93, 149, 208
    theme, 18, 43, 48, 172
Intouchables/Untouchable (Olivier Nakache and Eric Toledano, France 2011), 6
Irène (Ivan Calbérac, France 2002), 39–45, 69, 104, 152
Irigaray, Luce, 24, 145
Islam, 29, 50, 54–55, 105, 117
It Happened One Night (Frank Capra, USA 1934), 75, 179

J'me sens pas belle (Bernard Jeanjean, France 2004), 39, 40

Jamais le premier soir (Melissa Drigeard, France 2014), 210
Jameson, Fredric, 146, 194
Jaoui, Agnès, 62, 73, 84–85, 103, 105, 134, 135–136
Jarvie, Ian, 4
Je crois que je l'aime/Could This Be Love? (Pierre Jolivet, France 2007), 187, 190
Je ne suis pas là pour être aimé/Not Here To Be Loved (Stéphane Brizé, France 2005), 79
Je préfère qu'on reste amis (Olivier Nakache and Eric Toledano, France 2005), 43, 115–116
Je reste!/I'm staying! (Diane Kurys, France 2003), 63, 71, 143
Je vais te manquer/You'll Miss Me (Amanda Sthers, France 2009), 36, 47, 54, 119, 120, 147, 152
Je vous trouve très beau/You are so Beautiful (Isabelle Mergault, France 2006), 24, 93, 99–100, 106, 175, 190
Jeffers McDonald, Tamar, 5, 8, 74, 89, 113
Jermyn, Deborah, 17, 172, 185
Jeunet, Jean-Pierre, 2, 4, 30–34
Jeux de l'amour, Les/Games of Love, The (Philippe de Broca, France 1960), 21
Jewishness, 53–55, 126, 149–150, 157, 208
Jules et Jim/Jules and Jim (François Truffaut, France 1962), 163
Jupon Rouge, Le/Manuela's Loves (Geneviève Lefebvre, France 1987), 150

Jusqu'à toi (Jennifer Devoldère, France/Canada, 2009), 189

Kaganski, Serge, 30
Kaplan, E. Ann, 130, 137, 143–145, 147, 148
Keaton, Buster, 18, 194
King, Geoff, 8, 19, 23, 25, 106
Kinship (*see* Family, the)
Klapisch, Cédric, 84, 130, 135, 157, 200, 205–206
Kramer vs. Kramer (Robert Benton, USA 1979), 139
Kristeva, Julia, 24, 145
Kruger, Diane, 211
Krutnik, Frank, 4, 5, 8, 19, 26, 37, 67–75, 106, 174–175
Kuisel, Richard, 189, 213
Kurys, Diane, 63, 92

L'Enfant/The Child (Jean-Pierre and Luc Dardenne, 2007), 209
Laisse tes mains sur mes hanches/Leave Your Hands on My Hips (Chantal Lauby, France 2003), 146
Lakoff, George, 19
Lamome, Stéphanie, 195–197
language, 37, 116, 175–179, 187–189
Laroque, Michèle, 62
Lauby, Chantal, 42, 100, 103
Laughter, 8, 55, 70, 96
Le Bihan, Samuel, 98
Leahy, Sarah, 147
Léaud, Jean-Pierre, 126, 207
Lemercier, Valérie, 63, 96, 99

Let's Hope It's a Girl/Speriamo che sia femmina (Mario Monicelli, Italy/France 1986), 149
Levinas, Emmanuel, 24
Lhermitte, Thierry, 60, 98, 100
Liaisons dangereuses, Les, 58
Libertinage (*see* Adultery)
Libido, the (*see* Desire)
Life According to Agfa/Ha Chayim Aply Agfa (Assi Dayan, Israel 1992), 46
Lincoln, Andrew, 183, 203
Lipovetsky, Gilles, 29
Literary studies, 7, 14–17, 19, 35
Literature, French, 34, 133
Lives, women's, 16, 34, 82, 106, 210
Living, urban, 28–40, 44, 49, 50, 56, 82, 88, 208
Lol (Laughing Out Loud) (Lisa Azuelos, France 2008), 24, 55, 139–143, 178–179, 199, 200
mother-daughter relations, 134, 138, 140–143, 146, 152, 161, 176
Loneliness (*see* Solitude)
Lotharios (*see* Adultery)
Love, companionate, 18, 58, 61, 68
Love Actually (Richard Curtis, UK/USA 2003), 182–183
Lubitsch, Ernst, 23, 68, 171, 193
Luhmann, Niklas, 58
Luxury (*see* Wealth)

Ma femme est une actrice/My Wife is an Actress (Yvan Attal, France 2001), 54, 77, 95, 97, 103, 111, 150–151, 171, 175, 187
Ma vie en l'air (Rémi Bezançon, France 2005), 103, 111, 113

Ma vie est un enfer/My Life is Hell (Josiane Balasko, France 1991), 96–97
Ma vie n'est pas une comédie romantique/It Had to Be You (Marc Gibaja, France 2007), 76, 180, 181–185, 187, 192
Machineness, 33–35, 55
Madame Bovary, 16, 34
Made in Hong Kong/Xianggang Zhiao (Fruit Chan, Hong Kong 1997), 46
Mademoiselle Chambon (Stéphane Brizé, France 2009), 71, 79, 103
Magnolia (Paul Thomas Anderson, USA 2000), 47
Maid in Manhattan (Wayne Wang, USA 2002), 91
Maïwenn, 16
Maltby, Richard, 20
Manhattan (Woody Allen, USA 1979), 172, 203
Mar Azcona, María del, 44, 47–49, 72, 79, 132, 142, 158
Marceau, Sophie, 63, 94, 141–143, 155, 197, 208
Mariage Mixte (Alexandre Arcady, France 2004), 147
Mariages! (Valérie Guignabodet, France 2004), 23, 73, 77, 78, 97, 131, 136, 177, 178
Marivaux, 190
Marketing, 2, 5, 118, 172, 174, 190, 201
Marmottes, Les/Groundhogs, The (Élie Chouraqui, France 1993), 62, 75, 77, 132–134, 138, 145–147, 157, 175

Marriage, decline, 7, 9, 15, 74, 130, 212
incompatibility with romance, 58–59, 66, 79
Marshall, Tonie, 2, 12, 36, 86, 100
Masculinity, melodramatised, 106–110, 114–117, 121, 137, 188
Maternity (*see* Motherhood)
Mauvaise foi/Bad Faith (Roschdy Zem, France/Belgium, 2006), 149, 150, 161
Mazdon, Lucy, 23, 107, 130, 169, 207
Mazursky, Paul, 67
Meet cute, the, 37, 174, 182
Melodrama, 22, 60, 106–110, 117, 123, 133, 157–159, 195
Men, rich, 46, 106, 153, 206
see also Masculinity, melodramatised
Mensonges et trahisons et plus si affinités/The Story of My Life (Laurent Tirard, 2002), 40, 43, 71, 79, 111, 147, 150
Mergault, Isabelle, 24, 99
Methodology, 10–13
Meyers, Nancy, 100
Micmacs à tire-larigot/Micmacs (Jean-Pierre Jeunet, France 2009), 4
Midnight in Paris (Woody Allen, USA 2011), 37
Misogyny, 6, 16, 20, 99, 101, 109, 112, 141
Modern Love (Stéphane Kazandjian, France 2008), 47, 48, 77, 119
Modleski, Tania, 16, 107, 117, 126, 133–134, 136

Moine, Raphaëlle, 2, 5–6, 17, 22–25, 113, 132, 168, 170, 198
Molière (Laurent Tirard, France 2007), 205
Môme, La/La Vie en rose (Olivier Dahan, France/UK/Czech Republic 2007), 3
Montage sequences, 44, 95, 148, 154, 170–173, 202
Moore, Rick Clifton, (*see* Machineness)
Moreau, Yolande, 12, 22, 63–64, 97, 99
Morrissey, Jim, 31–34
Motherhood, 7, 127, 129–131, 138, 143–151, 161, 212
Mulvey, Laura, 19, 134
Music and Lyrics (Marc Lawrence, USA 2007), 92
Musicals, 38, 63, 77, 122, 125, 178, 188
My Best Friend's Wedding (P.J. Hogan, USA 1997), 117
Myth, beauty, 82, 91–100

Naturalism (*see* Realism)
Neale, Steve, 5, 8, 19, 20, 26, 67, 74, 78, 92
Neglect of the rom-com, scholarly, (*see* Deprecation of the rom-com)
Negra, Diane, 17, 41, 75, 78, 82, 104, 110
Nelly (Laure Duthilleul, France 2004), 143
Neurosis, 74, 76, 84, 89, 112, 163, 176, 180
New Extremism, 98–9

New Wave, the, 6, 21–22, 126, 163, 172, 193, 201
New York, 172, 185, 187, 212
Non-places, 35–36, 212
Nostalgia, 18, 75, 77, 177
Notting Hill (Roger Michell, UK/USA 1999), 147
Nouvelle Ève, La/New Eve, The (Catherine Corsini, France/Portugal 1999), 86, 95, 136, 193, 194

Olsin Lent, Tina, 18
On connaît la chanson/Same Old Song (Alain Resnais, France/UK/Switzerland 1997), 61, 83, 133, 191
One and only, the, 67, 78
Où avais-je la tête? (Nathalie Donnini, France 2007), 83, 85
Oury, Gérard, 156
Ozon, François, 118, 130

PaCS, the, 29, 117, 120, 125, 127
Palais Royal! (Valérie Lemercier, France 2005), 63, 95
Palmer, Tim, 15, 25, 179
Paradis, Vanessa, 203
Parenthood (Ron Howard, USA 1989), 137
Paris, realist portrayals of, 37–38, 125–126, 137
utopian portrayals of, 30–35, 45–46, 47, 77, 117, 123, 172
Parlez-moi de la pluie/Let's Talk About the Rain (Agnès Jaoui, France 2008), 85, 105
Parody, 42, 44, 111, 115, 204

Passe-passe/Off and Running (Tonie Marshall, France 2008), 99
Pastiche, 154, 169, 171–2, 178, 179, 203–205
Patriarchs, deficient, 31, 50, 54, 119, 122, 136–137, 142
Pédale douce (Gabriel Aghion, France 1996), 46, 61, 123–124, 133, 148, 149, 161, 175
Performance style, 93–96, 117–118, 125, 158, 202–203, 211
Performativity, 122–123, 168, 202–203
Pièce Montée/Wedding Cake, The (Denys Granier-Deferre, France 2010), 78
Plus beau métier du monde, Le/The Best Job in the World (Gérard Lauzier, France 1996), 60, 62
Politique des auteurs, the, 23
Populaire (Regis Roinsard, France 2012), 209
Post coïtum animal triste/After Sex (Brigitte Roüan, France 1997), 87
Post-feminism, 17, 75–76, 78, 81–85, 93
Post-modern, film techniques, 30, 36, 39, 43, 75, 80, 110–113, 181, 205
  intimacy and family, 43, 71, 144, 154, 203
  life, 29, 32, 34, 35, 47- 52, 80, 144, 167, 174
Post-romance (*see* Romance, discourse of)
Post-structuralism, 19

Pourquoi pas moi?/Why Not Me? (Stéphane Giusti, France 1999), 121, 125
Pouzadoux, Pascale, 143, 154, 197
Powrie, Phil, 11, 44, 45, 48, 117, 130, 139, 161
Prédal, René, 22
Pregnancy, 87, 126, 137, 146–147
Premier jour du reste de ta vie, Le (Rémi Bezançon, France 2008), 136, 199
Press, the, 23, 102, 145, 189–197, 200
Prête-moi ta main/I Do (Eric Lartigau, France 2006), 1, 43, 79, 94–95, 147, 173, 190–191, 199
Pretty Woman (Garry Marshall, USA 1990), 3, 76, 92, 93, 180–182, 197
Prévert, Jacques, 33
Professionalism (*see* Work)
Proliferation of the rom-com, 6, 75, 81, 166, 190
Promiscuity (*see* Sex, casual)
Prostitution, 42–43, 106, 108, 181, 210
Psychoanalysis, 35, 67, 69–70, 86, 131, 176

Quand j'étais chanteur/The Singer (Xavier Giannoli, France 2006), 190
Quand la mer monte/When the Sea Rises (Yolande Moreau, Gilles Porte, France 2004), 11, 21, 63–64, 78, 97, 175
Quatre cents coups, Les/400 Blows, The (François Truffaut, France 1959), 135, 163

Quatre étoiles (Christian Vincent, France 2006), 68, 73, 78, 93, 103, 175
Queerness (*see* Homosexuality)
Question humaine, La/Heartbeat Detector (Nicolas Klotz, France 2007), 42

Race, 30, 50, 54–57, 96, 149, 208
Radway, Janice, 16, 35
Rampling, Charlotte, 65, 101, 118
Rape, 46, 96, 111
Rappeneau, Jean-Pierre, 21
Realism, 16, 22, 29, 67, 132, 154, 172
Rebellion, female, 6, 82–85, 90, 96, 106, 108, 112
Recomposée, la famille, 130, 138–144, 157
Referentiality, 6, 75–77, 88, 132, 162–3, 174, 180–182
Reines d'un jour/Hell of a Day (Marion Vernoux, France 2001), 47, 48, 87, 96
Religion, 29, 50–56, 87, 126, 150
Remakes, 6, 197–201, 202
Reno, Jean, 83, 94, 180, 181, 199, 211
Reservoir Dogs (Quentin Tarantino, USA 1992), 179
Resnais, Alain, 62, 84, 191
Resolutions, maternal (*see* Motherhood)
Résultats du féminisme, Les/Consequences of Feminism, The (Alice Guy, France 1906), 81
Richard, Firmine, 83, 93
Rohmer, Eric, 21, 22

Roles, gender 1–9, 14, 75, 81–85, 121, 130, 209
  women in professional, 41, 92, 107, 154–155, 209
Rollet, Brigitte, on families, 130, 133, 157
  on men, 107, 114, 136–138, 207
  on women, 24, 35, 83, 87
Roman de Lulu, Le (Pierre-Olivier Scotto, France 2001), 77, 100, 103
Romance, discourse of, 11, 15, 22, 28–29, 40, 57–59, 66–67
  literary, 15, 35
  nervous, 14, 67, 74–75
  new, 74–76, 78, 89, 159, 175, 185, 209
Romuald et Juliette/Mama, There's a Man in Your Bed (Coline Serreau, France 1989), 2, 36, 83, 93, 103, 107, 147, 150, 171, 194
Rosello, Mireille, 31
Roudinesco, Élisabeth, 130, 139, 140
Rousseau, Jean-Jacques, 144
Rouve, Jean-Paul, 113, 115
Rowden, Terry, 166–168, 200
Rowe, Kathleen, 5, 18, 19, 62–63, 72, 82–83, 107–108, 112, 172
Ryan, Meg, 174, 180, 182, 211

Sagnier, Ludivine, 212
Salvadori, Pierre, 2, 190
Satire, 15, 63, 96, 119
Scatton-Tessier, Michelle, 31, 34, 35
Schatz, Thomas, 18, 106

Se souvenir des belles choses/Beautiful Memories (Zabou Breitman, France 2001), 8
Sedgwick, Eve Kosofsky, 150
Seduction, 58, 86, 92–94, 141–142, 155, 201–205, 208
Seigner, Mathilde, 73, 90, 112, 139, 205
Sellier, Geneviève, 5, 6, 21, 25, 59, 84, 136
Serreau, Coline, 2, 8, 83, 108, 130, 171
Settings, festive, 50, 78, 156–159, 162
　holiday, 45, 64, 65, 78, 114, 122–125
Sex and the City (Darren Star Productions/HBO/Sex and the City Productions, 1998–2004), 65, 75, 195
Sex and the City 2 (Michael Patrick King, USA 2010), 17, 75, 89
Sex and the City: The Movie (Michael Patrick King, USA 2008), 17, 75, 89
　casual, 59, 67, 68, 74, 86–87, 111, 199
Sex, and intimacy, 39, 60, 79, 85, 86, 111, 179
　marginalisation of, 33, 78, 85, 96, 99, 183
　modern, 39, 42, 44, 64, 65–68, 85–89, 98, 115
　scenes, 68, 69, 70, 99, 184
Sexism, 25, 94–96, 106, 111, 139, 196
Short Cuts (Robert Altman, USA 1993), 47

Si c'était lui/Perfect Match (Anne-Marie Étienne, France 2007), 71, 100–101, 152
Si je t'aime, prends garde à toi/Beware of my Love (Jeanne Labrune, France 2002), 87
singlehood, 9, 30, 39, 86, 182
Singles (Cameron Crowe, USA 1992), 49
Singly, François de, 210
Sinon, oui (Claire Simon, France/Canada, 1997), 145
Slapstick (*see* Farce)
Sleepless in Seattle (Nora Ephron, USA 1993), 8, 181, 182
Smoking, 84, 95, 163
Smoking/No Smoking (Alain Resnais, France/Italy/Switzerland 1993), 191
Solitude, 29–40, 44, 49, 56, 82, 210
Songs, love, 75, 76, 123, 175–179
Sorlin, Pierre, 4, 24
Sous le soleil (TF1, 1996–2008), 105
Spectators (*see* Audiences)
Sphere, domestic, 90, 130, 154–155, 182, 184
　private, 212
　public, 82, 87, 105, 129, 212
Spirituality, 28, 29, 50–54, 56, 210
Splendid, le (*see Café théâtre*)
Stacey, Jackie, 15, 19, 71, 91–92, 98, 134
Star Trek (Desilu Productions/Norway Corporation/Paramount Television, 1966–1969), 184
Stars, 9, 94–100, 131, 168, 174, 199, 210
Stone, Lawrence, 58

Stories, relationship, 67, 73, 74, 79
Storm/Sturm (Hans-Christian Schmid, Germany/Denmark/ Netherlands/Sweden/Bosnia & Herzogovina, 2009), 207
Stratégie de la poussette, La/Stroller Strategy, The (Clement Michel, 2012), 209
Structures, dyadic, 45, 49, 70, 90, 196, 209
   choral *see* ensemble
   ensemble, 44–50, 70–73, 79, 131–134, 144, 200, 208
   mosaic (*see* ensemble)
   multi-protagonist (*see* ensemble)
   triangular, 58, 72, 126
Sturges, Preston, 18, 195
Style, French, 59, 62, 66, 83, 131, 170
   US, 82–83, 88, 116, 174, 179
Sullivan's Travels (Preston Sturges, USA 1941), 18, 194
Superbad (Greg Mottola, USA 2007), 116
Swamp, The/Ciénaga, La (Lucrecia Martel, Argentina/France/ Spain 2001), 45

Tarr, Carrie, 11, 26, 50, 88, 96, 123, 138, 145–146
Tasker, Yvonne, 11, 17, 41, 75, 78, 92, 104, 110, 174
Tati, Jacques, 18
Tautou, Audrey, 22, 35, 39, 45, 51, 84, 94, 100, 170, 199, 201
Technology, 28, 33–35, 40–44, 145, 176–177
Teenpic, the, 55, 141–142, 178

Television, 24, 105, 133, 177, 194–195, 196
Tellement proches (Olivier Nakache and Eric Toledano, France 2009), 136, 138, 146
Tenue de soirée/Ménage (Bertrand Blier, France 1986), 109
Themes, dark, 7, 38, 80, 157, 200
There's Something About Mary (Bobby and Peter Farrelly, USA 1998), 192
Thompson, Danièle
   director, 2, 12, 37, 41, 45, 65, 156–165, 181, 193, 195–198
   writer, 62, 76, 147
Thompson, Sharon, 134, 171
Thriller, the, 25
Timsit, Patrick, 96, 123
Tirez sur le pianiste/Shoot the Piano Player! (François Truffaut, France 1960), 172
Toi et moi (Julie Lopes-Curval, France 2006), 103 151, 190, 194, 195
Tout ce qui brille/All That Glitters (Hervé Mimram and Géraldine Nakache, France 2010), 48
Tout pour plaire (Cécile Telerman, France/Belgium 2005), 90, 103, 151, 154
Toutes les filles sont folles/All Girls are Crazy (Pascale Pouzadoux, France 2003), 71
Transience, places of (*see* Non-places)
Transnationalism, 48, 166–169, 180–186, 194–201, 213
Transporter 2 (Louis Leterrier, France/USA 2005), 201

Transporter 3 (Olivier Megaton, France/UK/USA 2008), 201
Transporter, The (Louis Leterrier and Corey Yuen, France/USA 2003), 201
Transvestite (*see* Drag)
Tricheuse/ So Woman! (Jean-François Davy, France 2009), 39, 104
Tröhler, Margrit, 46–49, 132–134
Trois hommes et un couffin/ Three Men and a Cradle (Coline Serreau, France 1985), 130
Trop belle pour toi/ Too Beautiful For You (Bertrand Blier, France 1989), 101
Truffaut, François, 21, 22, 126, 135, 163, 172
Truth About Cats and Dogs, The (Michael Lehmann, USA 1996), 175, 209
Tudor, Andrew, 4

Un air de famille/ Family Resemblances (Cédric Klapisch, France 1996), 84, 135, 137, 157
Un bonheur n'arrive jamais seul/ Happiness Never Comes Alone (James Huth, France 2012), 207
Un divan à New York/ A Couch in New York (Chantal Akerman, USA 1996), 70, 83, 98, 171, 176, 178, 189
Un grand cri d'amour (Josiane Balasko, France 1998), 71, 77
Un plan parfait/ A Perfect Plan (Pascal Chaumeil, 2012), 209

Un week-end sur deux/ Every Other Weekend (Nicole Garcia, France 1990), 139, 209
Une femme en blanc (Escazal Films, 1997), 105
Une semaine sur deux (et la moitié des vacances scolaires) (Ivan Calbérac, France 2009), 134, 138, 147, 161
Une vie à t'attendre (Thierry Klifa, France 2004), 100
Utopianism, 18, 45, 98, 115, 116, 118, 125, 127, 150

Vanderschelden, Isabelle, 23, 25, 26, 31–33
Vénus Beauté (Institut)/ Venus Beauty Salon (Tonie Marshall, France 1999)
  reception, 12, 22
  romance, 39, 50–51, 73, 77–78, 86, 98, 100, 102, 103
  urban loneliness, 36, 39, 50, 88
Vérité ou presque, La/ True Enough (Sam Karmann, France 2007), 65, 66, 119, 121
Vernoux, Marion, 47, 48, 87, 126
Viard, Arnaud, 36
Viard, Karin, 86, 87, 96, 109
Viewers (*see* Audiences)
Vincendeau, Ginette, 5, 6, 25, 31, 174, 198, 206
Les Voleurs/ Thieves (André Téchiné, France 1996), 47

Wealth, 48, 76–78, 92, 94, 153, 206 (*see also* Men, rich)

Wedding Crashers (David Dobkin, USA 2005), 115
West, Mae, 83
When Harry Met Sally (Rob Reiner, USA 1989), 3, 31, 71, 75, 76, 179, 180, 182
Wittig, Monique, 24
Wolf, Naomi, 92
Woman, the unruly (*see* Rebellion, female)
Women (*see* lives, women's, and filmmakers, female)
Women, The (George Cukor, USA 1939)
Work, 33, 40–42, 51, 90, 93, 103–106 (*see also* Roles, women in professional)

Wright-Wexman, Virginia, 4
Wrong partner, the, 73, 119, 157, 158, 174, 206

Y'aura t'il de la neige à Noël?/Will It Snow for Christmas? (Sandrine Veysset, France 1996), 62
Young, Mallory, 26, 27

Zèbre, Le/The Oddball (Jean Poiret, France 1992), 60, 98
Zem, Roschdy, 50, 54–55, 150
Žižek, Slavoj, 42

www.ingramcontent.com/pod-product-compliance
Lightning Source LLC
Chambersburg PA
CBHW070023010526
44117CB00011B/1686